CHANGING JAPANESE SUBURBIA

Japanese Studies
General Editor: Yoshio Sugimoto

Images of Japanese Society: *Ross E. Mouer and Yoshio Sugimoto*
An Intellectual History of Wartime Japan: *Shunsuke Tsurumi*
Changing Japanese Suburbia: *Eyal Ben-Ari*
A Cultural History of Postwar Japan: *Shunsuke Tsurumi*
Beyond Computopia: *Tessa Morris-Suzuki*
Constructs for Understanding Japan: *Yoshio Sugimoto and Ross E. Mouer*
Japanese Models of Conflict Resolution: *S. N. Eisenstadt and Eyal Ben-Ari*

Forthcoming

Enterprise Unionism in Japan: *Hirosuke Kawanishi*
Group Psychology of the Japanese in Wartime: *Toshio Iritani*
The Rise of the Japanese Corporate System: *Koji Matsumoto*
Science, Technology and Society in Postwar Japan: *Shigeru Nakayama*
Transferred Development: Western Technology and the Industrialisation of Japan: *Ian Inkster*

CHANGING JAPANESE SUBURBIA

A Study of Two Present-Day Localities

Eyal Ben-Ari

KEGAN PAUL INTERNATIONAL
London and New York

First published in 1991 by
Kegan Paul International Ltd
PO Box 256, London WC1B 3SW, England

Distributed by
John Wiley & Sons Ltd
Southern Cross Trading Estate
1 Oldlands Way, Bognor Regis,
West Sussex, PO22 9SA, England

Routledge, Chapman & Hall Inc
29 West 35th Street
New York, NY 10001, USA

The Canterbury Press Pty Ltd
Unit 2, 71 Rushdale Street
Scoresby, Victoria 3179, Australia

© Eyal Ben-Ari 1991

The publishers gratefully acknowledge the assistance of the Japan Foundation
in the publication of this volume.

Phototypeset in Times 10/12pt.
by Intype, London

Printed in Great Britain by T. J. Press Ltd, Padstow, Cornwall

British Library Cataloguing in Publication Data
Ben-Ari, E. (Eyal), *1953–*
    Changing Japanese suburbia. – (Japanese studies).
    1. Japan. Suburbs. Social aspects
    I. Title   II. Series
    307.7′4′0952

    ISBN 0–7103–0381–5

Library of Congress Cataloging-in-Publication Data
Ben-Ari, Eyal, 1953–
    Changing Japanese suburbia: a study of two present-day localities
/ Eyal Ben-Ari.
        p.   cm. — (Japanese studies)
    Includes bibliographical references and index.
    ISBN 0–7103–0381–5
    1. Suburbs—Japan—Case studies.   2. Community organization—
Japan—Case studies.   3. Suburban life—Japan—Case studies.
    4. Neighborhood—Japan—Case studies. I. Title. II. Series.
    HT352.J346   1991
    307.74′0952—dc20   90–43778
                                                                   CIP

Contents

Illustrations

Tables

Figures

Maps

Preface

This book, based on fieldwork carried out in Japan between 1981 and 1983, is a study of two residential communities in the context of Japan's post-war urban and social developments. Rather than attempting a comprehensive ethnographic account of the two communities studied, it represents an effort to examine some questions bearing upon the changing qualities and dynamics of such localities. These questions, which arose while doing my fieldwork and analysing the data, sprang from the contrast I could not help but note between the dominant social scientific approaches to Japanese society which had shaped my view of the plight of post-war villages and neighbourhoods and what I was actually experiencing in the communities I was studying. The accepted views tend to lay the blame for the breakdown or dissolution of local communities on the macro forces of urbanization and modernization or on the transfer of community orientations and modes of organization to the workplace. What I saw, however, were two communities marked not only by thriving local activity but also by a high capacity to undertake joint ventures. I was thus faced with a need somehow to explain the discrepancy between the rather bleak portrayal in the literature and the more favourable circumstances I had encountered. A few words about the two communities, and about my initial attempts to account for their peculiarities, may contribute to an understanding of how this explanation – or rather the questions leading to it – were formulated.

Yamanaka, a commuter village, and Hieidaira, a new suburban housing estate, are set against the picturesque Hieizan mountain chain to the east of Kyoto's northern suburbs (see Maps 1 and 2). Together they comprise an independent administrative district (*gakku*) within the city of Otsu in Shiga Prefecture.[1] Yamanaka, which has a population of 230 people, appears to be nestled into

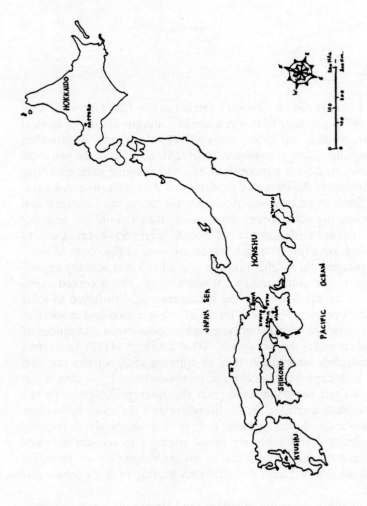

Map 1 Japan: major islands and cities

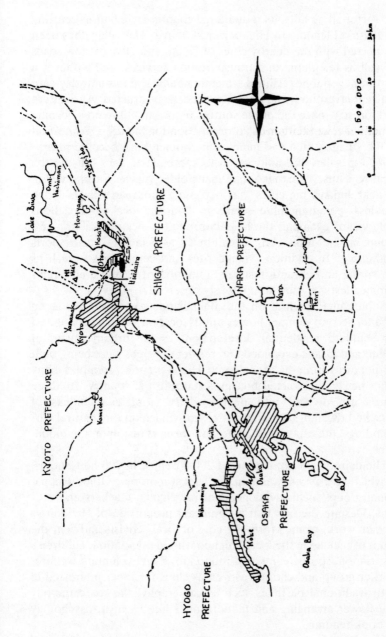

Map 2   Kansai: major prefectures and cities

the surrounding hills, its rather large country-style houses centring on the road leading to Hieidaira just above. The village has been connected with the nearby cities of Kyoto and Otsu by new roads as well as telephone and transportation services, and within it a host of new public facilities – meeting halls, gymnasium, day-care centre, playground, and pool – have been constructed. Agriculture and forestry, once the prime sources of income, have now become either a weekend affair or an occupation for the aged. Almost all of the village's men and many of its women have become *sararii-man*, i.e. salaried employees who commute to jobs outside the locality. Thus, Yamanaka, like many older villages located within or near Japan's big cities, has become a suburban village. None the less, communal life seems to flourish; local organizations include, for example, the neighbourhood association, a women's group, an old-folks club, a children's association, and a sports committee. In addition, village rites and ceremonies – such as the spring and autumn festivals, initiation rites, and a children's summer festival – are scrupulously observed.

Suburban Hieidaira, on the other hand, was developed as an area for second summer homes but its location made it economical for standard residential development as the urban centres of Kyoto and Osaka expanded and residential areas were being built further away from the urban cores. Hieidaira now resembles many other newly constructed housing estates in the country. Its three wards are divided into neat, orderly rectangular blocks of detached dwellings. In contrast to the village and its natural surroundings, the estate appears to have been thrust upon the mountains.

Hieidaira has a population of 2,400 people in 700 households, of which *sarariiman* make up the largest minority. Other occupational groups include independent merchants, teachers and artisans. Despite the fact that a significant proportion of Hieidaira's women work, women form the core of local activists and bear the brunt of managing the local neighbourhood association, children's association, sports teams, old-folks club, PTA, voluntary welfare-worker group and chorus, as well as clubs for those interested in both traditional pastimes such as calligraphy, the tea ceremony and flower arranging and modern ones like English, psychology or book-reading.

Hieidaira has undergone great change in its short history. Because it was shoddily developed, the citizens found they had to organize and fight for what are considered minimum public facilities in a residential estate. Successful movements for the establishment of educational facilities – school, kindergarten, day-care centre – were followed by pressure on the developer and on the Otsu city government to provide new roads, a new water system, community and meeting halls, a fire brigade and a bus system.

Hieidaira and Yamanaka only became an independent administrative unit in 1977, upon construction of a school that serves them both. Until then they had belonged to a unit encompassing other communities some four kilometres away. This amalgamation demanded a new need for co-operation and unity not only in local organizations but also vis-à-vis local government. Thus, for example, the two communities have set up a joint neighbourhood association which presents demands to and receives budgetary supplements from city officials as an autonomous administrative entity; they participate in united welfare organizations to support the elderly of the district, and in such combined activities like bazaars, summer camps or sports days – all of which slowly engender a new sense of sharing in a common fate and new joint customs.

This is not to say that becoming an independent administrative district has not posed problems; for the political interests and social circumstances of the two communities are dissimilar. The prime need in Hieidaira – as in many newly built suburban estates – has been a viable infrastructure (water, roads, transportation) and public facilities. And, like other urban and suburban localities marked by partial involvement and limited commitment to community affairs, it takes much time and effort to mobilize Hieidaira's populace. The prime concern in Yamanaka, however, has been to find the delicate balance between 'opening-up' and continuing as a separate social and cultural entity. The villagers point to their relative solidarity, intimacy and potential for concerted action vis-à-vis the 'anonymous' suburban estate, and voice their fears of being swallowed up by the larger locality.

It was while doing fieldwork in Hieidaira and Yamanaka that I began to be bothered by the discrepancy mentioned above: academic portrayals – and my own personal expectations – to the contrary, these two localities did seem to evince a continuing potential for some kind of community 'involvement'. The reason for this, as I discovered, is that the citizens of both communities have involved themselves in a host of matters which bear directly upon their central concerns: the struggle for the necessary environmental and public facilities, the establishment of new organizational arrangements for providing aid and assistance to the elderly or generating local solidarity and a sense of belonging to the territorial unit. The residents of Hieidaira and Yamanaka did, of course, have to overcome a variety of difficulties in order to achieve both their instrumental ends and less tangible notions and affects. This meant that they had to recruit local activists, set up channels of communications, define joint goals and engage government officials. Yet, especially during analysis of my data, I became aware that these difficulties pointed less to the inherent weakness of these two localities than to their changing forms of communal activities, and the complexity and scale of the environment within which they are embedded.

It is out of this background that I gradually began to formulate the three sets of questions which have guided my analysis. The first set has to do with the nature of the embeddedness of local communities within wider urban and administrative systems: how the growing dependence of localities on external agencies and structures is related to their continued capacity for independent actions and activities; the place of local voluntary organizations in managing the collective response to and negotiations and relations with these external agencies and structures. The second set of questions is related to the changing internal qualities and processes of local communities: how the 'artificiality' – in terms of a lack of prior natural social networks – of neighbourhoods such as Hieidaira or the amalgamated Hieidaira–Yamanaka district shapes the emergence of a community consciousness and a definition of collective goals; how does an aggregate of strangers – each with prior commitments and ties and orientations external to the locality – turn into a collective unit based on the mobilization of community-wide resources. The third set of questions involves the place of cultural models of group and community organization: how the historical Japanese models of local associations and group formation guide the construction of post-war organizational frameworks for communal activities and action; whether what we are witnessing is new models emerging out of the encounter between older models and the new circumstances of local communities.

With the aim of placing this study within the wider context of social science work on Japan, I therefore interrupted my writing to carry out a rereading of many such studies. This was when another consideration – related to the whole literature on the Japanese company or enterprise – began to take shape. For what I found was that often implicit in this literature are questions regarding 'what happens at home'. These questions entail not only a set of (important) descriptive questions about what men do after work and how the large groups of housewives, children and the elderly, who spend most of their time in the locality, occupy themselves. These involve further inquiries into the company––local community contrast as one between two kinds of organizing social frameworks, i.e. two interrelated models of social organizations. From this vantage point the book can be read in two complementary ways: as an ethnographic complement to the excellent corpus of studies on the 'company', or as an in-depth, but theoretically informed, examination of the qualities and dynamics of Japan's modern communities.

A Note on Language Conventions

All Japanese words are romanized according to the modified Hepburn system. Long vowels, however, are rendered as a double letter rather than with a superscript bar.

People's names are given in the Japanese order with the personal name following the patronym. Names of prefectures, cities, and references have been rendered without long vowels.

Acknowledgments

The origins of this volume lie in a Ph.D. thesis which I submitted to the Department of Social Anthropology at the University of Cambridge. The book, however, represents a revision of the thesis, a significant expansion of many points only alluded to in the dissertation, and an addition of five new chapters.

In essence this is a study of two communities in Japan. My deepest thanks go to the people of these communities: Hieidaira and Yamanaka. They accepted me into their homes, and shared with me their lives and experiences. I am also very grateful to a large number of teachers at local educational facilities and to officials from the Otsu City Office who gave me of their time.

While in Japan I was supported by the Otsuki Peace Fellowship of the Japan Christian Friends of Israel. The help and kindness of the Friends extended well beyond financial support.

The two years of research in Cambridge were supported by the Lady Davis Foundation and by the British Friends of the Hebrew University through the following: Michael and Anna Wix Fellowship Trust, Anglo Jewish Association, the Humanitarian Trust, Harper-Wolfson Fund, and Sherman Fund. Grants for fieldwork expenses were gratefully received from the Audrey Richards and the William Wyse Funds of the Department of Anthropology and from St John's College of the University of Cambridge.

In Jerusalem I have been supported by the Harry S. Truman Institute and by the Koret Foundation. The people at the Truman Institute – directors and staff – have extended numerous kinds of assistance as well as creating a very pleasant atmosphere for work.

For comments, advice and discussions on various parts of the book I would like to thank Victor Azarya, Marcus Banks, Erik Cohen, Don Handelman, Ehud Harari, Shlomo Hasson, Haim Hazan, Joy Hendry, Reuven Kahane, David Lewis, Gilbert Lewis, Robert J. Smith and Rachel Wasserfall. At Osaka University, Kurumi Sugita and Hirosato Kimizuka gave me much academic and personal support and helped me tackle the university bureaucracy. Special thanks go to D. Hassett and M. Winter, who painstakingly went over the volume, provided a wealth of comments, and valiantly tried to curb my zeal for sociological abstractions and American jargon.

In England my supervisor, Esther Goody, provided much needed support and important advice while I was in the field and when I was in Cambridge. In Israel six former teachers (now colleagues) have given me their time and encouragement for over a decade: Victor Azarya, Erik Cohen, Harvey Goldberg, Don Handelman, Reuven Kahame and Ehud Harari. In the hectic and sometimes contentious academic world this is far from a taken-for-granted matter.

Eran and Ehud in moving across the three cultures – Israeli, Japanese and English – with such ease helped me keep a decent perspective on things. Edna, *be'ahavah bishvilekh*.

Part One
INTRODUCTION

1 Introduction: Approaches and Problems

Interpretations of modern Japanese communities

Most analyses of Japan's modern residential communities contend with a set of basic questions about these localities' potential for community 'involvement'. This potential is explored in areas such as political action, the provision of mutual aid and assistance or the creation of local identity and solidarity. These studies also tend to draw their theoretical premises and analytical orientations from one of two main interpretive models, both of which stress the inevitable weakening and dissolution of local communities. According to one such rendition, which is theoretically akin to the 'breakdown of community' approach that appeared in the United States a few decades ago, the breakdown of traditional localities results from the few major macro-social trends that appear whenever a society modernizes. Another account emphasizes the cultural continuity, social integration and 'groupishness' of traditional localities, but in non-territorial social units. In this 'transfer of community' approach the weakening of local communities is said to result from the transfer of a community's peculiar characteristics to such social collectivities as the Japanese 'company' rather than from the negative effects of modernization directly.

Both approaches provide good general analyses of the basic changes undergone by modern Japanese communities. They place a sound stress on the comprehension of local developments within wider social and historical trends, and introduce a comparative emphasis by exploring different types of localities (rural, urban, suburban). Yet, when the arguments used in these approaches are examined, the theoretical shortcomings of conceptualizing modern Japanese communities as inevitably breaking down become clear.

3

The breakdown of community approach

While the 'transfer of community' approach is probably more popular among Western academics, most social critics and scholars in Japan have situated their understanding of today's communities within the scheme of 'loss' or 'breakdown' of community (Irokawa, 1978: 253; Allinson, 1978:458). Fukutake, one of the most influential and sophisticated of these scholars, provides a good introduction to this approach (1982:131). He links his assertions to the changes Japan has undergone in the post-war phase of modernization:

Rapid industrialization, accelerated change in agriculture, and the continuation of urbanization could not fail to bring great changes to the local communities of villages and urban wards – changes of such magnitude as to make understandable that one should hear talk of neighborhood societies having 'form, but no content', or of 'community disintegration' or 'community dissolution'.

Fukutake's analysis sounds uncannily like Stein's (1960) treatment of the 'eclipse' of modern American localities, which he saw as the outcome of urbanization, industrialization and bureaucratization. In essence, both depict a unilinear and inevitable transition from *Gemeinschaft* to *Gesellschaft*; one that takes place in all local communities found in societies that modernize successfully. Thus, the pre-war *Gemeinschaft*-like community Fukutake portrays is the Japanese version of what was long ago termed the 'natural community' (Suttles, 1972:8ff.). While he admits that such communities – the *Kyoodootai*[1] – differed in their rural and urban guises, Fukutake nevertheless claims (with a large measure of accuracy) that these 'natural entities' shared a number of important features that were seriously weakened by the impact of modernization.

The rural village, 'the mold in which the modern Japanese were formed' (Fukutake, 1982:105), was marked by strong sentiments of mutual obligation and loyalty based on agricultural co-operation and reciprocal assistance, as well as by self-sufficiency in production and consumption. They were given wide leeway in local autonomy and self-government, and they were characterized by a unitary nature symbolized in the village shrine and rituals, the continuous identification with and awareness of belonging to the village as a territorial unit, and the pervasiveness of hierarchical structures based on land ownership, the renting of land and exchange of wage labour.

While urban neighbourhoods were not marked by the same community character as rural villages, they were nevertheless quite well integrated and tightly patterned. The Tokugawa-era (1600–1868) traditions of residents selecting ward officials, sharing communal work for the upkeep of roads and shrines, and deciding about local affairs in ward meetings continued. Moreover, the formal organizations set up in these neighbourhoods tended to resemble rural hamlets in many respects: their membership comprised households rather than individuals and affiliation was automatic or semi-automatic; their functions spread over a wide range of activities; and they organized festivals and maintained shrines in ways reminiscent of such practices in villages. All in all, cities tended to have more of a village than an urban character. Thus, Fukutake concludes (1982:34):

> It often used to be said that even the great city of Tokyo was one great village, and exaggeration though that might be . . . it nevertheless has a measure of truth. The microsocial character of prewar Japan, in both rural and urban areas, really was a structure of village and neighborhood units of such a tightly solidary character that talk of 'one great village' does not seem entirely out of keeping.

While the closed, solidary properties of 'natural communities' began to break down in the pre-war period, it was only after the war that their final demise became imminent. The central agents of change were economic and political: the expansion of industrial development which brought factories and housing estates out to the country; the creation of new political and administrative units dominated by big cities but encompassing older localities; the widening of transportation and communications networks which effectively enlarged the average citizen's life-sphere; the growing occupational heterogeneity of local populations – resident commuters in villages and new categories of white- and blue-collar workers in urban neighbourhoods; and extensive geographical and social mobility.[2]

Fukutake provides two examples of community types that have

been hit hardest by these trends. Interestingly, not unlike the two localities I studied, they are the commuter village and the housing estate. The effects on villages incorporated into expanding residential or industrial regions, and within which people turn more and more to non-farm occupations, were devastating. Hamlet organizations were reduced to little more than the lowest rung of government agencies, while local women's groups and youth associations barely survived. Religious practices, activities and funeral organizations declined, and communal rituals and gatherings weakened. Finally, co-operative ventures began to take on an inter- rather than intra-village character. In short, the picture Fukutake paints is one of the dissolution of the closely constrained co-operative character of rural villages.

In the towns and cities where these traits were weaker to begin with, the decline of local communities went further. Here the representative cases are large housing estates with no community tradition, which were often developed adjacent to or surrounding older, usually rural settlements. The residents of these new estates are no longer subject to the control of traditional leaders of urban neighbourhoods, who were mostly small businessmen and craftsmen who dominated the localities' affairs and associations. Although local organizations in these new areas act as collective representatives of the residents when struggling for environmental improvements, Fukutake dismisses them as acting out of self-interest rather than out of a concept of community or collective welfare. What has emerged here, he says, are settlements with little community sentiment or constraints, and an individualistic and egoistic local population that is not willing to join in co-operative activities.

The transfer of community approach

The 'transfer of community' approach is directly related to the 'group' or 'consensus' model of Japanese society. Throughout the post-war period this model has provided the central theoretical orientations for much of the social anthropological and sociological literature on Japan. Its clearest and most concise explication, found in Chie Nakane's *Japanese Society*, conceptualizes the model in social structural terms,[3] akin to the classic British social-anthropological tradition. According to Moeran (1985:107–8), the model:

assumes that people prefer to act within the framework of a group and that such a group will be hierarchically organized and run by a paternalistic leader. . . . The emphasis . . . is on harmony, and behaviour tends to be ritualized and formal in order to reduce or eliminate conflict or embarrassment. Ideally, in this kind of situation people are supposed to subordinate individual interests to group goals and to remain loyal to group causes. In return for their loyalty and devotion, the leader of the group treats his followers with benevolence and magnanimity [emphasis in original].

A number of further elements closely related to these peculiarities are an emphasis on the distinctiveness and exclusivity of the group (Smith, 1983:94), and a high degree of identity with, commitment to and acceptance of the group's authority.

As Nakane sees it, the pre-modern village – along with the 'historical' household (the *ie*) – is the prime example of how this group model works. For it was in this framework that the social structural principles – and the orientations, expectations and modes of interaction guided by these principles – found their clearest expression. She posits that the onset of industrialization and the concomitant mobility of people from such villages into urban areas brought little or no weakening of these organizing principles. Instead there ensued a process of transferral in which these principles were transplanted to the workplace. In other words, the separation of work from residence caused the community 'group' to translocate from the residential locality to the workplace. While her most important example is the company, it seems safe to assume that Nakane's model is also meant to apply to commercial firms, manufacturing plants, public bureaucracies or educational institutions.

In contrast to Fukutake, Nakane does not find that local residential communities are directly affected by the macro-trends of urbanization, industrialization and changes in agriculture. Instead, she views the dynamics and nature of such localities as a residue of the transfer of 'group' principles to the company. Nakane seems to view residential communities as lacking horizontal ties of sociability and mutual help, and as a place where friendships are partial and shallow because of the men's external orientations. She also views those who live in them as lacking the willingness and commitment to contribute money or time to the locality, and cannot see any real basis for the establishment of voluntary organizations due to weak identification with the area and the almost complete absence of prior social networks. Put somewhat strongly, Nakane thus views the residential community and the Japanese company as inverted images.

It is interesting that the only kind of residential community in which Nakane finds the principles and orientations of the group still operative is the company housing estate. For it is in these localities – where home and work coalesce – that one finds an urban territorial unit marked by closeness, solidarity, identification and a high degree of group consciousness. As Nakane talks not so much talk of the loss or breakdown of community as of its creation elsewhere – i.e. in non-territorial frameworks – she finds local communities in or near the big cities personally inconsequential and theoretically irrelevant.

Appraisal

There is no doubt that both of the above schemes have much academic and popular appeal. The appeal of Fukutake's model lies as much in its critique of a society in which the effects of industrialization and urbanization have gone unchecked as for its quest for the warmth and intimacy of the traditional community.[4] What captivates in Nakane's approach is its reassuring stress on the cultural continuity that underlies apparent ruptures and its self-congratulatory note on Japan's successful adaptation to its modern circumstances.

But the reality of modern Japanese communities is much too complex to be subsumed under the elegant but all-too-neat dichotomies of *Gemeinschaft* and *Gesellschaft*, or territorial and non-territorial social units. This is not to deny both scholars' important insistence on understanding modern localities in their historical and macro-sociological contexts or their underscoring of the major ways in which change has occurred. For there is no doubt that Japanese communities of the 1970s and 1980s are 'weaker' – i.e. less integrated, less capable of collective action – than the communities of the pre- and immediate post-war periods.

What is suggested, however, is a need to move beyond these approaches. This implies examining some of the premises underlying such interpretations, for example their suggestions regarding the passivity of local communities in the face of external encroachments; bringing out some of the wider theoretical concepts utilized by these schemes in order to discuss such issues as the relationships between groups and individuals or the relative importance given to conflict or integration; and 'teasing out' the new modes and potentials for co-operation and collective action that have emerged rather than situating the exploration of modern communities in the context of their decline. In other words, there is a need for a subtle theoretical shift in emphasis: from a stress on the breakdown of older forms to the development of new ones; not just the new forms of the Japanese company but also those of the local community. Finally, a greater degree of analytical precision must be introduced into Fukutake and Nakane's perceptive analysis of the experiences of different localities, i.e. it is important to spell out the dimensions along which they vary and change.

The emergence of 'communities of limited liability'

There are a number of insights which point to the ways in which modern Japanese localities are changing. First, it should be recognized that preoccupation with local affairs now varies according to the relevance of different issues to different segments of the local population: in other words, participation in local affairs has become selective. In the early 1960s Johnson (1963:223) showed how involvement with the rural hamlet had begun to be carried not by the community as a whole but by certain groups, especially women and children. Writing about a white-collar residential suburb of Tokyo, Vogel (1963: chap. VI) describes the tendency towards separate involvement on the part of men on the one hand and women and children on the other: the man in his 'company gang' and the two other groups in local affairs.[5] This last point highlights how, rather than having disappeared, participation in local affairs has become more specialized: i.e. it has come to depend more and more on a locale's ability to serve the interests of specific community groups.

The second element, often hinted at in research on the Japanese 'company' (Clark, 1979:196ff.; Rohlen, 1974), is made most explicit by Nakane (1973:63), who shows that because at least part of the traditional community's sentiments and loyalties have been transferred to workplace, commitment to the modern residential community has lessened. Thus, for example, Kiefer (1976a:287) notes that men in a white-collar housing estate have not become community-minded due to the 'quasi-kinship ethos' of Japanese organizations, in which 'the work environment makes heavier demands on the employee's time and loyalty than are made on his American counterpart.' Yet, by adding that one does find greater community involvement on the part of men in, for example, blue-collar estates, Kiefer underlines the fact that this element is a variable.[6] The essential point here is that while the high level of engagement with and obligations towards 'the company' and workmates makes for a much more circumscribed concern with their residential communities, the concern is not totally absent.

The third changing facet of local Japanese communities is their increasing dependence on external government agencies. In part, this trend is a reflection of the amalgamation of smaller areal units – hamlets, urban neighbourhoods – into bigger political and administrative districts. But it also reflects greater complexity and scale. For, since World War II the management and provision of services supplied to localities have had to become 'collective' and 'big' because of the nature and scale of these services. The steady appropriation of the supply of local services by large and complex organizations has led almost all aspects of local communities today to become not only embedded within, but also increasingly integrated into wider urban and state systems, for example, schools, public utilities, local authorities, the welfare bureaucracy, commercial firms, or transportation and communications enterprises.

This increased dependency on external agencies and organizations does not, however, imply their total passivity or submissiveness. Indeed, anthropologists have long been aware of the fourth element: an increase in the local community's capacity to react and consciously adapt to changing external circumstances. Bedford (1980) and Omori (1976) provide evidence of this reactive capacity in relation to the economic activities undertaken by rural hamlets, while Yoshida (1964) documents the ruralities' efforts to combat tendencies towards community disorganization. Krauss and Simcock (1980:196) note that suburban estates were the locus of organized protest against the lack of environmental amenities and facilities. Thus, political activity in present-day localities evinces a rather high degree of self-conscious purposefulness aimed at responding to forces beyond the community. This is not to deny the adaptive capacity of the traditional *buraku* (village), but rather to stress that today this capacity has a much more conscious and intentional character.

In many senses then, modern Japanese communities situated in or near big cities and towns are not very different from similar localities in other advanced industrial societies (Greer, 1972: chap. 7; Abrams *et al.*, 1981). For, like these other localities, they have become 'communities of limited liability' (Janowitz, 1967; Hunter, 1978), i.e. more specialized, dependent and volitional. Underlying this conceptualization is the view that an individual's attachment to and relationship with the local community is based on two interrelated elements: their social investment in the territory (through childrearing and home-ownership), and their ability to work towards the solution to their problems through organized action. Limited liability does not mean limited capacity; rather it implies limited participation in two closely related senses: (1) only some individuals or households – the 'invested' – are communally and socially active, and (2) when a community does not meet these peoples' (economic, social *and* emotional) investments with suitable rewards, they may withdraw either physically or emotionally. Individuals, then, 'associate with neighbors and belong to localized voluntary associations because their mutual investments bring them into contact, or they perceive common interests which require their collective organization to protect the turf' (Guest, 1984:9).

Local organizations and community potential

The nature of 'communities of limited liability' is perhaps most clearly understood through an examination of what has come to 'constitute' the community, local voluntary organizations – for example, tenant unions, residents' committees, ward or neighbourhood associations or special-purpose groups. Norbeck (1977; 1967; 1962) has most clearly and consistently documented the growing importance of what he terms common-interest associations in Japan. Although such organizations have a long history there,[7] their most significant growth has come with modernization and the decline in the scope and functions of kinship and local hierarchical structures that this has entailed. Put in rather abstract terms, the role of voluntary groups in the modern Japanese context could be understood as follows: collective co-operation and action in the traditional community were based on kinship, joint residence and common sentiments, as well as on the total commitment of all members. In modern localities such activity is dependent on an orientation to limited, usually instrumental goals, and on the involvement of only part of the local population. Thus the role of voluntary organizations in the internal community processes and the ways in which a diverse array of locals are recruited into concerted action is central. In other words, because the resources (time, money, status, involvement, expertise, leadership) necessary for engaging in external relations or conflict must be organized for collective purposes, and because these resources are distributed differentially among the local population, local groups can generally best effect community-wide efforts at mobilization and communication.

Another aspect of these organizations that should be stressed is their role in managing the 'community of limited liability's' external relations. For it is primarily these organizations who initiate the collective response to, and manage the negotiations and relations with the community's external 'advocates and adversaries' (Suttles, 1972), e.g. government agencies and bureaucracies, public utilities, private companies, the media, elected officials, and other communities. This function seems especially important because all public services and facilities are only available to individuals on the basis of residence in a geographically delimited area, and because the scale of most such services means that they can only be undertaken by 'big government' or 'big business'.

Turning back to a wider perspective, it seems that there is a rather general convergence between advanced industrialized societies in regard to the development of voluntary organizations. These similarities should not, however, be overstressed. For, while there is a broad likeness between the Japanese and other pathways to modernity, in several crucial respects the Japanese experience is a peculiar outcome of its own cultural and historical contexts. First, there is the tendency for Japanese associations and organizations to be spatially or territorially based. Relating this to the historico-cultural definition of 'village consciousness' that has developed in Japan, Fukutake (1982:34) contrasts Japan's territorial relation with the socio-relational definition found in India and China. Other scholars have observed that, in contrast to Africa where voluntary organizations have tended to be based on ethnic affiliation, and to the prevalence of class- or church-based associations in America and Western Europe, Japanese common-interest organizations are closely associated with territorial units (Norbeck, 1962:81–2; Taira, 1978:141).[8]

The second attribute that seems to be typical of many Japanese local organizations is their strong connection with various levels of government and public administration. Some local associations – e.g. traffic safety committees and voluntary welfare workers – were established by governmental agencies. Others – like old-folks clubs – were established in the wake of strong encouragement by the national bureaucracies. Still others – like women's groups and children's associations – are sub-divisions of wider (usually city or prefectural) organizations.[9]

Third, is the persistence of these local organizations. In contrast to the American experience (Suttles, 1972:102–3), where local groups tend to be rather ephemeral, Japanese associations seem much more durable. This is not to assert that Japanese organizations do not change or wane; the longitudinal studies of Norbeck (1977) and Smith (1978) document the decline of certain local associations during the post-war period. It is, however, to emphasize that while the organizational life-spans of many American movements can be measured in years, in Japan they are often measured in decades.

The existence of a host of territorially based organizations and associations with close links to the state raises questions about the quality of such locally organized groups that lead to further questions about the very nature of modern Japanese communities. Thus, scholars from within the 'breakdown of community' approach (Matsushita, 1978:179), have focused on the issue of local autonomy, asking whether close links with the state and its extensions by community organizations does not imply an openness to manipulation; i.e. whether it implies the lack of any real potential for local initiative, or the absence of conditions conducive to the development of a critically aware citizenship. In a related vein, others (Taira, 1978:150; Takabatake, 1978:192), concentrating on the issue of organizational design and dependency, ask whether local organizations have not become little more than administrative subcontractors for government, whether they have not become administrative extensions for effectuating state programmes 'on the cheap'. At heart, then, these are questions about the place of 'community' in the context of giant bureaucracies, about the modes of control and dependency that have developed, about the potential for independent and co-operative action on behalf of the area within which people live and about the capacity of modern localities to develop territorial identity and solidarity. These questions seem especially relevant in relation to suburban residential communities like the ones which form the focus of this book.

Suburban residential communities

While a few Japanese suburbs were developed during the first decades of this century (Kamachi, 1971), it was only after the war that they began to achieve considerable importance. National patterns of population migration and settlement were a prime factor in their expansion; growth of jobs and the opportunity to earn higher incomes that accompanied Japan's reindustrialization from the mid-1950s produced rapid increases in migration into the major metropolitan areas. A 'layering' or 'doughnut effect' (Glickman, 1979:19ff.; Ito *et al.*, 1979:265–6) began to take place a decade later, as the general trend towards metropolitan growth continued. This meant that the cores of the major cities began to lose population and the outer sub-regions and suburbs began to grow in expanding circles. According to one estimate (Allinson, 1979:5) these suburbs today encompass at least a third of Japan's total population.

The importance of Japan's post-war suburbs goes beyond their mere quantitative expansion, for the major transformation undergone by the country's occupational structure finds expression in these regions. From a society dominated by independent producers, Japan has become one dominated by employees, above all by employees in the tertiary sector.[10] The most significant spatial expression of this trend has, of course, been in the major metropolitan areas where the new corps of *sarariiman*, Japan's

14

version of the 'organization man', have settled in the suburbs (Takeuchi, 1982:10–12; Allinson, 1979:6).

Although Japanese suburbs are far from homogeneous or uniform in terms of settlement types, two kinds of residential areas are seen as important in understanding the post-war developments of local communities: (1) older rural villages or hamlets – much like Yamanaka – which are situated near urban centres, have been amalgamated into new administrative units since the 1950s, and most of whose local inhabitants have left agricultural pursuits for some kind of wage employment outside (e.g. Omori, 1976; Norbeck, 1977); (2) new housing estates (*danchi*) of either individual houses – like Hieidaira – or apartment blocks that have been developed by private or public companies, whose populace mostly is made up of white-collar workers who commute to their places of work (e.g. Keifer, 1976a and 1976b; Ames, 1981:52–4).

The questions raised above about the nature of modern Japanese communities seem especially pertinent for these two types of suburban settlements. This is because built into the very 'situation' of Japanese residential suburbia are a number of attributes which – at least at first sight – would seem potential mitigaters against the development of local autonomy as well as strengtheners of the community groups' dependence on external entities. Although these attributes are common to residential suburbs throughout the advanced industrial world, their peculiar manifestation in Japan seems to intensify a number of tendencies.

As Frankenberg (1965:198) noted, problems of separation between work and home are more likely to arise in such suburban communities. Thus, one would expect serious obstacles to the emergence of any collective effort among local populations where most of the men have strong orientations towards external entities, which would only be heightened by the purported Japanese propensity for cultivating a 'company community' (Vogel, 1979:6). Thus in Japan the obstacles are not limited to practicalities such as finding time to devote to neighbourhood affairs, but also involve the emotional and symbolic involvement with an alternative to the locality.

Further, the 'artificial' or 'contrived' character of such suburban communities would lead one to expect that their creation by external entities – government, public or private – would render them open to manipulation from the outside, and that the 'natural'

15

social networks so crucial to co-operative activity and the creation of local identity would also be absent.

Finally, there is the heterogeneity of the suburban communities. In contrast to the class homogeneity of such settlements in America (Fischer, 1976:211), a number of scholars have remarked on the social diversity of Japanese suburbia (Smith, 1979:95; Allinson, 1979; Krauss and Simcock, 1980:209). Thus, while such communities in Japan are very broadly 'middle-class', this label masks a vast array of occupations, including small-scale entrepreneurs, grey-collar workers (bus drivers and waitresses, for example) and the new blue- and white-collar workers of large organizations. Given the importance of shared characteristics as a basis for neighbourhood co-operation and participation in the United States (Gans, 1972:52–3), one would therefore anticipate problems in Japanese suburbs. That is, one would expect difficulties to arise when there is no common base for collective and concerted action.

When linked back to the assertions of the 'breakdown of community' and 'transfer of community' approaches, these attributes seem to raise interrelated questions regarding: the implications of external and internal investments and commitments for the way people or households in the community strike up local relationships, utilize situational strategies or create and manipulate identities; the mechanisms by which a locality is transformed from an aggregate of individual strangers into a more-or-less organized collectivity with a potential for 'self-consciousness' and concerted action; the place of historico-cultural models – e.g. of community associations or urban movements – in providing guiding images or exemplars for modern local organizations; and, finally, whether new types of group orientedness or varying modes of group formation – of which 'company' and 'community' are two examples – are now emerging in Japan.

On reading the book

The main part of this work, comprising four case studies, is presented after a short ethnographic profile of Hieidaira and Yamanaka. The first study deals primarily with 'community action' in Hieidaira vis-à-vis the development of the suburban housing estate. In it I trace out the processes by which the citizens discovered the shoddy nature of the development, their organization into local political movements, the petitioning of the developer as well as city and prefectural authorities, and local movements' success in securing the required environmental and urban facilities. The focus is on local organizations – especially neighbourhood associations – their formation and activities.

The theoretical centre of attention in this study is on community action in suburban communities of limited liability. This involves an examination of the independent capacity of local communities to react to the external political and economic forces impinging on them – i.e. to their determining, limit-setting environment. This, in turn, involves an analytical focus on both external and internal dimensions. The 'external' processes by which the estate emerged as a 'polity' is related to the wider struggle for urban and environmental facilities through an analysis of the efforts that local organizations used to enter the city's political arena, gain recognition, set an agenda and forge links with other political actors. This entails exploring the effects of citizens' movements on the local political scene: their legitimization of new modes of political participation, their alteration of public debate and their influence on local government officials. 'Internally', I explore the creation and maintenance of communication and mobilization networks among the local residents by tracing out the organizational skills that the new groups of white-collar and professional workers brought to the struggle and by a more 'cultural' or 'symbolic' analysis of the way critical issues as well as models of organizational participation were perceived and then acted upon by the locals.

The next two case studies are devoted chiefly to community care in the two localities. The cases presented involve two types of local welfare organizations: voluntary welfare workers and old-folks clubs. Here the discussion follows the rise of the aged as a social problem, the unfolding of 'community care' as explicit government policy, the kinds of aid and assistance provided by the two local organizations and their ties to the city government and informal networks of the communities.

At the heart of the discussion here is an exploration of the way in which the dependence of older people is 'managed' by a mix of public and private entities. The increasing dependence by formal agencies on community resources is related to the important awareness that local groups such as old-folks clubs and voluntary welfare workers are characterized by an interstitial existence, i.e. that these community oganizations stand between the more bureaucratized welfare provided by statutory agencies and the more informal community networks of kin, friends and neighbours. My examination of how these organizations are operated and activated takes into account their diverse links of co-operation, support and control with both the formal and informal spheres.

The final study which is devoted to the potential for community identity and solidarity is based on an exploration of how this potential is created at the annual sports field-day in which residents of both Yamanaka and Hieidaira participate. The case study outlines the organization of the sports committee, preparations for the field-day, recruitment of organizers and participants, the competitions and activities involved on the day itself and the meeting held to review and conclude its success.

Here the analytical focus is on the communal mechanisms for creating local solidarity and identity against a background of the problems involved in generating such sentiments in artificially created territorial units like the Hieidaira–Yamanaka school district. By examining the sports field-day in terms of its relation to and 'borrowings' from traditional village rituals and more modern drinking 'occasions', I show how the special characteristics of these mechanisms facilitate the inculcation of solidarity and identity, and potentiate the coming together of the locals. Finally, there is a note on the implication of this case study for individual–group ties in Japan.

A concluding chapter gives the theoretical and comparative implications of the book as a whole in greater detail and relates the analysis to the growing controversy in Japanese studies about the utility and limitations of the dominant 'group' model of Japanese society.

Part Two
ETHNOGRAPHY

2 The Two Communities: An Ethnographic Profile

This chapter aims to provide a detailed introduction to the two communities. For reasons of space, I restrict myself to a number of segments which illuminate rather than explore in depth the main ethnographic points.

Hieidaira (lit. 'the plain of Hiei') and Yamanaka (lit. 'middle of the mountains') partake of an essential dualism that characterizes many suburban communities. For while they are linked politically and administratively to the city of Otsu (pop. 224,000), it is to the neighbouring giant of Kyoto (pop. 1.5 million) that most of the local residents are oriented.[1] It is to Otsu that they look for the supply of public services (schools, libraries, welfare aid) and the major utilities (water, gas, electricity, telephones). But it is predominantly to Kyoto that they turn for jobs, higher education opportunities, and the provision of daily needs like medical care, shopping and entertainment.

While this basic dualism colours many of their social features, in important respects the two communities offer a contrast. As most local residents would have it, this is a contrast between the old and the new – i.e. between a settlement deeply rooted in its 'rural' history and moulded by long-standing customs and intimacy, and an artificial one characterized by a certain 'urban' impersonality and an individualistic stress on 'doing your own thing'. Such a portrayal, however, does not do full justice to the difference between the two communities. For given that the estate is ten times the size of the village, differences in size and scale seem no less important. An understanding of Hieidaira and Yamanaka, then, involves taking into account all three elements: the suburban dualism, the contrast between the 'old and the new', and the differences of size and scale.

Location and physical appearance

The two settlements are situated in the southern part of the Hiei-zan mountain chain that stretches between Kyoto and Otsu (see Map 2). They are surrounded by dense green forests that are criss-crossed by little streams and hiking paths. Hieidaira lies on a saddle at a height of about 340 to 400 metres, and affords from its eastern side a mangificent view of Lake Biwa and the surrounding mountains. Yamanaka is located a few hundred metres to the west of the estate along a small river leading to Kyoto's northern suburbs.

The physical appearance of Yamanaka is much like that of many mountain villages of the linear type (Shimode, 1968:104), in that the location of the roads as well as the placement of dwellings and public buildings are dictated by topographical features. The main road that runs up to the village along the river is joined at four or five places by paths that themselves stretch along smaller streams (see Map 3). The steep mountains which surround the village and which make it impossible to expand have 'joined' with the rights of property ownership in ensuring that the location of most dwellings has not changed much since the war. It is for much the same reasons that the village's last remaining rice field as well as the small vegetable gardens – tended by the elderly and some housewives – have not changed their location for decades.

The buildings themselves have, however, changed. Reflecting the greater affluence of Yamanakaites, all the thatch-roofed houses of yesteryear have been replaced by modern dwellings of wood with tiled roofs. Interspersed among the residences are a number of public and communal structures. These include: a pre-war factory making cloth; three Buddhist temples which, because no priests live in Yamanaka, are used only on ceremonial occasions; a few storehouses which are rented out by the locals to Kyoto firms; a new playground for young children which has been built where the old day-care centre lay; and a fire station housing a fire engine, fire-fighting equipment and a siren that still sounds the signal for the noon break the farmers used to take. Just off the main road is the local Shinto shrine, where the main communal rites are held, and which is cleaned in turns by all of the village households. Near the exit that leads to the suburban

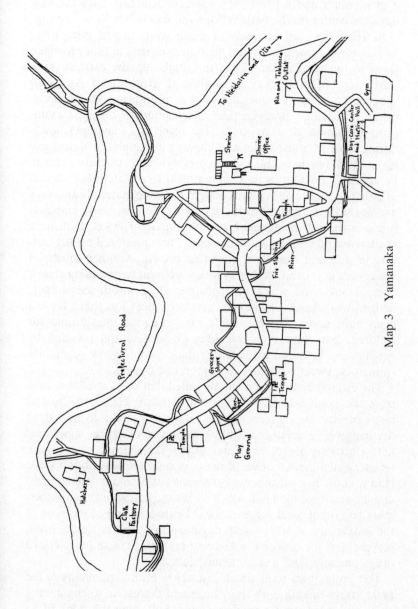

Map 3   Yamanaka

estate lie four public facilities built in the last fifteen years: a pool, a gymnasium and a two-storey concrete structure with the new day-care centre on the bottom floor and meeting halls on the top.

In Hieidaira vast amounts of earth were carved out of the mountains in some places, and filled-in in others, in order to make possible the rectangular blocks that make up the estate's three wards (see Map 4). Yet in contrast to British and American suburbs where most homes are built in a uniform style by developers, Hieidaira's dwellings (like many suburban Japanese examples) are almost all owner-built. The result is a sometimes bewildering array of house styles and building materials. In almost any given block one may find a cheap prefabricated structure that can be assembled within 24 to 48 hours, next to a custom-built house of either Japanese or Western design. Building materials also vary and include concrete, bricks or wood. Yet the most common house is the rather standard structure made of wood, built on a shallow foundation to allow flexibility, and plastered on the outside in different shades of cream or brown. Another source of variety are gates and the fences which are built surrounding almost every house, and which are constructed of wood, metal rails, hedgerows or bricks. Here and there are empty lots that have not been built upon. These provide the occasional playground for children, but more often are sites of horticultural invasion by neighbours. In these 'extended gardens' people grow vegetables (tomatoes, sweet potatoes, cucumbers) or flowers.

The estate's centre – if it can be called that – is a road that runs from the point where the three wards meet. Here are situated maps of Hieidaira which visitors refer to in order to find their destinations,[2] a small fire-fighting station, post office, supermarket, electricity store, *sake* and liquor shop, *sushi* eatery, rice retailer and a branch office of the developer (which still has some land to sell). Just off this road are some coffee shops, restaurants, and the small meeting hall which serves the neighbourhood association and other local organizations. Dotted around other parts of the estate are a school and day-nurseries, sports fields, pool, playgrounds for children, a three-storey guest house for a Tokyo drug company, and a small tennis club.

The prefectural road which just skirts both settlements is the main artery linking both the village and the estate to the nearby cities and major transportation routes. Following the track of an old mountain path, this narrow road winds its tortuous way up

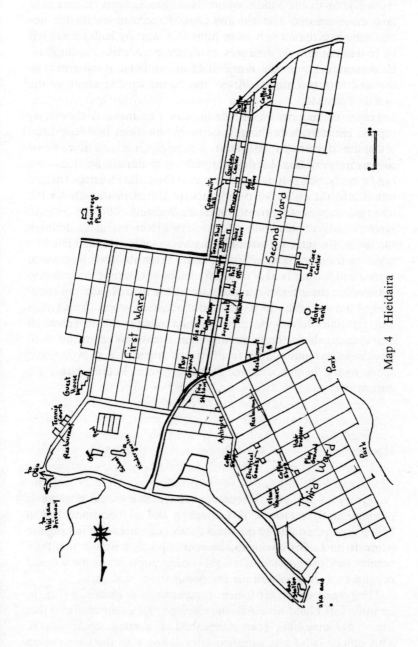

Map 4 Hieidaira

from Kyoto to the saddle where Hieidaira is located, and then goes down again to the lake and Otsu. Paved only in 1960, it has become since then a very busy route. On any given day it is used by tourist coaches on their way to the temple complex of Mt Hiei, by commuters from the north of Otsu, by holiday sojourners to the lake and its leisure facilities, and by the local residents of the two settlements.

Travel in and out of Hieidaira and Yamanaka is mostly by private car, on one of the new improved bus lines that have been inaugurated between Hieidaira and both Otsu and Kyoto,[3] or more rarely by taxi. It is a short 10- or 15-minute bus ride to a big Japan National Railroads station in Otsu. It is a further fifteen minutes to the centre of the city where the main stations for the national as well as private lines are located. The bus ride to Kyoto's outskirts also only takes ten or fifteen minutes, although the trip to the main private railway stations of Keihan and Hankyu takes about three quarters of an hour. From the train stations of Kyoto and Otsu it is easy to reach almost any part of the country.

Other traffic arteries are quite accessible as well. The construction of a new bypass to Kyoto's south-eastern wards (Yamashina and Fushimi) has made these a good deal easier to reach. It has also cut down the travelling time it takes to reach the main Osaka–Tokyo expressway to fifteen minutes by car. Additional roads to the neighbouring prefectures (Nara, Fukui, Aichi) are also nearby.

History

A history of the area where the village and estate now lie is predominantly a history of Yamanaka and its 'location'. For in being situated on one of the main roads (*yamankagoe*) linking the ports on Lake Biwa with the ancient capital of Kyoto, this little hamlet saw the passing of all the major political, economic and religious forces who vied for the domination of Kyoto.

The origins of the settlement remain unclear (Inoue, 1972). In an interview I held with him, the Otsu city historian ventured that the village may have been established by a minor court official. This official, who was banished after siding with the losing camp in the Jinshin Uprising of 672, had a name that later recurs in documented evidence about Yamanaka. Some of the older inhabitants of the village suggest – perhaps half-mischieviously – that Yamanaka was started by robbers and other criminal elements who sought refuge in the mountains, away from the authority of the emperor and aristocracy. What does seem clear, however, is that the village functioned for hundreds of years as a resting place. Sporting a small inn, Yamanaka served as a stop both for pilgrims on their way to the temples of Hiei, and for the transporters of rice who carried shipments from the lake to the capital city.

The first actual mention of Yamanaka in historical documents (Otsu-shi, 1978:422ff) occurs in an account of the struggle between Oda Nobunaga – the first of Japan's three unifiers – and the temple forces of Mt Hiei in the late sixteenth century. When Nobunaga succeeded in subduing these forces he ordered the whole temple complex as well as the surrounding mountain forests to be burnt down. Most of the village (and with it all prior documentation) was also razed and then given to a minor vassal. This vassal built small forts in the village and on an adjoining mountain, presumably to reinforce his lord's control over the transport route.

This venture, however, was only short-lived, due to the construction a few years later of the Tokaido: what became the main traffic route to link Edo (Tokyo) in the east with Osaka and Kyoto in the west. Begun by Toyotomi Hideyoshi – the second of the three unifiers – and completed by the Tokugawa shoguns, the Tokaido followed a river that led from the lake's southern tip, around the mountains, and all the way to Osaka. As a result the mountain road passing through Yamanaka became little more than a secondary route, and the village stagnated. Although it still provided a resting place for the few pilgrims who ventured up to the temple complex which was being rebuilt above, and for some people who travelled over the mountains from the lake, Yamanaka seems to have changed very little throughout the Tokugawa period (1600–1868).

With the beginnings of modernization in the Meiji period (1868–1911) Yamanaka began to change again. In 1880 the village had a population of 410 people in 86 households, 79 of which were engaged in agriculture or forestry (Shiga Ken, 1880). The main activities of these families were the cultivation of tea and mountain rice, and the collection of firewood which was sold mainly in Kyoto. The other seven households operated the local

27

inn and provided a porter service (*shafu*) for the travellers passing
through the mountains.

During the first two decades of this century small industrial
establishments began to be set up along the river running from
Yamanaka to Kyoto. A few of these were located within the
village. Run on water power, this small-scale industry included
the cleaning and processing of rice, manufacture of glue, or more
specialized concerns like wiring and gold plating. Later a small
factory producing cloth for the Imperial Navy was also established
in Yamanaka. All of these small factories drew some of the villagers away from agriculture and forestry. Some older Yamanakaites recall that at the beginning this was mostly short-term work
undertaken to supplement income from agriculture. But as these
establishments grew a significant minority began to turn to salaried
employment as a full-time job.

The 1930s saw further changes. First, some of the small industrial establishments – including Yamanaka's cloth factory – were
electrified, and those that did not soon closed down. Second,
Yamanaka was amalgamated into the city of Otsu. The official
designation of the village changed from Yamanaka-*mura* to Yam-
anaka-*choo*, denoting its – at least nominal – urban status. In
effect, while it joined five other such settlements in a larger administrative district (*Shiga*),[4] in many respects Yamanaka remained
quite independent. This is because it continued to maintain its
own local associations and to deal with the city authorities directly.

According to local testiments about ten of Yamanaka's young
men were killed during World War II. But the general consensus
is that Yamanaka's lot was in other respects rather fortunate.
Because of its proximity to Kyoto it suffered none of the bombings
and strafings incurred by such settlements close to other big cities.[5]
Moreover, while limited, the food supply – mainly mountain rice
and home-grown vegetables – sufficed not only for the locals but
for some of their relatives who moved in from Kyoto for the
duration of the war. The American Occupation is remembered as
being rather benign. The factory that had supplied cloth to the
navy was closed (to reopen a few years later); but apart from that
the only direct link of the villagers with the Americans were the
occasional gifts of chewing gum and chocolate the soldiers
bestowed on Yamanaka's children.

The rest of Yamanaka's post-war history is treated in other
sections of this chapter and in Part III.

Population

With a total population of 2,404 people in 748 households (Table 1) the school district of Hieidaira–Yamanaka is the fourth smallest out of 24 such administrative units in the city. The rapid growth of the estate, however, makes the district also one of the fastest growing ones. This is due both to the yearly in-migration of families into the estate and to the natural increases among its young families. Although five 'new' families have moved into Yamanaka in the past decade (all of them with a commuting head of household), the trend is one of a gradual but steady decline. This is related to three processes: the natural attrition of an ageing population; the move of five families out to the neighbouring estate and the migration of others to Osaka, Kyoto and Otsu; and the tendency for all young people – except eldest sons – to leave the village.

Table 1 Number of households and population in Hieidaira and Yamanaka by wards: 1971–82

Area Year	Yamanaka House-holds	Pop.	1st Ward House-holds	Pop.	2nd Ward House-holds	Pop.	3rd Ward House-holds	Pop.	Total House-holds	Pop.
1971									161	473*
1972									205	651
1973									248	765
1974									302	959
1975	69	247	116	309	180	565	18	57	383	1178
1976	81	265	129	330	219	669	28	92	457	1356
1977	72	260	125	347	236	719	54	178	487	1504
1978	74	276	138	369	254	784	76	251	542	1680
1979	72	261	155	431	263	830	111	356	601	1878
1980	71	253	159	445	276	892	163	511	669	2101
1981	70	249	172	485	280	915	191	603	713	2252
1982	62	229	185	532	284	945	228	731	759	2437

* There are no separate figures for Hieidaira and Yamanaka for the years 1971–4.
Source: Otsu City Citizens Registration Office.

While the average number of people per household for the whole school district is 3.21,[6] this number masks internal differences. The relevant averages are: Yamanaka 3.67, the estate's first ward 2.88, the second ward 3.32, and the third ward 3.32. These figures are related to the contrasting history of each subarea, and will be dealt with in Part Three, but they also give a good indication of the type of household found in each place. The figure for the village reflects the predominance of extended families, where three and sometimes four generations live together. The figure would be higher were it not for the presence of ten households which consist of an elderly single person or couple living alone. The average for the first ward, on the other hand, is related to the presence of a sizeable minority of pensioners living – usually as a couple – alone. Finally the fact that the averages for the second and third wards are higher than the relevant figure for the district as a whole is related to the presence of a greater proportion of young couples with children in these sub-areas.[7]

Turning now to place of birth and previous place of residence, the data collected about Hieidaira by both Motoyama (1982) and myself[8] point to a number of interesting features. Although over 60 per cent of the estate's population was born in the Kansai area,[9] it is on the whole quite heterogeneous in terms of place of birth (Table 2). There are sizeable minorities (above 5 per cent) from places as far away as the Tokyo, Nagoya or Hiroshima areas.

Table 2 Place of birth of Hieidaira residents

	Motoyama		Ben-Ari	
	Number	%	Number	%
Kyoto Prefecture	35	46.1	37	37
Shiga Prefecture	6	7.9	10	10
Kansai (except Kyoto)	9	11.8	14	14
Kanto (Tokyo Area)	5	6.6	10	10
Chubu (Nagoya Area)	10	13.2	7	7
Chukoku (Hiroshima)	3	3.9	7	7
Kyushu	4	5.3	5	5
Shikoku	–	–	5	5
Tohoku (North Japan)	1	1.3	2	2
Overseas	1	1.3	3	3
No answer	2	2.6	–	–
Total	76	100	100	100

The data becomes more interesting, however, when previous place of residence is taken into account (Table 3). The most prominent feature here is that about 75 per cent of all the sub-urbanites moved to Hieidaira from within Kyoto prefecture, suggesting that the move to the estate was the second of a two-step process. This was corroborated in family interviews. Most people who were born outside Kyoto said they had originally come to the city because of the educational opportunities it offered (universities, colleges and special technical schools). Then when they had found jobs and married, they looked for housing in one of the cheaper residential quarters surrounding the city. Hieidaira was thus usually chosen out of similar areas to the north and south of Kyoto (Fushimi, Uji, Arashiyama, Iwakura) or around the lake in Shiga (Kusatsu, Yasu, Moriyama, Omi-Hachiman or north Otsu).

Table 3 Previous residence of Hieidaira residents

	Motoyama Number	%	Ben-Ari Number	%
Kyoto Prefecture	58	76.4	54	74
Shiga Prefecture	9	11.8	9	12.3
Kansai (excl. above)	6	7.9	7	9.6
Kanto	–	–	3	4.1
Other	3	2.9	–	–
Total	76	100	73	100

For many the move to Hieidaira represents the culmination of efforts to become houseowners. Fully 94 per cent of the houses in the district are owned by their occupants, while only 6 per cent are rented from private or company landlords.[10] Hieidaira thus differs radically from the housing estates which are composed of apartment blocks. In these latter neighbourhoods in Japan not only are most dwellings rented, but the overall sentiments are those of transience (Kiefer, 1976a:292–3) – i.e. people conceive of their residence in these communities as an interim arrangement, until they move out and buy a house somewhere else. Indeed 25 (41 per cent) out of the 60 families for which I have this data lived, before moving to Hieidaira, in a rented apartment that was owned by a public or private company.

In Yamanaka, place of birth is strongly related to marriage patterns. Two features are apparent from Table 4 where data gathered on 26 village couples has been set out. On the one hand men – and these are almost always eldest sons – have continued to stay in the village in the past decades. Indeed of the three men born in Kyoto, two moved to the village as primary-school age children (one to his maternal, the other to his paternal, kin), and only a single man is an outside commuter now working in Otsu. On the other hand, the patterns of in-marriage have changed. While women used to come from within Yamanaka or the nearby hamlets of Otsu (Shiga-mura) or Kyoto (Kitashirakawa), from about 15 or 20 years ago they began to come from areas situated further away. Thus, for example, of the 5 women born in Yamanaka, 4 are over the age of fifty-seven, and the 4 women born in 'other' (Oita, Tottori, Shimane and Okayama) prefectures, are all under the age of forty-three. Moreover, the younger brides born in Kyoto or Shiga now tend to come from areas other than those that traditionally supplied women.

Table 4 Place of birth of Yamanaka residents

	Total	Men	Women
Yamanaka	28	23	5
Shiga Prefecture	7	—	7
Kyoto Prefecture	13	3	10
Other	4	—	4
Total	52	26	26

Yamanaka seems to have never suffered a bride famine (*yome kikin*), a term used to describe the difficult situation of many rural settlements in finding women ready to undertake all the duties and burdens associated with marrying a farmer (Murakami, 1978:197ff.). This is related to changes in the occupational structure of the village to which we now turn.

Work and employment

According to data gathered from the national census of 1980 (Table 5), 70 per cent of the district's working population are employed in the tertiary sector. That this is a high figure is apparent when the relevant proportions of tertiary-sector employees are considered for the city (62.1 per cent), prefecture (47.4 per cent) and the nation as a whole (54.2 per cent) (Asahi Shinbunsha,

Table 5a Size of labour force by economic sector and sex, Hieidaira and Yamanaka

	H-I District	Per Cent	(Otsu)*	Men	Women
Total	942	100	(100)	612	330
Primary	10	.1	(3.5)	7	3
Secondary	274	29	(34.2)	198	76
Tertiary	658	70	(2.1)	407	251

* Figures in parenthesis refer to percentage in city.
Source: Otsu-shi, 1982:53 based on the National Census, 1980

Table 5b Size of labour force by type of work and sex, Hieidaira and Yamanaka

	H-I District	Per Cent	(Otsu)*	Men	Women
Total	942	100	(100)	612	330
Agriculture & Fishing	10	.1	(3.5)	7	3
Building	69	7.3	(9.2)	56	13
Manufacturing	205	21.7	(24.1)	142	63
Wholesale & Retail	227	24	(22.7)	140	87
Banking & Insurance	29	3	(3.4)	17	12
Real Estate	23	2.4	(.7)	17	6
Communications & Transport	28	3	(6.1)	23	5
Electricity, Gas and Water	5	.5	(.8)	5	—
Public Servant	36	4	(5.2)	18	18
Service	310	33	(22.9)	187	123

* Figures in parenthesis refer to percentage in the city.
Source: Otsu-shi, 1982:53 based on the National Census, 1980

1983:42). According to my calculations, this figure places the district in fifth place out of 24 such city districts in terms of tertiary-sector employees. Moreover, because the 'construction' and 'manufacturing' categories include workers who do clerical or sales jobs as well, the actual number of people in the district who are employed in productive activity is even smaller. This can be seen most clearly in the data collected by Motoyama and myself (Table 6)[11] where the combined proportion of 'manufacturing' and 'construction' hovers around 5 per cent.

Turning now to a more specific examination of the estate (Table 6), the most apparent feature is that no one category dominates

Table 6 Type of employment of Hieidaira and Yamanaka residents

	Motoyama (Hieidaira)		Ben-Ari (Hieidaira)		Yamanaka	
	Number	%	Number	%	Number	%
Sales, service and clerical	21	22.8	51	27.5	24	38.7
Self-employed	24	26	40	21.6	8	12.9
Teachers	17	18.5	28	15.1	2	3.2
Professionals	4	4.3	14	7.5	–	
Manufacturing and construction	4	4.3	10	5.4	3	4.8
Housewives	–		30	16.2	14	22.5
Pensioners	–		12	6.4	10	16.1
Agriculture	–		–		1	1.6
No answer	22	23.9	–		–	
Total	92	99.8	185	99.7	62	99.8

the others. There are more or less similar proportions for the 'self-employed' and 'sales, service and clerical' categories, with 'housewives' and 'teachers' following closely behind. Another feature to which informants constantly directed my attention is the high combination of 'teaching' and 'professional' occupations. Although I have no comparable data about these categories in the other city districts, 21 or 22 per cent seem to be especially high figures.

An analysis of the breakdown of each category yields a further variety of vocations and job types. Thus, for example, one finds more than the quite ordinary range of retailers (clothes, foodstuffs, electrical goods, etc.) and owners of coffee shops and restaurants among the self-employed. In Hieidaira one finds many artisans who specialize in the painting, design and dyeing (and often marketing) of traditional kimono, or of Western-style clothing, as well as owners of print shops and antique stores, or advertising and public relations people who own and operate their own offices. The teaching category encompasses lecturers at national or private universities and colleges; primary, middle and high-school teachers, as well as people who teach in kindergartens. The 'housewives' category includes many women who as a sideline teach – more often than not for monetary remuneration – such things as the tea ceremony, flower arranging, music (piano, violin) or cooking. Finally 'professional' covers doctors, accountants or architects, as well as the 'semi-professions' like nursing or computer technicians.

A number of points merit underlining in relation to Yamanaka (Table 6). The first is something that I felt while doing fieldwork but which was only corroborated when the statistical compilation was finished. In comparison with the suburban estate, there is a lower proportion of working women, and a higher proportion of elderly pensioners in the village, although most women do take on occasional work from time to time. The second point is the predominance of the 'service, sales and clerical' category which accounts for 38.4 per cent. When combined with the lack of any professionals and the presence of only two teachers (one in a primary school, one in a kindergarten), this figure highlights the presence of 'company men' in the village. The few villagers who are classed as 'self-employed' run small businesses such as a rice store, carpentry works, a small mushroom factory and iron and electric workshops.

Indeed, without needlessly debunking the rather arbitrary categorization of the national census or my own questionnaires, one further observation should be made in relation to this last point. I became aware of this when a number of times people who were not employed by private enterprises nevertheless evinced attitudes towards their workplace that were similar to the attitudes of the first type of workers. Thus employees of city governments, a clerk at a national university, and a middle-level manager in one of the public utilities all called their workplace 'the company' (*kaisha*). This was not only to denote their salaried status. More importantly this underlined the similarity of working hours and conditions, and the obligations of socializing and deference that are common to most employees of large organizations. In terms of occupation, then, the most important dividing line seems to be whether one is a salaried employee of a middle or large organization – whether you are a *sarariiman* – or not. This has important consequences for both family and community, and we shall return to this presently. What is significant to note in this section, however, is the high proportion of non-*sarariiman* in Hieidaira: i.e. the great number of people who have flexible time schedules, and different kinds of obligations towards their workplace.

Lastly, the suburban nature of both the village and the estate is evident in Table 7. In both settlements more than half the population commutes to the city of Kyoto. In the next category are people who work in the community (either at home or at local establishments) and this is followed by a few people who work in Shiga Prefecture (actually in the city of Otsu).

Table 7 Place of work of Hieidaira and Yamanaka residents

| | Motoyama | | Ben-Ari (Hieidaira) | | Yamanaka | |
	Number	%	Number	%	Number	%
In area	13	14.1	39	32.5	10	29.4
Kyoto Prefecture	54	58.7	65	54.2	18	53
Shiga Prefecture	7	7.6	10	8.3	5	14.7
Osaka Prefecture	1	1.1	5	4.2	1	2.9
Other	—	—	1	0.8	—	—
No answer	17	18.5	—	—	—	—
Total	92	100	120	100	34	100

Income and earnings

Whether employed by private, public or government organizations, the monthly income of salaried employees is graded and grows according to a mix of educational achievement and length of service within the organization. Although there are differences between employers, a starting *sarariiman* with a college education earns about 150,000 or 160,000 Yen a month. By the time he is in his late 30s, married with two children and has already served about 15 years in the oganization, this employee would be earning a monthly salary of about 270,000 or 280,000 Yen. These sums are usually supplemented by other 'perks' in regard to which there are differences between employers. These include 'welfare' arrangements such as the provision of canteens and in-house shopping networks or help with health insurance or pension schemes. These also include the twice-yearly bonuses which can equal a few months' salary. In *sarariiman* families I was often told of the plans to use these bonuses for paying mortgages, buying a new car or furniture, or extending and improving the house.

Not surprisingly, I had difficulties in eliciting information about the earnings of the self-employed. While quoting a monthly, or even a yearly figure was difficult in a few cases because of income differentials between busy and slack periods, in most cases this was related, I suspect, to a certain concern that my data would inadvertently reach the tax authorities. Thus the majority of self-employed persons interviewed was either reticent about giving me any figures, outrightly refused, or gave me such an absurdly low figure as to make impossible any realistic assessment. Much the same kind of response was encountered when I questioned many of the women who were working on a side-line.

For all this, however, one should not jump to the conclusion that all of the self-employed wallow in material wealth. It is true that some of them – as the local supermarket owner avidly noted – have considerable buying power. Indeed this can be seen in some of the more lavish houses and gardens dotted around the estate, as well as the occasional foreign-made car (Mercedes, BMW) parked in one of the streets. But most of the self-employed live on a level not much different from families of *sarariiman* where both spouses are working. They buy the same goods at local stores, drive similar cars, and own the same type of houses.

All in all Hieidaira is not a poor neighbourhood. That over 90 per cent of the households own their own homes is one indicator of this. Other interesting indices are the complaints I heard from three different local merchants: a newspaper agent, a steakhouse owner who also sells meat, and the manageress of the *sake* and liquor store. All complained of the difficulties of finding local high-school or university students to do temporary or side jobs on an hourly rate (*arubaito*). In part this is a reflection of the demographic make-up of the estate's population where the 15–25-year-olds form a small group. But this also reflects the small number of families where teenage daughters or sons have to find jobs to supplement the household's income.

While the post-war salarification of Yamanaka's population has brought about a general levelling of incomes and earnings, the greater nationwide affluence of the past decades has brought about a gradual elevation of these. Some locals who come from what were the poorer families still vividly remember the differences between the 4–5 wealthier village households and the rest. These differences – in houses, foodstuffs or the clothing worn to local festivals – have all but disappeared. Now people eat the same food, live in more or less the same kind of houses and wear similar clothing for formal affairs. The greater general affluence, in turn, has produced the beginnings of a process best called 'keeping up with the Tanakas'. As one local pensioner related to me,

'It used to be, before the war that is, that everything was kept
very simple in the cemetery. Today everybody has one eye
on their neighbours and the way they're making the
tombstones much more fancy and elegant. Then they
themselves try to make them just as nice and beautiful. But
anyway it is important for the ancestors that their tombs be
maintained in a nice way.'

Shopping and services

Shopping was a serious difficulty during the suburban estate's first
few years. The general lack of local commercial facilities forced
the local residents to take frequent trips to the shopping centres
and markets of the nearby cities of Kyoto and Otsu. This proved
especially difficult for many of the elderly and some of the housewives who either did not drive or had no private cars.

The past nine years, however, have seen the opening of a host
of new facilities: a rice shop, pharmacy, *sake* and liquor store,
post office, gasoline station, newsagents, gas centre, electrical
goods stores, small garden centre, hairdresser, *sushi* (raw fish)
eatery, coffee shops and restaurants, and a supermarket. More
specialized stores have been opened for such things as antiques
or four-wheel drive vehicles. Just before leaving the field I also
heard of plans to open up a bakery and a stationery shop. In
addition, one local merchant operates a 'grocery on wheels' (actually a converted bus) chiefly for the benefit of the housebound
elderly, and two housewives run a service linking the estate and
dry-cleaning establishments in Kyoto. On a given day the modern
version of Japan's street vendors – motorized and hawking their
wares on gigantic loudspeakers – sell fish, *toofu* (bean curd),
fruits and vegetables. Less regularly peddlers who mend shoes and
leather goods, fix bicycles or sell socks and cheap clothing also
appear. In many respects, then, Hieidaira has come to resemble
other local residential areas in Japan where daily shopping is done
in neighbourhood shops located within walking distance.

Besides these, local residents are constantly beset by sales
agents and advertising matter (stuffed into their mailboxes), which
sell a whole range of goods and services. A sample from my

fieldnotes includes the following items suggested by salespeople: children's books, encyclopedias, cars, glass extensions to the house, new soft drinks, life insurance and savings programmes, pickles, newspaper subscriptions, garage roofs, electrical and gas heaters, or religious salvation (Jehovah's Witnesses). The things offered by the voluminous quantity of leaflets, letters, handbills and folders include the following: take-out food, cosmetics, films, cram schools, water softeners, cars, vitamins and drugs, women's clothing, air conditioning, rings, bags, videos, stoves, tables, kimono, houses, cutlery, restaurants, tea ceremony classes, or the services of a Buddhist pet cemetery.

An important marketing network which covers over 200 of the estate's households is the Consumer Co-operative (*Seikyoo*). The co-operative was set up in 1973 by a group of housewives who were looking for a way to overcome the lack of local shopping facilities. Since then the organization, which is affiliated to the city alliance of co-operatives,[12] has grown and is now comprised of 35 base groups (*han* or *kumi*) across the three wards. Members of these groups, which are usually made up of 5–7 households, join the co-operative by paying an initial sum of 3000 Yen which goes towards financing the various activities of the organization. These members take turns as 'organizers' or 'managers' (*unei-iin*) who are in charge of keeping account of the orders and money that are passed on to the city co-operative. The goods, mostly foodstuffs but more recently cosmetics, electrical goods or some clothing as well, arrive twice weekly on a small co-operative truck that visits all 35 groups in the estate. On these occasions the *unei-iin* usually stores or keeps the goods at her house until the other members of the group collect it.

Once a month the estate's *unei-iin* congregate in the meeting hall to decide about such matters as the creation of new base groups, the petitioning of the city organization to supply different kinds of goods, or the setting up of once-weekly open air markets to which people can come and buy without the need to order in advance. They also elect three deputies (*soodai*) – one from each ward – who run the co-operative on a day-to-day basis, and who are in charge of liaison with the city and regional associations.[13]

For the hard-core members of Hieidaira's 'Bran and Muesli Belt' *Seikyoo* is still too commercial. They belong to what one member called a half-ideological, half-ecological movement. The movement's name, '*Tsukaisute Jidai o Kangaeru Kai*' (lit. 'Association for considering the age in which things are used and thrown away') attests to its ideological origin. But today it has become a base for a marketing network for foods grown or made with no artificial chemicals. The network, which covers about 40 families in the estate, is much stricter than the consumer co-operative in its requirements for 'natural foods' which include fruit and vegetables, meat and eggs, noodles (*soba*), ketchup or soya sauce.

Yet other suburbanites grow their own vegetables and a bit of fruit in their own back yards or on small patches around the estate. One young couple has even begun to rent a small allotment from an elderly Yamanaka villager. They grow a variety of vegetables, such as carrots, cabbage, cucumbers, eggplant, lettuce, onions, peanuts, tomatoes, or soya beans.

Yet in spite of the existence of the new marketing facilities and networks, and the 'agricultural' activities of the locals, the bulk of shopping is done elsewhere. This goes not only for any out-of-the-ordinary outlets like speciality shops, department stores, or discount centres, but for everyday needs as well. Here again (Table 8) the predominant destination is Kyoto. Note that except for 'rice' – which presumably because of its weight is difficult to transport individually – for all the other kinds of services at least 30 per cent of the locals use Kyoto's facilities.[14]

Table 8 Location of shopping by type of goods: Hieidaira residents

	Otsu		The district		Kyoto		Total
	Number	%	Number	%	Number	%	Number
Fruits and vegetables	12	12.9	52	55.9	29	31.2	93
Meat and fish	12	13.2	38	41.75	41	45.05	91
Rice	—	—	52	94.8	6	5.2	58
Banking	16	23.5	—	—	52	76.5	68
Post office	12	17.6	36	53	20	29.4	68
Drinking and entertainment	7	11.3	16	25.8	39	62.9	62
Gasoline	5	7.9	32	50.8	26	41.3	63
Medical care	17	22.4	4	5.2	55	72.4	76

One more fact that merits attention in relation to Hieidaira is the extraordinarily high number of coffee shops and restaurants found on the estate. These make up fully 15 of the 32 commercial establishments in the neighbourhood. This proportion of 46.9 per cent – the city average is 20 per cent – ranks the area highest in the city (Otsu-shi, 1982:97–8).[15] This does not so much reflect the lack of 'regular' retail enterprises, as the advantageous location of the estate as seen by the owners of local cafes and eateries. Hieidaira not only stands on the way to the religious and tourist centre of Hiei and the leisure facilities of Biwa, but offers from many quiet spots beautiful views of the lake, mountains and forests, and the nearby cities (which take on a pleasant appearance from afar).

In Yamanaka the only regularly opened retailers are a tiny grocery store and a small outlet for rice and tobacco. The term 'retailer', however, lends these establishments the air of a fully fledged shop. In fact the grocery store is little more than a few shelves constructed in the entrance hall (*genkan*) of one of the houses, and is intended, as the woman who runs it told me, 'to keep her occupied' (*asobi*). The small outlet is run from their home by the wife and mother of a villager who owns a rice shop in Otsu. In addition the wife of another man operates a small hatchery with 80 hens, and supplies the village and a few of the estate's families with eggs. Street vendors, one of whom actually lives in the village, appear three or four times a week along the main street that runs through the settlement. As a consequence, the tendency to rely on service outlets outside the area – especially those in Kyoto – is even more pronounced in Yamanaka (Table 9).

Table 9 Location of shopping by type of goods: Yamanaka residents

	Otsu		The district		Kyoto		Total
	Number	%	Number	%	Number	%	Number
Fruits and vegetables	–	–	9	39.2	14	60.8	23
Meat and fish	–	–	5	27.8	13	72.2	18
Rice	–	–	16	94.1	1	5.9	17
Banking	2	12.5	–	–	14	87.5	16
Post office	2	8.3	2	8.3	20	83.3	24
Drinking and entertainment	4	23.5	2	11.8	11	64.7	17
Gasoline	–	–	8	57.1	6	42.9	14
Medical care	4	22.2	–	–	14	77.8	18

As a way to ease the difficulty of dependence on external facilities, the village has arranged for the payment of certain bills in a collective and co-ordinated way. On the first Wednesday of every month, representatives of each household converge on the big meeting hall above the day-care centre and pay their water and electricity bills, the shrine and neighbourhood association fees, the monthly payments for national, life, fire and accident insurance, and some of the aged receive their pensions. In addition, those who use her services pay the barber, while those persons who park their cars on part of the shrine's land pay a rather nominal parking fee. Except for the pensions, and life and accident insurance that are paid out by professionals from the Agricultural Co-operative (*Nookyoo*) all other payments are handled by representatives of local organizations: youth group, women's and neighbourhood associations, and the shrine deputies (*soodai*). Members of these organizations take turns in receiving the money, recording it in special notebooks, providing receipts, and forwarding it when relevant to the gas and water companies and to the city departments handling national insurance.

Another facility the neighbourhood association has arranged for is a live-in barber. An older divorcée, she offers her skills for a very low fee in return for free accommodation. In the past few years, however, the number of younger people coming to her small room for a haircut has decreased. This is because – as she half-apologetically observed – she does not offer the curly-hair type of permanent that is the latest fashion among the nation's youth.

Education

There are four formal institutions which cater for children in the district: a kindergarten (*yoochien*) and day-care centre (*hoikuen*) in Hieidaira; a day-care centre in Yamanaka; and a joint primary school (*shogakkoo*) which serves both the estate and the village.

The kindergarten caters for children between four and five years of age. While it is not covered by the law concerning compulsory education, many parents opt for the two-year course provided in this framework. The 66 pupils who attend the two grades of the kindergarten are taught by the school principal who also doubles as the kindergarten head, by his assistant, and by two home-room teachers. The actual school day is quite short – usually half-past nine until twelve – and the emphasis is on teaching through arts and crafts, games and music. There is very little stress on reading, writing and teaching maths skills, although if pupils show an interest in these they are encouraged to continue.

The day-care centre is located in another part of the suburban estate, and caters for children of working mothers (our son attended this centre for the period of fieldwork). Unlike the school or kindergarten which fall within the framework of the city's Board of Education, the centre comes under the jurisdiction of the municipality's welfare departments. The tuition is graded according to the parents' income and at its highest can reach a substantial sum of about 25,000 Yen a month. Its 45 children are arranged into three classes, and their ages vary from one to five. Although the centre is open daily from eight in the morning until five-thirty in the afternoon, only a minority of parents place their children there for the full nine and a half hours. The staff consists of the centre's head, her assistant, one home-room teacher each for the 4–5 and the 3–4-year-old groups, three teachers for the 1–3-year-old group, and two workers who do the cleaning and cooking. The attitude of the teachers is that the lot of the children – especially the younger ones – is rather pitiful or pitiable (*kawai-soo*). This is because of the 'enforced' separation from the mothers. Consequently the teaching staff attempt through the variety of activities at the centre to compensate for the absence of mother by granting a 'general education'. Such an education includes help with such things as dressing, table-manners or brushing teeth, as well as a stress on activities similar to those carried out in the kindergarten.

Yamanaka's day-care centre runs along much the same lines as the estate's, but with two exceptions. First, it is much smaller: it caters for 16 pupils between the ages of three and five and has a staff of two. Second, under the formal city government definition the village has been declared a 'remote place' (*hekichi*). Thus any mother – working or not – has the right to send her children to the centre, and most do. Indeed, because most of the children's mothers do not work, the opening hours are shorter and range between nine in the morning and four in the afternoon.

Once a child has reached the age of six she or he enters the district's primary school which is located at the northern edge of the estate and which was opened only in 1980.[16] Up until then Hieidaira's children attended a school some five kilometres away. Yamanaka's children attended a small village school that was established at the beginning of the century. This small school was marked by close teacher–pupil and teacher–parent relationships and provided a strong sense of village identity. Thus there were many apprehensions on the part of the villagers when the larger district school was opened. As it now appears, not only have Yamanaka's children become fully integrated into the larger institution but the parents of the two communities share and co-operate in many of the school's functions and activities.

With 326 pupils (June 1982), the school is the sixth smallest of 28 such city-run institutions. Its staff comprises 16 people: the principal and his assistant, a head teacher, a nurse (who also teaches health-related matters), an office clerk, one woman in charge of the grounds, and eleven home-room teachers (there are two classes each for each grade except the sixth which has one). The staff work long hours, from about eight in the morning to half-past five or six in the evening. Sometimes when there are special teacher's meetings they may even stay until nine o'clock at night. The teachers are expected to be either with their class, or running one of the many school activities and organizations (for example the students' union, or cooking, science, handicraft, music or sports clubs). When they are not doing these things they are usually at their desks in the staff room preparing lessons, helping each other or discussing problems that arise.

The new three-storey school building is well equipped. It is built in the same general architectural style that the Ministry of Education dictates throughout the country, with a lightish brown exterior, large functional windows, and light, almost stark, grounds. Each home room has large blackboards, a television, charts describing the school routine and lists of duties to be carried out, musical instruments and beautifully written lists of Chinese characters to be learned during the school year. In addition there are also a large gymnasium and wide playing fields. Both are used not only by the school but by many community organizations like the women's volleyball team, youth sports clubs, sports committee or the old-folks clubs.

Twice a year the school holds an open-day. On these occasions parents have an opportunity to attend a lesson given by their children's home-room teachers, to meet the teachers in short group discussions, and to attend general meetings held by the PTA. These open-days are almost always held on Sundays in order to give a chance for working fathers and mothers to attend.

The attitude to school varies somewhat between Yamanaka and

Hieidaira. Although things have begun to change in the village, there is still a strong feeling that such school concerns as curriculum, activities or discipline should be left to the discretion of the teaching staff. Yamanaka parents tend to show more respect to the teachers, and to look upon participation in school functions and the PTA as part of a general duty to help out in community matters. Many of the parents in Hieidaira hold the same kind of notions, but the estate also has a sizeable group with contrasting attitudes. Among these people not only is the parent–teacher tie seen as a relationship between equals, but most have an expectation that the schoolteacher be responsive to their demands and requests in regard to classroom matters.

Upon graduation from primary school, the children of the two communities go on to different middle schools (*chuugakkoo*). Hieidaira's schoolchildren commute by bus to an institution that is located in Otsu proper, about 6 kilometres away. With over one thousand children, this school is the fourth largest middle school in the city, and draws to it the student population of four (primary) school districts (Otsu-shi, 1982:213). Because there is no direct bus route linking Yamanaka with Otsu, the children of the village attend a Kyoto middle school.

The Yamanakaites for their part see this arrangement as having great advantages beyond the ease of commuting to the big city. A number of villagers emphasized that because the life-chances of most of them are closely linked to Kyoto (job and higher education opportunities), it is beneficial to become integrated into the big city's school sysem already at the middle-school level. One consequence of these circumstances is that while Yamanaka's children attend cram-schools, study the textbooks and are oriented towards the entrance examinations of Kyoto's high schools, Hieidaira's children tend much more towards the facilities of Shiga Prefecture and the city of Otsu.

High-school attendance is much more varied. There are scores of city, national and private high schools in Kyoto and Otsu. While some of the estate's children switch at this level to Kyoto's institutions, the general pattern of orientation towards Otsu persists.

At the university level the overwhelming orientation is towards Kyoto. Shiga, which has only two institutes of higher education, is no match for the big city which has 21 universities and colleges and scores of other technical, professional and specialized schools, and teacher-training colleges.

Table 10 Educational achievement of Hieidaira and Yamanaka residents

| | Hieidaira | | Yamanaka | |
	Number	%	Number	%
Middle school	10	8	12	38.7
High school	45	36.3	14	45.2
Academic*	60	48.4	4	12.9
Technical and further education	9	7.3	1	3.2
Total	124	100	31	100

* Includes university, college, junior college and teacher-training institutes.

There are differences between the village and the estate in regard to the adult population's educational achievement. As is evident from Table 10, the contrast is between a middle- or high-school education in Yamanaka, and a high-school or academic education in Hieidaira. An interesting corroboration of these findings were the inadvertent observations of one of the local newsagents. We were talking of the difficulties of delivering newspapers and journals in the estate when he said:

'You know, people in Hieidaira are more educated, they read all sorts of newspapers and magazines. Sometimes I get mixed up because I can't remember who ordered what and when. People here order the usual Yomiuri and Mainichi papers that I deliver in the morning and the evening, as well as the Sunday editions of these newspapers and the weeklies and monthlies they publish. I also deliver the *Supotsu Hoochi* published by the Yomiuri group and the *Supotsu Nippon* published by the Mainichi. In addition, I deliver newspapers in more specialized lines like *Tsuri Niyuzu* (Fishing News), *Juutaku Shinbun* (Housing Newspaper), *Tooshi Shooken Shinbun* (Investments and Securities Newspaper), one on the electrical goods trade, the Japanese version of the *Economist*, as well as a few medical journals. Ah, I also bring a number of families those magazines for children in primary and middle school. Sometimes I get so loaded down with all of these that my scooter can hardly move.'

Despite the differences between the educational achievements of the villagers and the suburbanites their aspirations for their male children's educational success do not differ markedly. In both communities one finds what one quick-witted Hieidairaite rendered into English as 'education-crazy mama' (*kyooiku mama*). The four university graduates that appear in Table 10 in Yamanaka are all under forty and are very much a model that people want their children to emulate. For the villagers well realize that a university education is the best 'ticket' to a good job as a *sarariiman*, with the security and welfare benefits and yearly wage increments this entails.

In Hieidaira many families share the same kind of view, although some may express it in a more sophisticated way. Our neighbour, who had recently moved to Hieidaira from Yokohama due to his taking up a post in a Kyoto university, once said to me:

'In Japan your advancement in life, your ability to earn money is directly related to your educational level. That's why if you ask me about my dream for our son it's that he'll progress and do well at school. Then afterwards, once he's finished college or university, he can decide what he'd like to do. He'll have the money and the resources to be freer in doing what he likes.'

It is in relation to the expectations of daughters that the people of the two communities differ. In Hieidaira many parents differentiate only slightly between boys and girls, expecting boys to do just that bit better in school and university. In Yamanaka by contrast most parents – young and old – see their daughters' future in 'traditional' terms. Thus one mother in her mid-30s answered my questions in the following way:

'I really have no aspirations for my two daughters because they're girls. I want them to be healthy and enjoy themselves. And when they grow older to become good brides and mothers and take good care of their families.'

Changing Japanese Suburbia

Local organizations and clubs

Local organizations in the Hieidaira–Yamanaka district carry out
a wide range of activities. These include varied concerns as social
welfare, fire-fighting, traffic safety, sports, commerce, religion, or
special programmes for women and for children (Table 11). As a
detailed analysis of the 'workings' – i.e. mobilization patterns,
activities, decision-making, division of labour and links to external
agencies – of the neighbourhood associations, voluntary welfare
workers, old-folks' clubs, and the sports committee, is given in
other parts of the book, and as the religious organizations are
dealt with in a later section, I restrict myself to a few general
comments here.

Despite the gradual opening up of the village, it is still marked
by wide participation in the organizations and affairs of both the
village and the school district. While it is not the *hyaku paasento*
(100 per cent) participation purported by some villagers, there
does seem to be extensive involvement with, and a sharing in,
public and communal activities. This is especially apparent against
the difficulties in Hieidaira of recruiting organizational officers
and engaging people in community affairs.

Thus, for example, the teams fielded by the village turn out to
a woman or man to such meets as softball tourneys, sports field-
days (*undookai*), or gate-ball competitions (a game roughly like
croquet). More often than not these teams bring with them family
and friends who form a highly encouraging and vociferous corp
of fans. One member of the district's sports committee explained
that the Yamanakaites not only know already who is best at
different sports (running, pitching, volleyball), but are also familiar with each others' working schedules so that they can make
the most of the village's athletic resources.

By contrast, both the size of Hieidaira and the presence of
many new families make the recruitment of full teams more difficult. Sports meets are advertised in the monthly letters of the
neighbourhood association and on noticeboards dotted around
the neighbourhood. But the sports committee also has to make
special efforts to contact people personally in order to ensure the
appearance of a full roster of teams. Indeed, despite its small size,
Yamanaka has constantly beaten the three Hieidaira wards in all
of the five sports field-days that have been held to date.

Table 11 Local organizations and associations in Hieidaira and
Yamanaka by level of affiliation

Name of organization	Hieidaira	Yamanaka	Joint affiliation	City affiliation
Neighbourhood association (*Jichi Kai*)	X	X		
Neighbourhood association alliance (*Jichi Kai Rengookai*)			X	X
Voluntary fire brigade (*Shooboodan*)	X	X		X
Traffic safety committee (*Kootsu Anzen Kyoo Kai*)			X	X
Women's association (*Fujin Kai*)	X	X		X
Children's association (*Kodomo Kai*)	X	X	X	X
Sports association (*Taiku Shinkoo Kai*)	X	X	X	X
Children's sports teams (*Supotsu Shoonendan*)			X	X
PTA			X	X
Shop owners' association (*Shooten Kai*)	X			
Social welfare council (*Shakai Fukushi Kyoogi Kai*)			X	X
Voluntary welfare workers (*Minsei-iin*)	X	X	X	X
Old-folks club (*Roojin Kai*)	X	X	X	X
Anti-delinquency group (*Seishoonen Iku Kai*)			X	X
Single mothers' association (*Boshi no Nozomi-Kai*)			X	X
Widows' association		X		
Youth association (*Seinen Kai*)		X		
Men's association		X		
Shrine deputies (*Soodai*)		X		
Pilgrimage association (*Ise Ko*)		X		
Buddhist parish group (*Dan Ka*)		X		

The voluntary fire brigades (*shooboodan*) that are set up (separately) in the village and the estate provide another illustration of

this contrast. These organizations are established in order to provide an on-the-spot (and often crucial) auxiliary service to the city
fire department. They have uniforms, fire engines, equipment,
and hold regular (monthly or bi-monthly) training sessions and a
fire safety drive each year at the end of December. Yet while the
village with 62 households fills its rota of 30 brigade members
to the man, the estate's 45-member brigade encounters constant
difficulties. This is not only in making sure that people turn out
to the practice sessions, but in recruiting them into the brigade in
the first place.

Although its population accounts for only 9.5 per cent of the
district's total populace, Yamanaka provides about 25 per cent of
the officers of the joint estate–village organizations. Indeed,
because of the settlement's small size and the limited number of
potential organizational activists this involves, membership and
participation in different community organizations tend to overlap. Thus it is not uncommon to find villagers who serve concurrently in two or three local organized groups. One villager, for
example, was at one and the same time: head of the anti-delinquency association, assistant head of the sports committee, head
of the village children's association, an officer of the school's PTA,
and head of the PTA in Yamanaka's day-care centre. He did all
this while commuting three hours each day, five times a week, to
a job in Osaka. It is no wonder that after a period he began to
experience gastric problems and was told by a doctor not only to
take it easy but to curtail what someone suggested was his prime
aid and energizer – drink.

While this is an extreme case, it nevertheless underlines an
element that – as we shall see again in the next section – is an
especially difficult one for the younger members of the village.
For in Yamanaka there is quite a strong sentiment of obligation
in affiliation with, and participation in, local organized activity.
As one astute resident of the estate put it when we discussed
Yamanaka, in the village it is very difficult 'not to join' community
activities. For the villagers are bound not only by the general
public expectations that they participate, but also by more specific
obligations towards individuals who ask them to join such activities. This is not to deny that many of the villagers find a great
deal of satisfaction and a sense of fulfilment in undertaking organizational roles, nor is this to deny that some see it as 'fun', or
'important' or 'required' to participate. Rather this is to under-

score the persistence of a strong sentiment that collective interests still take precedence over individual preferences.

The different sentiments which pervade Hieidaira were brought home to me most clearly in relation to a softball team that had been set up around 1980. One team member explained that it had begun as a very informal arrangement among 9 or 10 neighbours living along one of the third ward's streets. After a while the men who were playing together more or less regularly decided to chip in and buy themselves bright red and white shirts and wear them at their weekly meets. This 'act' did not, however, create a group towards which they felt obligations in a way similar to the Yam-anakaites. As the same team member explained, individuals feel that even if they belong to a team that has been playing for some years, they have the privilege of declining to participate if they have other plans. That is, people not only feel much less of a need to conform to group obligations, there is even a more positive sentiment: there is a freedom 'not to join' in Hieidaira.

While it is true that some people don't like to or don't want to join, the complaints I occasionally heard from the estate's community leaders about problems in finding willing and able people for local organizations should be put in perspective, for much of these difficulties are related to the sheer quantity of activity in Hieidaira. The estate's organizations and associations recruit close to *300* people every year for a variety of roles ranging from coaches for the youth sports teams through to people who hang up banners in the traffic safety committee's annual safety drive. Such complaints – as one cynical observer noted – should be ascribed to the estate's rather 'overabundant' oganizational life than just to the lack of willing residents.

The overwhelming majority of organizers of and participants in local organizations, associations and committees are women. Men may be chosen – quite frequently in fact – to lead such bodies as the PTA, children's committee or social welfare council. But it is the women who not only bear the brunt of the actual physical and technical aspects of organization, but actually decide about organizational priorities and budgetary allocations.

Many of these activists are – to borrow from Pharr (1976:322) – Neo-traditional women who continue to have a strong ideology calling on them to subordinate all other major life activities to the role of wife and mother. For these persons community activity is seen as a natural extension of care for the family, and contribution to the locality is seen as helping to build a 'good' environment for the development of their children. Others are New-women (*ibid.*) who still want to be wives and mothers but want to develop other interests as well. For these individuals community activity is related not only to their children, but is often seen as an avenue for self-realization and personal enjoyment.

Three groups stand out as the prime participants in clubs within and ouside the district: women (overwhelmingly housewives), pensioners, and children (Tables 12 and 13). The clubs in which women participate include both 'traditional' and 'modern' interests. Among the traditional are flower arranging, calligraphy, the tea ceremony and the recitation of Chinese poems. Examples of more modern ones are a psychology discussion group which dealt in one of its sessions with the relation between the territorial behaviour of animals and that of human beings, or the reading circle where one of the books the members read while fieldwork was being carried out was the Japanese translation of *The Sensuous Woman*. The affiliation of pensioners in clubs will be dealt with in Part IV. Club membership among children is on the whole related to those kinds of activities that are not offered locally at the school or the children's sports teams: for example, ballet, dance, ice-skating or swimming.

Table 12 Clubs within the Hieidaira–Yamanaka district with which local residents are affiliated

	Women	Children	Men	Pensioners
Abacus		X		
Baseball			X	
Calligraphy	X	X		X
Education of children	X			
Flower arranging	X			X
Motorcycles and cars			X	
Music	X	X		X
Painting	X	X		X
Pottery	X			X
Psychology	X			
Reading circle	X			
Shigin (Chinese poems)	X			X
Tea ceremony	X			X
Volleyball	X			

These lists *do not* include clubs that are conducted within local organizations (like the old-folks clubs) or schools.

Table 13 Clubs outside the Hieidaira–Yamanaka district with which
local residents are affiliated

	Women	Children	Men	Pensioners
Ballet		X		
Baseball			X	
Calligraphy	X			X
Cub scouts		X		
Dance		X		
Dyeing	X			
Golf			X	
Ice-skating		X		
Painting	X			X
Shigin (Chinese poems)	X			X
Soccer			X	
Swimming		X		

These lists *do not* include clubs that are conducted within companies or
labour unions.

Local ties: kin relations and neighbours

Yamanakaites are proud of the fact that the village has managed
to retain much of the close-knit character it traditionally had. This
character is maintained by a combination of intertwining kin and
friendship networks, and by the strong sense of the importance
of participating in village affairs that was mentioned before. That
five surnames account for about 60 per cent of all local family
names attests to the presence of kin relations that often reach
back for generations. These ties are constantly maintained through
mutual visiting and gift-giving during festivals, and by such customs as attendance at each other's Buddhist services for the dead
(*hooji*). Indeed, one woman who had married the oldest son of a
village family in the mid-1970s mentioned two types of problems
that in-marrying brides encounter. On the one hand they must
learn the various kin connections between local households. On
the other, they must face the constraints of always having to be
a family representative and the consequent difficulties of initiating
contacts as individuals that this entails.

Things are changing in this respect, however. In the last twenty
years only one couple has married within the village. As the older

53

generation pass away it is to be expected that ties based on kin relations will slowly but steadily weaken. As one 35-year-old villager told me, relations with distant family in Yamanaka are growing thin (*usui*).

At the beginning of fieldwork I was struck by what seemed to be fictive-kin relations between village men. For example many young men call older males *ani* – the informal and rather intimate word for older brother. Moreover, many times during interviews men would characterize their ties with other village males as brother or sibling (*kyoodai*) relationships. When questioned more closely, however, many admitted that such ties are limited to certain age-groups. As it turns out they are part of the relationships that emerged among people who attended the little village school at more or less the same time. These people – the men and some of the older women born and married in Yamanaka – tend to remain close for the rest of their lives. Many form small circles of friends and go out together, visit each other's homes for the occasional meal or drink, or take part in regular occasions where the Japanese version of mah-jong is played.

Here again things are changing. Among younger couples the trend is towards an addition to 'school' ties, an addition of acquaintanceships and contacts based on affiliation with external entities like the workplace or outside clubs and associations. Indicative of these new ties were a number of co-workers of villagers who had been invited with me to view Yamanaka's festivals and to visit local homes.

At the same time there are negative aspects to the small size of Yamanaka and to the close kin and friendship networks of the village, for these circumstances make for a situation in which any local occurrence quickly becomes part of the village's 'public knowledge'. As one 45-year-old villager employed in the public sector noted:

'The minute someone does anything shameful (*haji*) it
becomes immediately known. For example, if a couple have
an argument because of the husband's unfaithfulness, the
whole village is informed by the next day.'

This situation seems irksome not only to those young people – in-marrying women and a few couples who have settled in Yamanaka from the outside – who are used to the greater anonymity of urban neighbourhoods. It is at times also extremely annoying to many of the younger village-born men who have not only been exposed to such external norms of behaviour, but are increasingly coming to place a higher value on the expression of individual taste and interests.

A related point that was often remarked upon by the younger village couples pertains to the growing alternatives such people have for social contact outside Yamanaka. For many of these, the great amount of social intercourse (*tsukiai*) based on kinship represents an increasingly burdensome outlay in terms of time, attention and money (for gifts). One 40-year-old man, who as eldest son had stayed on in Yamanaka, complained how ten of his Sundays in 1981 had to be devoted to various functions with village kin.

Yet for all that, the villagers remain proud of the rather intimate flavour of relationships within Yamanaka. Nowhere is this more evident than in the way they contrast the rich communal life in the village with the rather tenuous one in the estate. The comments of one 80-year-old villager about Hieidaira well illustrate the image Yamanakaites have in regard to social relations in the estate:

'Hieidaira is actually a little Tokyo. It's like Tokyo in that you have people from all over the country. They're all so occupied with their jobs or businesses that there is almost nobody willing to invest his time in the neighbourhood association. Well, what do you want, they're all first generation in the estate, there's no feeling of community (*furusato*), and little contact between the people.'

This is an exaggerated view. As the supermarket owner noted when we discussed shoplifting from his store, Hieidaira is still small enough for people's reputation to be spoilt if word gets out about their indiscretions. Moreover, while it is true that there are less solidary links and less social contact for Hieidaira *as a whole*, this does not mean that intimate ties with much mutual assistance do not exist. What is apparent in this suburban neighbourhood is the emergence of distinctive smaller groups within which these ties operate. The two most common bases for the development of such groups are territorial – i.e. smaller, more limited areas of the estate – or organizational – i.e. on the basis of shared affiliation in a local association or club.

One example of the 'territorial' base of group formation is a social circle that began in 1979 in one of the streets of the third ward. In a family interview one of the participants in this group of 4 or 5 families related how it began like 'a gathering of women around the well of an old village', for it was through the sharing of information and the talk about children that the wives began to become friendly. Then, as mutual visiting between the women increased, the husbands were eventually also drawn in. Now most socializing that is done in the evenings or at weekends is done by family units and includes going out together for picnics or inviting each other for meals and the occasional barbecue. No less importantly, the group is a base for much mutual help and assistance: not only for the borrowing of the proverbial cup of soya sauce (in Japan it is not sugar), but also for taking and fetching children from school, minding babies, cooking for someone who has become sick, or providing emotional support in times of personal problems.

Another circle which consists of 6 or 7 women dotted around the first two wards provides an illustration of the 'organizational' base. Formed more or less around 1976, this group first became acquainted through the PTA. Although this circle has been in existence for close to seven years, it is still very much a women's group with little socializing between the husbands. This does not mean, however, that the men do not figure in the provision of aid. Thus, for example, when the husband of one of the women fell ill one evening, his wife immediately called one of her friends from the circle. This friend's husband – a doctor in Kyoto – arranged for the ill man to be admitted to his hospital that evening without going through the usual bureaucratic complications.

In my fieldnotes I have seven recorded cases of another type of relationship found in the estate. These are ties among extended families in which the grandparents, while living quite nearby, do not reside with their children and grandchildren. Locals invoked a popular saying when describing this arrangement; they said the parents live within a distance where the soup doesn't get cold (*miso shiru samenai kyori*). That is, living at such a distance that if you take a bowl of hot soup you have prepared for the parents it won't get cold on the way. The advantage of this arrangement lies in its granting a measure of independence and privacy for both families, while preserving the relative physical proximity which is important for the provision of mutual aid and assistance.

Related to the sentiment of the right 'not to join' local estate organizations is that of the right 'not to neighbour'. I was given an excellent example of this sentiment when I asked an elderly professor of Buddhist studies about his ideas of an ideal neighbour. Before replying he took out a book of Chinese proverbs and – translating it painstakingly into English – read me one by Confucius: 'The communication of gentlemen is like water.' Giving a little chuckle he continued:

'It isn't like milk or juice you see. This kind of communication is brief and frank (*assari*). It involves little interference in each other's affairs and no real commitment.'

This rather wide leeway for privacy and independence is at the bottom of the emergence of a category of people whose number it is very difficult to measure – social isolates. Beyond little more than a formal affiliation with the neighbourhood association, these people have almost no contact with their neighbours or other locals.

Religious life

It is in the religious sphere more than in any other that the two communities of Hieidaira and Yamanaka provide a clear exemplification of the differences between the 'traditional' and the 'modern'. While much of Yamanaka's communal life is still dictated by the local versions of the 'established' religions (Shinto and Buddhism), Hieidaira is very much – to borrow from Peter Berger – a supermarket of religions.

Maintained by a fixed number of hereditary parish families, the three little Buddhist temples of Yamanaka are supported respectively by 25, 20 and 15 households each.[17] Because of their small size the temples cannot support live-in priests, and thus resort to inviting such religious functionaries for the special occasions they are needed. These invitations are usually directed to the three head temples in Kyoto with which the local temples are affiliated. The three head temples belong to the following sects: Joodo-shu, Joodo Shin-shu and Shingon-shu. There seems to be no competition between the temples for each other's devotees, and there are no signs of the appearance of cleavages based on Buddhist affiliation within the village.

The Shinto shrine, rather than the Buddhist temples, is the symbolic centre of the village and the locus of its main religious rites and festivals. The shrine is 'managed' by a committee of deputies (*soodai*) who arrange for the cleaning of the grounds, the procurement of *sake* and ritual food that is consumed during festivals, the maintenance of the office and religious structures, and for the invitation of a Shinto priest who comes in for the 4 or 5 main ritual occasions of the year. One village household does hold an hereditary Shinto role: its eldest male is the 'keeper of the shrine' (*miyamori*). But as this role is quite low in the Shinto hierarchy this man cannot (and is not trained to) carry out the ritually more important functions of purification and prayer. Many of the rites, like the autumn and spring festivals, reflect Yamanaka's agricultural legacy. Others, like the boys' and girls' initiation rites, or the festival day for children who have become three, five or seven years old (*shichigosan*), are related to stages of the life-cycle. In recent times, in addition to the usual prayers calling for health, fire-safety and success in material pursuits, special prayers for success in school or university entrance examinations have also been added.

The salarification of Yamanaka's populace has had its effect on religious festivals in a way similar to its effect on other community activities. Whereas festivals used to be held on set days during the year, now they are held 'on the first' or 'on the third' Sunday of the appropriate month. This is true not only for the Shinto-related occasions, but also for such functions as the Buddhist services for the dead.

Yet the salarification of the village has not led to any real weakening of religious observance and participation. The village elders sometimes complain of the physical feebleness of the youngsters who, because they no longer farm, find it difficult to carry the holy carriage in its yearly trip around Yamanaka. But these older persons are also aware of the fact that in contrast to other communities, Yamanaka has not yet felt the need to hire special porters to carry the holy carriage. The young men of the hamlet appear in full numbers to carry out this task.

The prime participants in religious activities and the major caretakers of religious affairs are women, usually older ones. It is they who come on the monthly 'pilgrimage' to the village shrine, who make most of the arrangements for the Buddhist services for the dead, and who maintain the family tombstones and cemetery. It is also women who clean, maintain and pray before the Shinto god-shelves (*Kamidana*) and family altars (*Butsudan*) that are found in most households.

In Hieidaira one finds an array of religions, sects and religious functionaries. All the major Buddhist sects are represented: Pure Land Zen, Tendai or Nichiren, for example. Local Christians belong to Catholic as well as seven or eight different Protestant churches. In addition Hieidaira sports a suburban shaman (who exorcises fox spirits, I was told), two Finnish missionary families who belong to a Pentecostal church, and a plot of land that is to be turned into a Zen monastery. Finally, a number of families consider themselves – or so they said during family interviews – to be agnostics or atheists.

The situation is in fact more complicated than this for, given the Japanese propensity for inclusion rather than exclusion in religious matters, one finds many families where two or three religions or sects intermingle. One couple, now in their late thirties, provide a concrete example of a popular description of Japanese religious tolerance. When born, they were both taken – the husband in Osaka and the wife in Okayama – to Shinto shrines for dedication ceremonies; they were married in a Catholic church in Nagasaki; and they expect to have a Buddhist funeral in Otsu when they die.

Coupled with such tolerance is a general wariness of imposing any kind of religious uniformity on the estate and its residents. The neighbourhood association, for example, discontinued – after it was alerted to the fact by one of the association's members – the distribution of a bi-monthly newsletter which a nearby shrine (Ohmi Jingu) had tried to send with the community organization's regular notices. I encountered similar sentiments when I questioned various locals who had helped organize the summer children's festival (*Jizoobon*). In reply to my queries about the prayers and offerings that were made to the stone image of the Buddhist God of Children (*Jizoosan*), almost all took pains to explain that this was not really a matter of a religious nature, but rather one connected with some general notion of the benefit for children.

Yet for all this one does hear talk of the need for some kind of religious centre in the estate: a (presumably Buddhist) cemetery or a Shinto shrine. Such talk is not limited only to the elderly. Various suggestions such as a link-up with Yamanaka's shrine, or an importation of a 'branch' deity from one of the big neighbouring shrines (Ohmi Jingu or Hiyoshi Taisha) were heard among others from a 50-year-old university professor of Chinese history, and an artist in her early thirties. Such suggestions were usually couched in terms of children's need for a religious atmosphere or some kind of spiritual experience. Similar sentiments probably underlay other proposals, such as the writings of a local estate history, or the publication of my findings in popular form. This, as though to create a corpus of documents which would validate – in a way local histories do for older communities – the emergence of a locality with some kind of traditional 'depth'.

This, then, is the essential background for an understanding of the two communities. In the following chapters I explore in depth some of the more general points raised here and in the Introduction.

Part Three
THE POLITICS OF DEVELOPMENT

3 Introduction

The development of the suburban estate of Hieidaira in the late 1960s formed part of the tremendous post-war expansion of new residential areas housing Japan's new corp of salaried employees and professionals. Unfortunately, like other estates developed during this suburban boom, Hieidaira was constructed rather shoddily. It lacked during its first few years almost all of what were then considered essential public amenities and facilities for a new residential area. Moreover, both the internal social character of the neighbourhood, as well as its dependence on external political and economic agencies, seemed unfavourable for the initiation of a collective effort aimed at rectifying this situation. Internally, not only was there a lack of any kind of community organization, but the attributes of the recently arrived middle-class population seemed to limit the potential for such a movement: a lack of sentimental or prior associational basis for cohesion; weak identification with the area; and the absence of mutual neighbour obligations and loyalty. Externally the suburb was dependent on large-scale and complex organizations (the developer, city and prefectural administrations, Boards of Education, public utilities, transport companies) for the provision of essential services and facilities.

Yet within a few short years, the local residents achieved remarkable success in mounting a collective struggle for, and securing the establishment of, not just one or two of these services, but a whole array of them: a school, a kindergarten, a day-care centre, a community meeting hall, parks and playgrounds, a bus service, and new roads. This came about through the suburbanites' success in setting up a representative community organization, and a community-wide network of communications and mobilization. They then pressured the developer into supplying the land needed for public facilities, and lobbied the city and prefectural authorities for the supply of these goods and services.

When seen against a background of the relevant research which has been carried out in Japan, Hieidaira's experience of community action raises a number of issues for analysis. An examination of studies dealing with collective political action in the context of middle-class suburban estates (like Hieidaira) reveals only a sprinkling of comments or discussions that are often polemical. Studies of local Japanese political associations or territorially based political action have been overwhelmingly analyses of rural localities (Norbeck, 1967; Smith, 1978; Steiner, 1968), or, as in the West, studies of the urban poor and ethnic minorities (Cornell, 1967; Taira, 1968–9; De Vos and Wagatsuma, 1966). Indeed, even Vogel's semi-classic *Japan's New Middle Class* (1963) deals with suburban politics only in an incidental manner, and generally dismisses such community involvement as unimportant for the new corps of white-collar workers (*ibid*.:98; see also Allinson, 1979:12). One recent exception is Allinson's (1979) excellent analysis of politics and social change in two suburban towns near Tokyo. But his book, like most of the articles in another compilation (Steiner *et al.*, 1980), tends to deal primarily with city-level politics and developments. Both kinds of studies – on rural settlements and on city-level politics – provide a good background for an exploration of community action in residential estates. This is both in terms of providing a comparative perspective from other types of communities, and portraying the wider context within which such community action takes place. Such studies are no substitute, however, for detailed cases which trace out the specific processes and elements involved in such collective political action.

This lack in the literature is all the more surprising in view of the post-war increase in the number of Japanese white-collar employees and professionals,[1] and the accompanying growth of the residential areas where these have come to live. In the Japanese literature, the basic portrayal of these new middle-class housing estates – either of individual houses (like Hieidaira) or apartment blocks – is situated within the 'breakdown of community' schema or within the approach stressing the 'transference of community to the company'. These estates, created as they are by combinations of giant private and public bodies, are seen as passive objects of business and administration, and as lacking any real potential for local collective political action. Almost every aspect of these (to borrow from Suttles, 1972:243) 'enacted communities' is seen to be affected by external forces: their name chosen by realtors; location dependent on central planning; placement within limited cost gradients done by builders; and most importantly the provision of public facilities and services dependent on the goodwill of developers and government. Internally they are said to be marked by: a prevalence of secondary relations between residents, and an egoistic and individualistic ethos that is manifested in a reluctance to join in co-operative activity (Fukutake, 1982:137); lack of social consciousness and political apathy (Koschmann, 1978:17); strong orientation (especially among the men) to outside work and friendship ties (Kiefer, 1976a:288, 1976b:26; Nakane, 1973:131); and a marked weakness of community sentiments (Nakane, 1973:63). The underlying attitude toward community action in such neighbourhoods seems to be one of a mix of indifference and (especially with Fukutake) at times contempt. Such action is seen either as marginal, as an unimportant phase in Japan's political development, or as rooted in selfish desires for material betterment that are divorced from serious critiques of Japan's central institutions.

Yet despite this view, a long series of other studies has brought out the new potential that the new middle class possesses. These studies stress how part of the middle class that has emerged since the war (that is professionals and white-collar workers) has contributed significantly to organized activity aimed at a confrontation with and opposition to the giants of government and business. The new attitudes towards authority and participation that this new element of the middle class carries have been most clearly underscored in studies of labour relations (Koshiro, 1979; Passin, 1975a; Rohlen, 1974), and citizens and consumer movements (Kirkpatrick, 1975; Krauss and Simcock, 1980; Maki, 1976; McKean, 1981). It is especially these latter studies of citizens' groups that have pointed to an explosion of protest that has occurred in Japanese suburban estates since the mid–1960s and to the new mode of political participation that is found in those areas where tertiary-sector employees are more numerous (Tsurutani, 1977:198; Krauss and Simcock, 1980:196).

In part an outgrowth of the wider political ideals and civic sentiments that have swept Japan since that period, in part a reflection of new attitudes to work, and the importance now attached to home and the family, and in part linked to the formidable organizational capabilities the new middle class has brought with it, this protest has expressed itself in many ways. Concretely in a new conception of community action (Watanuki, 1966); an opposition to local conservative 'powers'; a proclivity to act out political dissatisfaction (White, 1976:105);[2] a new kind of internal movement egalitarianism and democracy (Nakamura, 1968:201); and the struggle for more public expenditure on urban infrastructure (Bennett and Levine, 1976). The inhabitants of these new residential estates have successfully organized themselves in movements opposed to such projects as the location of nearby industrial plants or highway interchanges or, as in the case of Hieidaira, lobbied for provision of essential services such as sewers, parks, or sidewalks (Krauss and Simcock, 1980:196).

Much of the relevant research, then, seems to revolve around the emergence of 'community autonomy' in these new residential estates: the capacity of such communities to act and struggle independently as political groups. Given the scale and level of organization of the modern state and its extensions, and given that 'created' suburban communities are highly dependent on external entities for the supply of goods and services, such localities rarely (if ever) have an independent ability basically to restructure their environment. Yet at the same time this dependence does not imply that the environment is fully determinative, for much is left to the initiative and active struggle of the locals. Thus, as mentioned in the book's introduction, an examination of community autonomy involves both the study of the internal mobilization and communication patterns of these communities and the way they handle relations with their external advocates and adversaries. In the following chapter these issues will be examined through a detailed case study of community action in Hieidaira.

4 Development of the Estate

The land: forests, fields and real estate

At the end of World War II, the bulk of the land where Hieidaira now stands was common forest land, and a few patches of field where mountain rice was grown. The forests, under the existing legal framework, were owned conjointly by the six hamlets (*aza*) of Shiga Village (*mura*).[1] The rice fields were owned privately by some of the villagers of the nearest hamlet: Yamanaka. During the war and for a number of years afterwards, acute difficulties in procuring charcoal and oil made the selling of firewood an extremely profitable business. Well aware of this, the villagers cut and collected wood from the forest, and then carried it off (on their backs or on carts) to the cities of Kyoto and Otsu where it was sold.

For a short while, as a consequence of the American Occupation's policy of land reclamation – aimed at increased food production and provision of jobs for the demobilized (Dore, 1959:182) – attempts were made to convert some of the forest land into plots of sweet potatoes and other vegetables. But soon these efforts were abandoned. As in other parts of the country, this was due to the low quality of the soil and to the fact that all the areas where farming was possible were already being cultivated.

The organization in charge of the reclamation effort and maintenance of the forests (e.g. thinning, setting up water barriers, clearing trails), was the Shiga Forest Association (*Otsu Shi Shiga Shinrin Kumiai*).[2] A juridical body (*hoojin*) in charge of the village's common property (*kyooyuu zaisan*), it had 538 members from the six hamlets, and managed an area of over 300 hectares (3 million square metres).

From the mid-1950s two trends related to Japan's industrial

rebuilding led to the gradual abandonment of forestry and other agricultural activities. The first was the increased gasification and electrification of the country. A pre-war trend which had been halted by the war (Minami, 1976), the widening of the gas and electricity networks began again in the major urban centres and quickly spread to areas near them. Hence as the use of wood as a source of fuel became obsolete, and as its low quality ruled out its use for house or furniture construction, so did the local occupation with forestry. The second trend was the opening up of new work opportunities in the nearby cities. Salaried jobs, less physically strenuous, with fixed hours and promise of long-term security, compared favourably with agriculture and forestry. In growing numbers, Shiga Village's men began to enter and commute to the urban job markets of Kyoto and Otsu. Agriculture more and more came to be viewed as either a weekend affair, or something to be left to housewives or the elderly who stayed at home. In sum, the changes in energy consumption, the unsuccessful attempts at land reclamation, and the widening of job opportunities in nearby cities, all contributed to a gradual change in the perception of forest lands. Once seen as the primary source of livelihood, they now came to be viewed as worthless or useless.

At the same time, however, the realty companies operating in the Kyoto–Osaka region began to see these forest lands differently. The area's physical features – rolling hills, scenic forests, view of the lake, and locational advantages (near enough to the region's major cities for ready access) – afforded potential in a different sense: as real estate for the leisure industry. Accordingly, the Forest Association was first approached by the real estate arm of the giant Keihan Railroad Company in 1957. The ensuing negotiations centred on over one million square metres which the realtor wanted as part of a much larger project aimed at developing a combination of tourism and pilgrimage centre. As soon as the selling of the land was completed, the project began to be built and was finally completed in 1959 (Bring, 1978:13). Known as the Mount Hiei Driveway (*Hieizan Doraibue*), it is now a large complex which includes cable cars, restaurants, hotel, children's playgrounds, observatory and a (tolled) parkway leading to the temple centre on top of the mountain range.

Again in 1958, the Association was approached, this time by the developer of golf courses. After short negotiations some 600,000 square metres were sold to the firm. Subsequently the construction of the area's first 18-hole golf course was begun, and finally opened in June 1961 (Kansai Gorufu Gaido Mappu, 1982).

To facilitate the inflow of tourists, pilgrims, and golfers that came into the area, the roads to Kyoto and Otsu were widened and asphalted. This in effect removed the last difficulties of commuting for the villagers – travel time by car or bus was considerably shortened.

Developments in the regional housing market began to determine the use of the remaining forest lands. In ways similar to the Tokyo–Yokohama and Nagoya regions, the Kobe–Osaka–Kyoto conurbation had been growing steadily since the mid-1950s. The housing shortages created by this growth were at first alleviated by the construction of residential areas in or near to the major cities. But the effects of the general economic recovery and stability were soon felt. The availability of funds for investment brought about a rapid rise in centrally located land prices (Sargent, 1975:242). Thus, for example, between 1955 and 1970 land prices rose by 14 times, or by a yearly average of 19.2 per cent (Matsumoto, 1982:3). These trends, and the construction of new transportation routes outwards from the centres, contributed to a suburban boom. New dormitory communities began to pop up further and further away from the cities of Kobe, Osaka and Kyoto. Owing to the shortage of land, these were developed either on the site of existing rural settlements (themselves becoming 'dormitory villages'), or through the clearing and conversion of surrounding forests and agricultural land. In the Kyoto area (Akamatsu and Yamamoto, 1971:313ff.) the new suburban developments occurred first south of the city, and later in the north, with the construction of residential neighbourhoods at the foot of Mt Hiei (see Map 2). As in America (Steiner, 1981:224), and Europe (Berry, 1973:chap. 4), the tremendous post-war pressures to develop a substantial number of residential units within a very limited period led to shoddy developments: uncontrolled land use (Matsumoto, 1982:3), haphazard provision of public facilities and amenities, use of substandard building materials, and improper real estate dealings (Kamachi, 1971).

Well aware of these problems, a now much more astute Shiga Forest Association was understandably wary of the residential developers that began to approach it in the mid-1960s. These firms were one by one investigated (e.g. credit situation, previous projects), and then promptly rejected. They gave an impression

– as one living member of the Association's steering committee put it – of being fakes (*inchiki*), swindlers (*sagi*), or what the Americans would call 'shady dealers' (*sanbyaku daigen*).

Then, in July 1966, a first meeting was held between the Association's representatives and the head of a large residential developing company based in Tokyo.[3] From the beginning, according to another member of the steering committee, the relationship with this firm stood in contrast to previous experience. A native of the village who had gone to Tokyo and reached the executive level of the National Telephone and Telegraph Company had acted as a go-between. It was he who initially vouched for the solidity (*katasa*) of the developer. A Taiwanese enterprise named Tonan Shoji Kabushiki Gaisha, it was run by a Taiwanese national who had been educated at an elite Japanese university in the pre-war period. Originally set up in 1952, the company had since then developed residential areas first around Tokyo, and then outwards to the north (Sendai, Utsunomiya) and west (Hamamatsu). It was now looking to expand into the Kyoto area, and had already scouted and rejected some places around Moriyama and Otsu cities. Tonan Shoji, well aware of the area's potential for leisure-oriented developments, proposed in this initial meeting to build a suburb of summer homes, on an area of about 165 hectares.

In the coming months the developer courted the village representatives. Meetings were held, and a study trip to Tochigi Prefecture (where the company had already built an area on a scale similar to what it now proposed) was arranged. The company president, apparently a warm and forthright man, gradually won over the trust of the steering committee.

Before the land sale was finalized, however, general meetings were held in each hamlet. The progress of the Forest Association–Developer negotiations was reported on and discussed. Some older villagers recall that a few people voiced apprehension at selling ancestral land. The ancestors, such people said, would be depressed, they would be 'sick at heart' to learn of the sale. But the vast majority, fearful it would lose what seemed a very good financial opportunity, were in favour of the sale. Among these were children of Association members who had left the village, but who under the new post-war laws – bequeathing all inheritance (including rights in common land) to all siblings equally – were entitled to a say. These naturally were less eager to support village affairs, and wanted to use the projected income for other purposes. Thus the drive for a quick profit, coupled with the by then strong perception of the uselessness of the land, led to a general agreement that the land was to be sold to Tonan Shoji.[4]

The situation where almost all the land was owned by and negotiated through one association made the process of buying the land a short one. This stands in contrast to the experience of other developers in Japan (Kamachi, 1971:80), and America (Steiner, 1981:138), where because of piecemeal ownership this took much time. By December 1966 (just six months later) Tonan Shoji had bought 97 per cent of the rights of the Forest Association covering almost twice the area of the planned suburb: a total of about a million and a half square metres. Direct liquidation of the Association was ruled out because under the Forest Law management of the forest land not included in the suburb could not be carried out by a residential developing company. Thus Tonan Shoji continued to control the forest lands through its ownership of the Association's shares.

In order to complete the purchase of a final few hundred square metres needed for the third stage of the suburb's development, Tonan Shoji approached the rice-field owners in Yamanaka. After short negotiations the required land here too was secured. While there are conflicting statements in regard to the price of the land, it seems that it was about 330 Yen per square metre. In any case when divided among the 500 or so households who shared the common rights, this did not add up to much. In the words of one man, 'we lived it up for a short while – we drank, we ate, and we bought a few things for the house – and then the money was gone.'

Preparations and development

The developer next approached the city and prefectural administrations in order to secure approval for the proposed development.[5] Based on a concept of phased development (*dankaihatsu*), under this system of residential land control a developer applied for approval under one law or set of regulations before proceeding on to the next. As the area had been declared a 'natural park' in 1950, Tonan Shoji first applied (at the beginning of 1967) for a development permit under the Natural Parks Law. This was promptly granted in April, and within the next year and a half the company applied for and was given approval under the Residential Land Development Law, and the Urban Planning Law. Following further negotiations with local government officials, a Development Guidance Deed was signed. While confirming the legality of the proposed project, this document, which was shown to me by a city official, nevertheless clearly stipulated that all construction and provision of public facilities by the developer be carried out under the direction of prefectural and city officials.

On the basis of preliminary proposals and layouts drawn up during and after the negotiations that led to the purchase of the land, a general master plan was evolved which was heavily oriented towards 'physical' development. After the clearing of the forests and the levelling of the ground were finished, the suburb would be built in three stages, each of which would take roughly between two and two-and-a-half years. Each stage would also see the completion of one of the three wards (*choo*) that would eventually comprise the whole area. The developer would undertake – through subcontracting out the actual work to various building and construction companies – the provision of the local infrastructure: water, sewerage and drainage, roads and street lighting. Parallel to this it would initiate contacts with and secure the services of the public corporations supplying gas, electricity and telephones.

At this time too the developer completed and then began to implement a marketing and public relations campaign (through newspapers, the publication of pamphlets, and the placing of ads on trains and buses in the Kyoto region). A number of people who were then working for the company's Hieidaira branch mentioned that several aspects of the planning of the area, including the way in which the development was promoted, were influenced by the company president's 1964 trip to America. There he had been taken up by the idea of suburbs as centres of leisure. This, he thought, required planning and constructing a complex (tennis courts and club, pools, restaurants) which would be used both by local residents and by visitors. These ideas were also incorporated into the master plan, and lands allocated for the leisure complex.

The next step was the creation of an image for the area. After reviewing a number of suggestions, the president chose a name he himself had conceived: Hieidaira. The first two characters figured in the name Hieizan (Mt Hiei), a nationally famous historical sight, which is also a prominent pilgrimage centre for Tendai Buddhism. The last character (*taira*), usually means flat, level or plain, but in the post-war context takes on the nuance of heights or plains (as in the American suburbs of Crestwood Heights or White Plains). Such a name, he reasoned, would give the area a note of renown, a hint of newness, and a strong visual identity – one associated with the forest-covered mountains of the area. The two catch phrases used in the early ads emphasized this last aspect: '*Biwako no mieru koogen bessoochi*' (Lake Biwa Heights – a summer homes area), and '*Kansai no Karuizawa*' (The Kansai Karuizawa). Both attempted to use well known names or resort centres (Lake Biwa in the Kyoto and Karuizawa in the Tokyo areas) to evoke the environmental images of clean air, green forests, an abundance of space and vague references to a 'leisured life-style'. The ads used such terms as *yuttari* (calm, composed), *shizukasa* (quietness, calmness), *hisho ni* (summering), or *kenkoo raifu* (healthy life), to describe the area. These were also intended as a contrast to the shortcomings and difficulties that were coming to be associated with urban life in Japan.

Beginning in March 1967 and completed in early 1970, the suburb's first ward was thus developed primarily as a summer homes area. The lots, ranging between 330 sq.m and 400 sq.m, were rather large by Japanese standards, and the price per square metre, although rising during the period from 6,000 Yen to 15,000 Yen, was still cheaper than urban land in Kyoto or Otsu. Nevertheless from the beginning only a few bought the lots – and the small number of prefabs the developer had constructed – as summer homes. Increasingly, two types of people – both cognizant of an already rising rate of land prices – started purchasing plots. A small minority of rather well-to-do Kyotoites and Osakaites bought up land as an investment. According to the estimate of a company employee this amounted to about 10 per cent of the total land sales. The majority of newcomers, however, saw another advantage to the area, apart from the relatively low price of the land: its proximity to Kyoto. This group saw Hieidaira as a place in which to reside on a permanent basis, and from which to commute to the big city nearby. With the arrival of this group, the process of becoming an 'ordinary' residential suburban community started.[6]

As the second ward began to be developed, a number of trends amplified this process. First, chiefly as a consequence of corporate purchase, land prices in the urban centres rose sharply (Sargent, 1975:241; Matsumoto, 1982:3). This forced many who were seeking housing in the cities to look further afield. Whereas the first ring of dormitory communities had been built about ten to twenty kilometres from the city centres, now the second and third rings (some even forty or fifty kilometres away) began to be constructed (Glickman, 1979:22ff.). In this context Hieidaira – only 15–20 minutes by bus or 8–10 minutes by car from the outskirts of Kyoto – compared favourably with other residential areas built further away along Lake Biwa (e.g. Moriyama, Kusatsu, Omihachiman, and northern Otsu).

The developer was also experiencing difficulties. As the head of Tonan Shoji's Hieidaira branch explained, the large size of the lots, and the rising price of land, began severely to limit the number of potential buyers. Slowly, Tonan Shoji came to feel that a change was needed. The original plans for large (and by now expensive) plots were to be modified. Thus the second ward was parcelled into smaller, more compact lots that, it was thought, would match the buying power of most middle-class people. It was on these lines that the second ward was developed. The smaller lots, varying between 200 sq.m and 230 sq.m, and priced between 12,000 Yen and 20,000 Yen per square metre, were just within reach of ordinary salaried workers. The newcomers now tended almost exclusively to be people seeking permanent residence in Hieidaira: mostly young married couples and a sizeable minority of retired people. As one local leader put it a few years later, from being a '*bessoo danchi*' (a summer homes area), Hieidaira now became a '*mai hommu danchi*' (a my-home housing estate). This connotes not only an estate of settled house-owning commuters, but also the emergence of a sense among the residents that they had a certain stake in the locality.

All of this was followed by a further shift in the promotion and advertising efforts. Now, on top of the leisure-oriented 'environmental' image of the suburb, was added a 'locational' one. Hieidaira's proximity to Kyoto and Otsu, and the accessibility to the major rail (Japan National Railroads, Keihan), bus and highway routes were stressed. Pamphlets and ads of the area now began to include little maps of the suburb's location in relation to these routes.

With more and more young families taking up residence in

the area, a number of issues faced by all 'ordinary' residential communities began to arise. Among the most important of these were schooling, public transportation (for children, the elderly, and housewives), day-care facilities (for children of working mothers), and parks for the children to play in. During the first few years – when the number of households was 30 or 40 – the citizens petitioned the developer about these matters directly, usually meeting at the latter's local offices.

At first a number of temporary solutions to the citizens' demands were found. After applying to the City's Board of Education, the children were given permission to attend a school in Otsu proper, some five kilometres away. But as the number of children swelled, the informal arrangements among the parents for ferrying the kids back and forth did not suffice. The Board was petitioned again, and the residents received the services of a charter bus on which the children commuted daily. Later, as the number of children continued to grow, a second and then a third bus were added. For the city this presented an increasingly heavy financial burden.

As the 1973–4 correspondence of the developer shows, solutions to the public transportation needs followed a similar path. For two or three years a small mini-bus owned and operated by the developer was provided. With a rather flexible timetable, it was used to transport people mainly to and from Kyoto during busy periods. Yet here again, as Hieidaira's population grew, the service was not sufficient. Tonan Shoji entered into negotiations with the Keihan Company and secured the services of a charter bus line. This line was more expensive than other regular lines, and offered only a limited number of buses to and from the estate.

Not even a temporary solution for the problem of day-care facilities or parks was found at first. No land had been allocated for a day-care centre in the area, and parents were told to rely on other city-run centres in Otsu. This in itself was problematical in that most mothers – as indeed most of the suburb's working population – were employed in Kyoto. The few parents that did send their children to such centres usually sent them to expensive privately run ones near their workplace. The children played in the streets, on as yet unbuilt (empty) lots, and in the surrounding hills. But proper facilities – especially swings and slides for the younger children – were still lacking. This situation existed while paid facilities (owned and run by Tonan Shoji), such as pools and tennis courts, were already built.

Establishment of a local study group

By 1972, with the number of households now about 100, these problems were growing acute. At the same time the developer, as a number of local residents told me, was growing less and less responsive to the citizens' pleas. Tonan Shoji, they began to feel, was more interested in providing services as a way of increasing the area's marketability than of improving the actual conditions of the residents. Furthermore, as the accountability of the company to the residents was weakening so the scale of such problems as schooling and transportation became such that it could not be handled on the citizens–developer level. It became increasingly clear to a small group of residents that some kind of citizens' representation had to be set up both to study the issues involved and to carry the residents' demands to government bodies. To that end, in mid-1972, an ad-hoc study group was established under the leadership of five or six highly active residents.

Although varied in terms of their occupations and background, members of this study group brought with them a wealth of political knowledge and experience. The core of the group consisted of the following members: a young university lecturer who had been active in student politics and since then become involved in various citizens' and civil rights movements, and in the Socialist Party; a retired civil servant who had served in Kyoto's progressive prefectural government; a white-collar employee in Kyoto with a background in union affairs and activism in the Communist Party; a carpentry contractor who owned a small business in Yamanaka, and an older university professor who was involved as a central member in Kyoto's intellectual circles. Other less central members included housewives, and a further number of university teachers and white-collar *sarariiman*.

As is evident from their various activities since 1972, the inclination and aptitude of this original group of people for public activism went beyond the establishment of the ad-hoc study group. Thus, for example, the carpentry contractor later became the head of the second ward's neighbourhood association, head of the district's children's association, and an officer of the PTA. The retired civil servant for his part has become (and still is) a central member of the district's alliance of neighbourhood associations and head of its traffic safety committee, as well as almost single-handedly setting up the estate's old-folks club. The university lecturer has been a member of the local environmental protection committee for the past ten years, as well as the head of the Japan–Seychelles Friendship Society, and a campaigner for Koreans' civil rights.

According to the carpentry contractor – and to two other people more peripheral to the original core of members – the establishment of the ad-hoc study group seems to owe much to the initiative and sense of enterprise shown by the young university lecturer. This man, who was just twenty-nine at the time, figured centrally in the investigations the group carried out, as well as in the formulation of letters and petitions that were later needed.

As its primary aim at this stage was to probe into the development of the suburban estate, there was no real need to broaden the ad-hoc group's membership. Looking back from the vantage point of the present, this seems to have been advantageous, for the small group that commenced its investigations in the late months of 1972 could work in a close and co-ordinated way.

Furthermore, the informal social networks that had emerged by that time sufficed as a means by which to inform even those people who were not directly involved, of the activity of the ad-hoc study group. For since Hieidaira's beginnings patterns of neighbouring, mutual child-minding, ferrying the children to school and chance acquaintances had created a vaguely defined but nevertheless quite vigorous network for discussion and deliberation. Thus, for example, one woman who had moved to Hieidaira at the beginning of 1972 recalled – perhaps with a hint of romanticism – the intimate flavour of social relationships during the estate's first few years:

There used to be a time, when the charter bus began to work, that we all went down to Kyoto together. Because there was no community hall during that time, we decided to turn the bus into one. But that was only when Hieidaira was small. . . . It was nice, though, not like Kyoto where you can live somewhere and not know somebody living a few houses away.

The young people more than others got to know each other during that time. Most of us moved here without grandparents so that we had to rely on each other for help. . . . There was a period when I knew the children's names of all the families that lived in the area.

'Fushigi' development

The group began by carefully reviewing the specific document-ation relating to Hieidaira's development. First they examined the relevant development guidelines and deeds, and the correspon-dence between Tonan Shoji and the local authorities. Next, they looked at part of the general literature on suburban residential construction by going over national laws and stipulated building minimums and safety features. What the group quickly discovered was not only that serious defects in building and construction were present, but also that in major instances the developer had contravened existing legal requirements.

Two examples of the defects they found are roads and sewerage. The roads, it turned out, were covered with too thin a paving, and thus within the first few harsh winters they began to crack and potholes appeared almost everywhere. Moreover, having been built too narrow, problems of restricted street parking and turning corners constantly occurred. The sewerage pipes leading from each residential unit to the main street lines were too narrow as well. This necessitated building a small and expensive purifi-cation plant outside each residence, so that the sewerage matter would be broken up before it entered the narrow connecting pipe. In addition the capacity of the new projected neighbourhood purification plant (finally completed in 1974) was sufficient to accommodate only one-third of the area's planned population. Other defects were deviations from building percentages, inade-quate water supply, problematic water pumping procedures, badly built rain drainage, and inadequate street lighting.

More seriously they found that Tonan Shoji had failed to allo-cate land and funds for all of the major public facilities to which the area was entitled under the existing legal framework: parks, community halls, a school, a kindergarten, a day-care centre, and playgrounds. This, it turned out, had come about through collusion between the developer and the main development approval authority, the prefectural governor. Under the existing set of regulations, a developer had to allocate land for public facilities if the planned area was to include more than 1,000 households. Tonan Shoji succeeded, however, in getting the prefecture to give official recognition to each ward as a separate entity. With the projected number of households for each such ward ranging between 600 and 700, as separate developments they did not reach this minimum of 1,000 households. One city official commenting about this state of affairs some ten years later ironically called the development *'fushigi'*. A term with Buddhist connotations, *fushigi* variously means 'mysterious', 'inexplicable', or a 'wonder'. As the study group delved deeper into this murky business, they were led first into uncovering the links between the developer and the prefectural government, and through that to the wider regional and national relationship between the building industry and government.

While it is extremely difficult to uncover all of the specific details of Tonan Shoji's collusion with the heads of the prefectural authorities, it appears that *uragane* (lit. money behind the back) was paid on a number of occasions paralleling the stages of development approval. It was paid first in order to get official recognition of each ward as a separate development project. Then, as some of the more specific plans were completed – for the water, roads and sewerage systems, for example – money or gifts again changed hands, this time for overlooking plans that were not up to the accepted standards. Later when local government officials came to the suburb for inspection of the actual construction process, gifts were again subtly pressed upon them. One further allegation I heard from only one informant was that, with the prefectural governor's knowledge, the suburb's land was intentionally given a lower estimate of value, and thus the developer received a form of 'tax break'.[7]

That this was not an isolated case of corrupt practices was clear. It was one example of the wider building industry–government network. From the national down to the local centres of power, this network had grown out of an interplay of circumstances: the pork-barrel character of Japanese politics; the virtually uninterrupted rule of the Liberal-Democrats since the war; and the flexible character of the development approval system. Under the pork-barrel type of arrangements, cabinet ministers, central members of the ruling Liberal-Democratic Party, and highly placed bureaucrats who controlled central government appropriations and policies, supplied funds for a variety of local improvements. Local politicians – such as prefectural governors, mayors, or members of the national Diet – secured these funds through 'direct pipelines' (*chokketsu*) of patronage ties to these central elites. Many such local leaders saw the 'noticeability' of actual facilities and public works as an advantage in symbolizing to their constituencies their success in securing central government allocations. Thus vast sums of money were poured into the construction of 'conspicuous' projects such as buildings, plazas, roads, tunnels, or canals. By allocating public contracts for such projects these local politicians began to strike 'agreements' with firms in the construction industry. These compacts, in turn, served as bases for further 'agreements' spreading from public contracts to private development projects (Kamachi, 1971:77). The lengthy and stable rule of the Liberal-Democrats served to solidify these links and what emerged was a relationship of what one of Yamanaka's leaders termed 'adhesion' (*yuchaku*) between building firms and local governments.

The weakness of the development approval system served to give local authorities great flexibility. Under the system three general laws served as a base for specific negotiations regarding each project. The Urban Planning Law dated back to 1919, and provided rather vague guidelines for zoning and land consolidation. The other two laws – the Residential Land Development Law and the Refuse Disposal Law – were not frameworks setting minimum standards, but ones aimed at prevention (against natural disasters and land and water deterioration). The actual quality of development – governing such things as building minimums, or the construction of public facilities – was determined by local authorities on the basis of standing rules, and the give-and-take of separate negotiations with each private developer.

In Shiga Prefecture this situation was especially rife (Yusa, 1975:151ff.). The Hieidaira affair was part of a much wider web of illicit practices, involving the prefectural governor, his top lieutenants, political parties, and major construction firms: Ueda Kensetsu and Kumagai Gumi. Kumagai Gumi was the company that won Tonan Shoji's subcontract for the initial development work in Hieidaira, i.e. the clearing of the forests and the levelling of the surrounding hills. Through investigations launched in the mid-1970s by the succeeding prefectural governor, it turned out that these were all involved in a vast ring of fixing land prices in the late-1960s and early 1970s (Ikemi, 1982:143ff.). One man, the prefectural comptroller (an executive advisor) was even convicted and sent to jail.[8]

It was against this background and on the basis of these findings that the study group began to consider its next course of action. And it is to this that we now turn in the next chapter: the rise of a much more explicitly political activism on the part of the residents.

5 The Rise of Citizen Activism

Citizen response

That the discovery of this situation – lack of facilities, faulty construction, unresponsiveness of the developer – led eventually to activism on the part of the residents should not be perceived as inevitable. As Orbell and Uno (1972:474–5) note, this rather easy assumption – of political activism as a natural response to an awareness of lack of neighbourhood quality – is at the base of much of the literature on community action. In exploring this point, a modified version of Hirschman's (1970) 'exit' or 'voice' model of reaction to community (and organizational) deterioration may be useful (Barry, 1974: Birch, 1975).

In Hirschman's own version of this model, reaction to a perceived deterioration of community quality (services, facilities, population make-up) would have entailed a simple choice – one between residential mobility ('exit'), or political action ('voice'). Put this way, the residents of Hieidaira, having become aware of the difficulties facing the suburb, could have chosen either an 'exit' option – moved from the neighbourhood in search of a suburb with better conditions – or a 'voice' option – stayed put and made an attempt to change things. Putting it this way, however, masks the complexity involved. For in effect the residents were faced with a series of analytically distinct decisions: between moving or staying, between remaining silent or voicing their demands, between individual or collective 'voice', and between the different organizational forms capable of carrying their collective expressions.

At the point where the locals became aware of the estate's low quality of development, they were faced with a first and above all an individual (or household) decision: between the options of

82

'exit' or 'stay'. Exit here supposes the availability of – and stay the lack of – both an outside community with a better quality, and the means needed to make the move. In both respects, the vast majority of Hieidairaites were at a disadvantage.

First, scarcely any areas reasonably close to the major cities were left untouched by urban problems. The literature on Japanese urbanism (e.g. Kamachi, 1971:77–8) confirms what the locals were keenly aware of: that the shortcomings of the 1960s urban sprawl were felt almost everywhere. Not only were the few areas left with a higher quality prohibitively expensive, but – as one resident who had moved to Hieidaira in 1971 emphasized – some residential developments were constructed in an even more questionable way than Hieidaira. These suburban estates were the locus of such problems as construction without public permission (on agricultural land, forests, or hills), shady dealers with weak credit bases, or 'decoy' sales (showing or advertising a well built house but selling a shoddy one). In the words of Krauss and Simcock (1980:210), 'unlike their more mobile American counterparts, the Japanese could not avoid environmental problems by fleeing to sheltered suburban enclaves and to completely undeveloped and isolated rural areas available in countries of much vaster land and space.'

But even if a more attractive alternative could be found, most residents found themselves 'locked into' the suburban estate (Laver, 1976:472). This was a point that was raised time and again in interviews with families who had arrived in Hieidaira in 1971 and 1972. They stressed that this was primarily a matter of personal finance. For the vast majority of people who had just succeeded in buying land before the prices skyrocketed, a move could not be realistically contemplated. The burden of paying back heavy long-term (20–30 years) mortgages, which most had taken out in order to buy house and land in the suburban estate, guaranteed this.[1]

Given that the option of 'exit' was severely limited, it is not surprising then that most of the residents opted to 'stay'. The next set of options were 'silence' or 'voice'. In opting for 'voice' in this context, a crucial factor was the emergence of a combination of a sense of legitimacy of expressing political demands, and a more concrete perception of the efficacy of such expressions. Against the Japanese background of political and economic values (a passive orientation to politics, a stress on group solidarity, and a deferential attitude to authority) both were not taken for granted. Indeed such values should, at least at first glance, have disposed the locals to depend on the 'usual' or 'accepted' conservative men of influence in order to 'voice' their demands for them. Furthermore, since the Meiji era there had also been a very strong national consensus around the 'production first' or 'growth first' policy (Vogel, 1975:xv). This consensus, which was about the importance of the nation's economic growth and which was coupled with a constant government emphasis on Japan's poverty and on the need to undertake great personal and collective sacrifices, should have had a similar effect. This consensus and willingness to undertake sacrifices in turn should have further disposed the locals to moderate their demands. Indeed a few, whether out of fatalistic resignation to yet another post-war difficulty (to be endured), or a traditional attitude of deference to and compliance with authority (or a combination of these), adopted a posture of reticence toward political activity.

But this was early 1973, and from the mid-1960s new attitudes and sentiments had begun to emerge. Variously called a 'sense of malaise' (Patrick, 1976:15), a 'spiritual crisis' (Hirschmeier, 1973:viii), a vague awareness of 'opacity and unease' (Yamazaki, 1984:8), 'a sense of disillusionment' (Sargent, 1975:228), or 'a turning away from modern traditional values' (Passin, 1975a:836), these new convictions spelt a growing rejection of, or at least a reflection upon 'growth first', and its attendant ills. This wide backlash against the problematic consequences of the post-war industrial and urban policies carried – in ways not unlike similar trends in Europe, America and Australia – both 'negative' and 'positive' themes.

On the one hand, the negative impact of many government-encouraged projects and programmes was stressed: pollution; land scarcity; housing shortages; shoddy urban development; traffic congestion; insufficient development of public amenities and the deterioration of existing amenities because of over-use; or the lack of basic social welfare schemes. The argument was that expenditure had for a long time been directed away from essential services, and that the concern with higher growth rates had come at the expense of infrastructure and the building of a better living environment (Linhart, 1975:198). This stress also included a strong opposition to the institutional arrangements within which these policies were pursued – the coalition of 'big' business and 'big' government (Matsumoto, 1978:31).

On the other hand, this movement carried more 'positive' themes: the need for greater degrees of local autonomy and discretion in handling services; greater participation in politics and decision-making (Matsushita, 1978:172); the provision of a new urban infrastructure (Cornell, 1981:27); the supply and initiation of welfare programmes on a level suited to the country's industrial development; a search for fulfilment at work and a new assertion of the importance of home and private life (Passin, 1975a; Tada, 1978); and a new stress on leisure and the right to enjoy it (Linhart, 1975).

These new political attitudes and civic sentiments that had emerged since the mid-1960s to pervade almost every public issue had their local corollary. Among the suburbanites a new perception of the efficacy and legitimacy of pursuing their demands was also felt. Not a vague or ill-defined perception, but one – as the activists of the time repeatedly emphasized in the interviews held with them – firmly rooted in the changing context of local politics, specifically in the rise of citizens' movements and the electoral victories of local progressive executives.

The new set of expectations from public life, which included not only the rejection and questioning of the 'growth first' policy but also a new stress on what has come to be called 'balanced growth', began to be carried by a host of new organizations on the local level. Arising out of specific groups aimed at securing compensation for pollution-induced diseases (e.g. mercury and cadmium poisoning), these movements began their political activity with rather traditional accommodating postures and attempts to work through the accepted political channels: for example through patronage ties, or pleas to local conservatives. But the lack of government, party, and business response pushed them increasingly into a more confrontational posture, and the use of extra-institutional modes of protest like the courts, media, sit-ins, or the use of outside advisors (see McKean, 1981; and Krauss and Simcock, 1980).

But then as the environmental issues spread, and the salience and legitimacy of citizen protest widened, the focus of indemnity changed. Now citizens' movements (*shimin undoo*) which saw environmental protest as part of a wider vision of activism, were joined by residents' movements (*juumin undoo*) based exclusively

on residents of an area and seeking redress for their own specific
self-interested grievances: for instance opposing the placing of
industrial plants or highway interchanges in their locality, or
demanding the provision of essential urban services by local
authorities (Krauss and Simcock, 1980:196–7). Indeed it appears
that this latter type – more urban-oriented and linked to a specific
area – formed the bulk of citizens' organizations in Japan (Reed,
1981:264).

The importance of these movements as 'models' or 'ideals'
(Krauss and Simcock, 1980) for the Hieidairaites cannot be overstressed. Most of the local residents had heard of such movements
through the vast amount of publicity they received in the newspapers and magazines of the time. Many others had actually participated – even before coming to Hieidaira – in a variety of
citizens' and residents' movements. One woman, for example,
told me that before moving to the estate she had been a member
of two campaigns that were centred in the apartment complex she
had resided in before (in Osaka): one was mounted in opposition
to rent rises, while the other was focused on the establishment of
a consumer co-operative (*seikyoo*). Another couple recalled that
when they lived in another area of Otsu they had helped a residents' drive for the construction of a shopping centre.[2]

Besides such 'external' experiences, in Hieidaira itself a residents' movement encompassing members from the estate, Yamanaka and a Kyoto neighbourhood (Kitashirakawa) had also been
organized. It mounted a drive against the illegal dumping and
burning of garbage by a Kyoto firm on a hill next to the estate.
Its successful campaign – the dumping was stopped – brought the
movement into contact with this commercial firm, the police, and
the governments of Otsu and Kyoto cities as well as Shiga and
Kyoto prefectures.[3] Thus many local leaders still talk of this period
as the beginnings of *juumin pawaa* (residents' power). In this
way they clearly underline the awareness that the persistence
and success of citizens' movements served not only to legitimize
participation in community organizations of local protest, but also
to emphasize the practical potential of such efforts.

At about the same time, changes in local politics were also
occurring. Clearly related to the rise of citizens' movements, the
nationwide electoral victories of local progressives were nevertheless an independent process. For the opposition parties (the social-
ists, communists, and social democrats) were the first to recognize

the great disaffection with Liberal-Democratic politics and policies, and to succeed in channelling them into electoral support. It
was the 'national local-government system' (Dunleavy, 1980) that
became the locus of expressing this disquiet. With 45 per cent of
the Japanese population living in a locality governed by a progressive local chief executive in the early 1970s (Samuels, 1982:631),
the widespread perceptions were both of a continued growth in
local reform power, and an anticipation that the post-war relations
between business and government would change. A significant
electoral victory in Shiga politics underscored this.

Supported by a progressive coalition, a former labour union
officer was voted into the Otsu City mayorship in October 1972
(Otsu-shi, 1982). In ways similar to other progressive-controlled
authorities (Tsurutani, 1977:204) he initiated a host of administrative reforms aimed at increasing the receptivity and sensitivity of
local government to citizens' demands. Thus, for instance, the
following measures were instituted: the establishment of new
administrative units for monitoring pollution, co-ordination of
citizens' activities, citizens' advice bureaux, or regular meetings
for consultation with neighbourhood associations (Shin Seikatsu
Undo Kyokai, 1982:45). This electoral victory signalled the rise
of, if not an actual ally, then at least a sympathetic supporter for
the residents of Hieidaira. The new political alignment thus not
only reinforced the influence of the citizens' movements ideals –
granting legitimacy and a sense of efficacy to citizens' 'voice' –
but more concretely it increased the perception among the locals
that a workable solution to their demands could be found.

However neither the acute lack of public facilities and services
in Hieidaira, nor the commonality of the problem for the whole
of the local population, nor the awareness of a legitimate and
efficacious way of rectifying the situation, could by themselves
give rise to an effective local movement. What were needed, then,
were the right organizational forms and resources for creating and
sustaining such a movement.

The dilemmas of community organization

As the members of the study group considered the specific organizational form their 'voice' would take, they came to appreciate that such an option – when compared to a move out of the neighbourhood – was problematical. In Orbell and Uno's (1972:471) terms they began to appreciate that such an option was 'messy'. It was 'messy' because the processes of aggregating and articulating citizen demands, mobilizing support, negotiating with outside bodies, and pursuing all of these until the demands were met, were both protracted and complex.

They began by reviewing the suburb's prior experience of organized action.[4] An arrangement on the lines of Hieidaira's first few years – direct residents–developer meetings – was out of the question. Now that the estate had more than a hundred households, such gatherings would be difficult from a practical point of view. Other individual efforts – writing, phoning, meeting politicians personally – would be disadvantageous in that they would not be recognized as representative of the community. The need for contact with the locality's external 'advocates' and 'adversaries' dictated, they reasoned, a comparatively small and cohesive body that could both manageably represent the locality, and communicate a greater sense of threat to the developer. As the resident who functioned as the 'advisor for educational affairs' to the citizens told me:

'We needed some kind of organization that could come into contact in a representative way with the developer, the city, and prefectural authorities. . . . Especially in new areas like ours there is a need for these kinds of organizations that can bargain and negotiate with government authorities. . . . Especially in regard to the whole problem of corruption, we knew that if we came as individuals we wouldn't be able to get anything done.'

Next, they thought, there was a possibility of organizing themselves into temporary movements or ad-hoc committees. This they had done a number of times, such as when they lobbied for a bus with which to commute to school, when they organized against the illegal dumping of garbage, or when they began to study the problems of the area's development. These groups were by now (at times still grudgingly) recognized by local officials, and some kind of reaction to their demands could be expected. But the scope of the problems – the lack not of just one service or facility but a host of them – and the expected length of time it would take to secure these, made such short-lived and makeshift efforts appear less effective. As the young university lecturer explained, unlike the groups that assembled now and then to deal with rather limited problems such as the redirection of a street, or the removal of a specific environmental hindrance, Hieidaira's problems necessitated a more enduring, a more persistent organizational form.

But there were further difficulties. Ad-hoc committees or movements were also limited in terms of the resources (time, money, expertise) they could muster for communication to and the mobilization of the citizenship. Two features of the growing population accentuated these problems. First, as more people moved into the area, the number of 'social isolates' as well as newcomers with few informal links in the locality was increasing. Second, Hieidaira like other areas in Japan (Bayley, 1976:17; Smith, 1970:5–6), and in contrast to most American residential areas (Orbell and Uno 1972:476), was while 'middle-class' nevertheless rather heterogeneous socially. Living now in the suburb were a mix of pensioners, merchants and self-employed, artisans, school and university teachers, professionals, as well as a sizeable group of salaried employees (predominantly white-collared). Thus on top of the communications problems posed by a large population, its heterogeneity and the existence of a number of people not integrated into the informal social circles of the estate would pose difficulties in organizing the residents into some kind of concerted action. In this context it would clearly be advantageous if an organization with regular means of communication (say publishing a weekly or monthly newsletter) could be established. This would facilitate, they thought, the integration of newcomers into the community, as well as provide a forum or focus for discussion of the locality's problems and needs.

Another logical possibility that was only hinted at by interviewees was a variant of the special-purpose group type of arrangement. Here the possibility would have been for a link-up between such groups and certain city and prefectural assemblymen. The latter could function as more permanent 'custodians' of community affairs, and a direct link to local authority funds and allocations. Looking at things in retrospect, however, it seems that Hieidaira was at the time as yet not big enough to be an independent electoral district. Such an assemblyman, while potentially helpful, would most probably have been more preoccupied with the larger, electorally more significant parts of the electoral zone.[5]

On the other hand, in a way similar to members of other citizens' organizations in Japan (Krauss and Simcock, 1980:221; Tsurutani, 1977:200), the locals were keenly aware of too close an association with political parties. Indeed, since the rise of citizens' movements less than a decade earlier, the political parties (especially those of the left) had seen in them potential rivals for public support, and subsequently strove to manipulate or co-opt such groups. The young university lecturer explained it thus:

'We thought that we didn't need the support of the Communist
Party. Because we could think for ourselves there was no
need for the Communist theories of politics or of power. The
influence of the Communist Party is strongest in those estates
where the residents have very little power. . . . The danger
with political parties is that things tend to get bogged down.
They tend to turn every success you have into the party's
success. It's like this Takada [a city assemblywoman
associated with the Communist Party] who always distributes
these letters about how she achieved things for Hieidaira.'

Moreover in the post-war context of Japanese local government, executive power (mayor, governor) had grown immensely in relation to city and prefectural legislatures (Nakagawa, 1980:191). With the local executive role based on a presidential rather than parliamentary model, the absence of local government vertical fragmentation (*tate wari gyoosei*), and the greater administrative specialization now found, it is not surprising that these executives and the heads of their bureaucracies control almost all important local policy making and budgetary allocations. An organization recognized by and capable of coming into contact with the local executives or their administrations was as important, reasoned the Hieidairaites, as one having political relations with local assemblymen.

In contrast to other industrial countries, in Japan there was a concrete cultural and historical organizational form that could answer most of the above considerations (Nakamura, 1968:205). Known variously as the *tonari gumi* (neighbourhood group), *burakukai* (hamlet association), *choonaikai* (urban ward or neighbourhood association), or as in Otsu city as *jichikai* (self-government association), these organizations were found in one form or another throughout the country (one recent estimate puts their national number at 270,000 – Shin Seikatsu Undo Kyokai, 1982:1). While they have no legal status under national law, these permanent, community-based associations both make demands on local government and aid and supplement public services. Based on semi-compulsory household membership, groups of between ten and twenty households are the basic units (*kumi* or *han*) of these *jichikai*, and furnish ready networks of community-wide recruitment and communications. In Otsu, the neighbourhood associations are linked to special administrative units in the City Office, and meetings between their leaders and administrators are held regularly. The revenue from small levies which these associations collect, and subsidies from the city and prefecture, provide a regular flow of money that is used at the discretion of the residents for a variety of local activities: for example, printing the association's announcements, trips for local clubs, or a sports field-day.

At the same time, however, the *choonaikai* or the *jichikai*'s popular image as an associational adjunct to local conservative political powers (essentially to politicians in or closely allied with the Liberal-Democratic Party), underlines the problematic character of the organization. Based on the five-household groups (*gonin gumi*) of the Tokugawa era, hamlet and ward associations were reintroduced in the pre-war period as administrative extensions of government.[6] The purpose of this hierarchical structure was explained 'as being the transmission of the *will* of those above to those below, and of the *feelings* of those below to those above' (Dore, 1959:104, emphasis in the original). More concretely these associations were used during the war to mobilize contributions for the military effort, digging shelters, rationing, civil defence, send-offs for soldiers, gathering comforts for the troops, and as a method of social control (through spying on neighbours and uncovering dissidents).

After the war, the American Occupation saw these organizations as auxiliaries of the totalitarian regime and attempted to abolish them through the Abolition of the *Choonaikai* Law (Nakagawa, 1980:157–8). Administrators in local government were directed by this law to refrain from using the *choonaikai* for any purpose. In their place local administrative branches (*shuchosho*) and police boxes (*chuuzaisho*) were opened to serve minimums of either 15,000 people or 8 square miles.

With the signing of the peace treaty in 1952, however, many associations were revived by residents of local urban and rural communities (according to one estimate about 80 per cent of them – Nakagawa, 1980:157–8). At the start, when they were resurrected for 'self-help' purposes – tipping the police, gathering contributions for local shrines, upkeep of street lights – the attitude of the civil administration was that of 'watchful non-intervention' (*hoonin seikan*), or at worst as something 'to be put up with' (*shikata ga nai*).

It is not surprising, then, that following this revival Japanese social critics of such local associations (for example, Isomura and Okuda, 1966:144) began to question their 'peculiarities'. These critics tended to decry their lack of independence from government, their being a repository of conservative values, and their inherent potential for a return to pre-war forms.[7] As Dore (in his introduction to Nakamura, 1968) eloquently puts it, among progressive Japanese

> The revival of *choonaikai* was to be deplored . . . a relic of
> the feudal past. The fact that households rather than
> individuals formed their constituent units . . . was a
> perpetuation of anti-individualistic familism. The assumption
> of automatic universal membership was an offence against
> liberty. . . . According to the typical stereotype, a *choonaikai*
> was composed of a small coterie of conservative and ambitious
> rogues, and an apathetic rank and file.

While these fears of the *choonaikai*'s 'pre-war' possibility have not materialized in the post-war period, other apprehensions have appeared. At root is the view that such associations, while positively increasing concern with, and participation in local affairs, have nevertheless a serious potential for being manipulated by 'big' government (i.e. formidable, large-scale, complex bureaucracies). Indeed as early as 1953, some groups in local and central government began to recognize the contributions these local associations could provide for city administrators (Steiner,

1965:223). In Otsu (Otsu-shi, 1973), the *burakukai* and *choonaikai* were formally re-established by the city authorities in 1954, and their name changed to *jichikai* the following year.[8] From that period and onwards, the Otsu City Office (as other local authorities) had actively encouraged the establishment of local *jichikai*, and used them for such purposes as communication of government notices to the citizens, public safety drives, public health campaigns, supplementary welfare activities, contributions to the Japanese Red Cross, maintenance of street lighting, and as sounding boards for planned city projects.

In considering the establishment of a local *jichikai*, Hieidaira's residents seem to have been well aware of these perils. One former civil servant now retired in the suburb noted that, seen as one aspect of the post-war enlargement of local government tasks and functions, the revival of the *jichikai* involves two problems. On the one hand there is an anxiety at returning to the wartime patterns. But also on a more practical plane, he added, there is a danger that these kind of associations would become little more than 'administrative subcontractors' (*shita uke gyoosei*) – voluntary organizations whose activities are aimed solely at easing the budgetary burdens of local government.

Yet at the same time the suburbanites were also aware of the more radical potential implicit in these local associations. For this was 1973, and for the past decade new sentiments had pervaded the neighbourhood associations of the new housing estates throughout the country. Externally less supportive, even opposed to the local conservative establishment (Krauss and Simcock, 1980:212; White, 1976:119), and internally more egalitarian and democratic (Nakamura, 1982; 1968:201), these organizations, with strong ideological and (sometimes) organizational links to the rising citizens' movements (McKean, 1981:chaps 6 and 7), had by then a long track record of success.

That an awareness of this new potential had filtered down even to those locals who were not part of the original group of activists, was impressed upon me in a conversation with an elderly pensioner who had stood on the sidelines, as it were, during this period. He emphasized what he saw as the new dimension that neighbourhood associations had taken on in the post-war period:

'You have to understand that in one sense the *jichikai* is the lowest rung of the city administration (*mattan soshiki*). In this way its a bit like the old pyramid that was part of the past militarism in the country. Then orders about what to do and how to act used to come down to the *jichikai* which would then communicate them to the citizens. But today it's equally important for the *jichikai* to communicate thoughts and feelings from the bottom to the top.'

These organizations, then, presented the Hieidairaites with a concrete model for effective action. This, both in terms of the less deferential, oppositional posture to local powers, but no less importantly in terms of the organizational forms that could carry their demands.

The Hieidaira *jichikai*

The first step in setting up the neighbourhood association was securing the approval of the city authorities. The ad-hoc study group thus approached the City Office section dealing with citizen's affairs, and formally asked that such an association be created. The city, which had been encouraging the establishment of such community organizations since the mid-1950s and which saw this occasion as a favourable opportunity for 'organizing' one of Otsu's new estates, readily agreed. Hieidaira's residents were then asked to assemble one evening and to elect – in the presence of city representatives – some people who were to become the first officers of the neighbourhood's *jichikai*. Not surprisingly the people elected were the central members of the study group who agreed to continue their community efforts within the more formal roles of the neighbourhood association.

One city bureaucrat who was only a minor official in the Citizens' Affairs Department in 1973 showed me the copy of guidelines for the *jichikai* (Otsu-shi, 1973) that was handed to the new association officers in Hieidaira. These stipulated in very general terms the following: the aims of the neighbourhood associations (the communication of municipality announcements, participation in fund-raising drives for such bodies as the Japanese Red Cross and co-operation in other kinds of administrative tasks); rules for electing association officers and representatives; and the type and amount of subsidies the *jichikai* would be eligible to receive from the city.

Next, with the small sums received from the municipality and the money collected from a small levy the *jichikai*'s constituent households began to pay, the association purchased some rudimentary equipment: cabinets, sofas, chairs, mats, heaters and stationery. It was only years later that the association bought a sophisticated photo-copying machine for its reports and newsletters. During that time it still used an old privately owned mimeograph machine that a member of the ad-hoc study group had in his possession. It also applied for and received the use of a telephone line and opened a bank account with the Post Office Bank.

From the developer, the association received the use of a small house that was converted into a community meeting hall. The structure remained, however, under Tonan Shoji's ownership and ultimate discretion.

A somewhat simplified organizational chart of the neighbourhood association and its affiliated organs is given in Figures 1 and 2. At the bottom of each ward's *jichikai* were territorial base groups (*kumi*) which covered the whole estate.[9] These were usually made up of between 8 and 10 households who rotated the post of group head or group representative (*kumi-choo*) between them on a yearly basis. These heads were in charge of relaying municipal and *jichikai* messages to all the groups' individual household members, and for collecting the small sums of the neighbourhood association's levy. These *kumi-choo* also elected the head and assistant head of each ward's *jichikai*. In addition the *kumi-choo* of all the estate formed the general representative assembly (*hyoogikai*), which elected the officers of the Hieidaira alliance of neighbourhood associations (*Hieidaira Jichi Rengookai*) which at that time meant in effect an alliance of the estate's first and second wards.

Figure 2 depicts the functional division of labour within the alliance of neighbourhood associations (which from this point and onwards will simply be referred to as the Hieidaira *jichikai* or the neighbourhood association). Here the main distinction was between the executive on the one hand, and the rest of the committees and associated organs on the other. The executive was made up of the following officers: the head of the association (the alliance) and his two assistants; a secretary who was in charge of

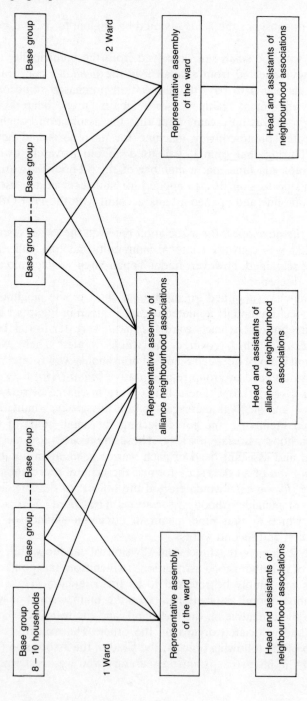

Figure 1 Organizational chart of the Hieidaira alliance of neighbour-hood associations: territorial division of labour

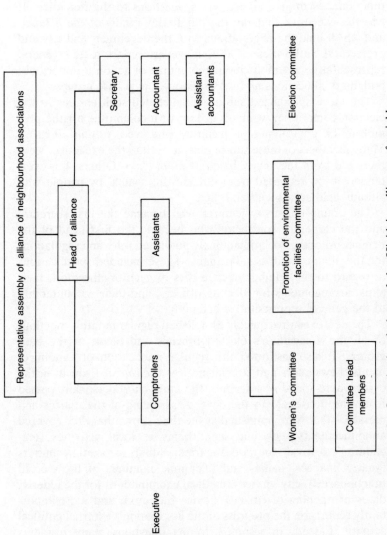

Figure 2 Organizational chart of the Hieidaira alliance of neighbourhood associations: functional division of labour

all the office, clerical and communications work; an accountant and his assistants; and four comptrollers (in the American sense of executive advisors) who were usually older individuals whose function was to give advice and suggestions to the executive. It was the executive that ran the day-to-day affairs of the *jichikai*, and which held the negotiations with the developer, and city and prefectural authorities. It did, however, report to the general representative assembly about the course of action it undertook, budgetary allocations and the creation of new base groups.

The more specialized sub-organs included such entities as the election committee, women's group, or a committee for the promotion of environmental facilities (*kankyoo suishin iinkai*).[10] Many members of these sub-organs, as well as the executive, were recruited from the yearly batch of *kumi-choo*. Others, however, tended to be recruited from outside this 'batch' by people who already held an association office.

The young university lecturer who became the first secretary and the carpentry contractor who became the first head of the neighbourhood association quickly published rules and regulations for the alliance and its sub-organs. These included specifications in regard to the number of members of each organization, their aims, arrangements for electing officers, and their accountability to the general representative assembly.

The new executive quickly established regular monthly meetings of all the association's elected officials and heads of the base groups. It also instituted the regular publication of announcements, newsletters and circular notices (*kairanban*) which, in the cases where speed was needed, the *kumi-choo* personally passed from one household to the next. A sampling of the notices and messages that were published at the time shows that they covered announcements regarding such things as local activities (e.g. children's festival, sports days, trips, clubs), association matters (yearly finances, names and telephone numbers of the elected functionaries), city services (medical examinations for the elderly, dates of opening of citizens' advice bureaux), and most importantly reports on the progress of the association's external political activity. Indeed, in response to my questions many residents admitted that their first introduction to the suburb's problems was through these regular messages of the *jichikai*. Even today when the salience of the suburb's problems has receded somewhat, most residents still read or at least skim through these regular announcements. In addition to this a number of notice boards were also erected around the estate (for example next to bus stations), so that even those few households that did not belong to the *jichikai* could be kept up to date.

This voluminous amount of formal communication thus augmented the patterns of information transferral and discussion that were part of the informal social networks that had emerged before.

Yet despite the fact that the *jichikai*'s communications network had been set up, information about the estate disseminated, and initial but regular contact with the local authorities and Tonan Shoji established, not all of the local population seemed to have actively supported the association's aims and tactics. For one thing, even within the group that contributed tangibly to the collective effort, people differed in the enthusiasm, time and skills they brought to such activities as the drafting and circulation of petitions. Thus while some recall that they lent a hand in the more technical side of mimeographing and distributing newsletters, others say that they only went along from time to time to the meetings of the association with the city authorities. Yet others seem to have entered these activities only half-heartedly. Thus one person who had moved to the estate from Otsu said that he participated out of a sense of obligation or courtesy (*giri*) to his neighbour who was one of the *jichikai*'s leaders. He added that he did this despite feeling that he himself was not especially capable in matters of public activism.

Moreover, according to the estimate of one local leader only half of the residents shared actively at any one time in the association's campaigns. Those who did not engage in the communal efforts were divided into three groups. The first, 'passive onlookers', were people who – whether out of previous experience, apprehension at the scale of the undertaking, or self-perceived lack of political knowledge – felt pessimistic about the local organization's potential for success. A second group comprised those who wanted a 'free ride'. Others, this group thought, would do all the dirty work while they could benefit from the results. The third group consisted of a few politically more conservative individuals. These, out of a distaste for protest politics or a personal dislike of some of the *jichikai*'s leaders, were hostile to the association. Such people tended to see in the *jichikai*'s attitudes a direct link with the radical politics of the 1960s. One of these conservative individuals characterized a central figure in the association (rather exaggeratedly), as 'radical, and insensitive to human feelings' and as one 'who had, during the students' rebellion of the late 60s, belonged to the Doshisha (University) pack who had worn helmets and attacked teachers and people.' Another older lady in dismissing unreservedly any kind of 'leftist' activity said that she 'does not care for petitions, dislikes citizens' movements, and hates the Communist Party.'

Yet in spite of the existence of these groups, and the fact that, even among the active supporters, not everyone provided enthusiastic and sustained contributions all of the time, the *jichikai* was to prove quite successful in the next few years.

Strategies and negotiations[11]

In the first meetings of the newly established *jichikai*, the activists realized that a number of interrelated efforts were needed in order to secure the services and facilities which were lacking. First, they would have to secure the recognition, by the progressive administration in Otsu, of Hieidaira as a political unit. In more analytical terms they seem to have realized that local self-definition had to be validated from the outside. Second, recognition of the community's demands had to be secured. That is, in the words of political science, the agenda had to be set. Third, acting in concert, the citizens and the local progressives would have to confront Tonan Shoji and secure the allocation of land and funds for the respective facilities. Finally, the citizens would have to turn to the local authorities and press for the supply of the actual services (the buildings, teachers, staff).

The stage of entry into the 'political market', as it were, proved to be rather easy. With the setting up of the *jichikai*, the city (and indirectly the prefectural) administration had not only given recognition to Hieidaira as a political unit, but also recognized the leadership of this organization as legitimate representatives of the community. The fact that the neighbourhood association was newly established also ensured that there were no 'barriers of entry' into this market. There were no previous local organizations (controlled, say, by conservatives) from which they had to wrest 'recognition' by locals and outsiders.

In 'setting the agenda', the *jichikai*'s direct link to the local government administrations also proved an advantage: no local assemblyman, or other party intermediary was needed. The neighbourhood association's leaders thus directly approached both the prefectural and the city authorities. But the reaction of these two governments differed greatly. The prefectural administration, which was still at that time under the rule of the corrupt Liberal-Democratic Governor, proved (not surprisingly) unreceptive to their demands. A newspaper account written a month or two after the *jichikai* approached the prefectural authorities relates the following (*Asahi Shinbun*, 10 March 1973). For one thing Hieidaira's leaders were not allowed to meet any highly placed official but only a sub-section chief (*kakarichoo*). Next, they were treated rather abruptly, with this sub-section chief raising his voice and telling them to leave the premises. The specific reason given by the newspaper for this 'eviction' throws light on the tactics used by the estate's neighbourhood association. It seems that Hieidaira's citizens tried to tape their conversation with the sub-section chief who became extremely angry at what he saw as an improper gesture and who subsequently asked them to leave. Another tactic I heard about from only one informant was that the head officers of the *jichikai* photographed all of the main bureaucrats who had taken part in the corrupt practices. But, most importantly, they were told that as there was no legal framework dictating the construction of public facilities when the estate was initially developed, the prefectural authorities could not put a binding request on Tonan Shoji to provide anything.

Despite this initial setback the citizens had a completely different experience with the progressive Mayor of Otsu who had taken up office in October 1972. As a series of newsletters published at that time by the neighbourhood association show, a working consensus gradually began to emerge out of the negotiations with this mayor and his administrators. The consensus covered both the right of the citizens to certain public facilities and amenities, and the immediate course of action needed to confront the estate's developer. Thus a letter issued by the neighbourhood association during the first week of March 1973, and addressed to the residents of the estate, reported the following:

At the beginning of the month our neighbourhood association formally petitioned and questioned the prefectural government about the lack of public facilities in the area. We gathered with a number of minor officials from the prefectural government in order to hear their reply. We went calmly and with complete faith in the prefectural governor and in his administrators. Their answer was, however, that it was impossible to do anything on our behalf because of the lack of legal provisions when the estate was developed.

Despite this paralysis of the prefectural government we approached the Otsu city authorities and began to study our problems with them. The mayor especially looked on the settlement of our difficulties in a positive and friendly way.

After four meetings with the city officials they said that as the municipality had full responsibility for roads and water works, they would find a solution to these problems. Further, the city will begin negotiations with a private bus company so that a study as to whether a regular bus line can be established to the estate will be conducted. We foresee that this will ease commuting to and from Hieidaira.

The municipality has also recognized the need in the estate for educational facilities and meeting halls. And we struck an agreement to complete the construction of these by 1976.

The letter goes on to report about the City Office's agreement to construct an administrative branch giving municipal services within neighbourhoods, and curved mirrors and road signs to help with Hieidaira's traffic safety.

The *jichikai*, as the contemporary association secretary told me, began to put direct pressure on the developer independently from the negotiations it had entered into with the municipality. According to him, two broad strategies for confronting Tonan Shoji were discussed. On the one hand, the new Hieidaira *jichikai* could have attempted to expose certain Tonan Shoji functionaries to the public prosecutor, hoped for their arrest and trial, and maybe procured some kind of compensation for the things the developer had not provided. But in the long run, they reasoned, such a strategy had a number of faults. First, the illegalities involved were reaching their limit under the statute of limitations. More importantly, they realized that with the developer still having a 'stake' in Hieidaira (it still owned land in the first two wards, and all of the as yet uncompleted third ward), struggling for a lump-sum compensation (in itself unsure) would not be prudent. Rather, as this man continued:

We decided to approach Tonan Shoji and combine threats of exposing their ethical wrongdoings to the newspapers, with promises not to do so if our demands were met. We supposed that they would be afraid that such an exposure would hurt their public image.

These threats were far from idle. For one thing, the post-war Japanese media – active in political muckraking and with a strong oppositional spirit (Passin, 1975b:259; Watanuki, 1975:135) – could be depended upon for support and aid. After all it was this group of Shiga journalists (see especially Shiga Janaaru, 1976) who had played a major role in uncovering the land scandals of the early 1970s. This 'reference public' (Lipsky, 1968), so crucial to the success of any modern movement, could provide potential support not only in exposing the immorality of the Tonan Shoji–prefecture connection as part of some abstract civic duty, but more crucially in the possibility of 'bad publicity' driving away the developer's potential customers. Or, in Hirschmanian terms, their own 'exit' effectively barred, the citizens could nevertheless have deterred others from buying land in the estate. This threat, then, made their bargaining position stronger and more credible.

The mayor and his City Office bureaucrats for their part also began to put pressure on Tonan Shoji. The bureaucrats, whether out of a feeling that they were at last freed from the previous conservative mayor, whether out of genuine sympathy with the citizens' claims, or whether out of anticipation of the new elected official's orientation, began openly to back the position of the suburban neighbourhood's *jichikai*. Tonan Shoji's development began to be called irresponsible (*sekinin ga nai*), and haphazard (*muchakucha*). An article from the Shiga edition of the national Asahi newspaper (*Asahi Shinbun*, 10 March 1973) summed up the city demands put to Tonan Shoji and the developer's reaction in the following report:

The development of a big estate for nearly 2,000 households is continuing without any public facilities. Representatives of the 300 households already living in this, the Hieidaira estate, have already met with city officials a number of times and demanded the provision of these facilities and amenities. . . . In a meeting yesterday city officials said that although there were no regulations stipulating the construction of such facilities when the estate was begun to be developed, this situation is proving to be very inconvenient for the residents. It has thus requested the developer to provide these facilities according to present guidelines for development. . . .

City officials further said that it is to be thought unusual that permission for such a development without facilities was given in the first place. This seems part, they further stated, of the background of unusual area development throughout the prefecture in the last few years.

Under the city's directives the developer Tonan Shoji (Rin Itoku – company president) was requested to provide land for the following: 25,000 sq. m for a primary school, 4,000 sq. m for parks, 1,000 sq. m for a citizen's centre, 2,100 sq. m for a day-care centre, and 1,500 sq. m for community meeting halls. It was requested to provide, then, 35,000 sq. m in all.

The residents of the estate are satisfied with the municipality request. But they are considering whether to introduce into their discussions with the city authorities a review of the way the permit for development was given to Tonan Shoji by the prefectural government. . . .

Otsu's mayor – Mr Yamada – stated that he requested Tonan Shoji to provide this land so that it would live up to its responsibility to the residents. . . .

As this newspaper article indicates, the strong bargaining position the City Office brought to the negotiations with the developer cannot be understood apart from the powers granted local government under the new national Development Approval System (*Kaihatsu Kyoka Seido*).

Itself an outgrowth of the new country-wide conception of balanced urban and industrial promotion, this system was based on a new Urban Planning Law, and such related laws as the Building Standards Law, or the Residential Land Transaction Law (Oshio, 1981). This new system stressed not only the prevention of hazards, but the more positive goals of controlled urban growth and the conservation of nature. This was to be done through initiating a host of more concrete measures: designation of controlled urban areas; strict limits on land use and building percentages; the clear differentiation and definition of real estate brokerage, transaction, and development; a system of publicizing land prices for the purposes of controlling price fluctuations; minimum engineering and allocation levels (e.g. sidewalks, parks); allowance within national minimums for local governments to set stricter limits; the probe of prospective developers by local governments (tax returns, financial situation, previous projects); and the establishment of new administrative units for the implementation of these.

As they were approved under a previous legal framework, city officials could do little directly in regard to Hieidaira's first two wards. But by threatening to withhold approval for the third ward they attempted to prod Tonan Shoji into providing the needed facilities and land for the whole suburban estate. In the idiom of local government, they threatened that no 'official seal' (*hanko*) would be given unless the developer took concrete steps to improve the situation.

This pressure was compounded by the election of a new prefectural governor within the next year. This man, who had been with the Ministry of Home Affairs and then mayor of a small city in Shiga, succeeded by a small minority in becoming the prefecture's first progressive governor (Asahi Shinbun, 1977:50–1). His election, and the subsequent administrative reforms he instituted,[12] spelt defeat for Tonan Shoji's conservative confederates. Within a few months of his election, this man too began to demand that Tonan Shoji furnish the missing public land and installations.

On top of the strong pressures put on it now by the city, prefecture and the *jichikai*, the developer was experiencing serious financial difficulties. Both the decline in private investment and public expenditure that followed the 1973 oil shock, and the continued rise of land prices, contributed to a sluggish state of the real estate market. Then a trend present since the mid-1960s (Kamachi, 1971:77–8) further exacerbated the situation. Partly in an effort at recovering public trust, and partly in an effort to squeeze out the smaller and medium-sized firms, the big developers (mostly those affiliated with Japan's giant conglomerates and railroad companies) began organizing the property sector into regional and national organizations such as the National Residential Areas Developers Alliance, or the National Association of Sellers of Residential Land. These associations evolved elaborate industry-wide codes of ethics in order to display their 'trustworthiness' to a wary public. But, more importantly, in confining the membership in these associations to firms above a certain size, they effectively limited access to the loans provided by the National Development Bank. Tonan Shoji thus found itself in constant difficulties in finding running capital for the business.

Having been rendered effectively powerless, the developer conceded and in the following years was prompted into providing: land and a small building (100 sq. m floor space) for a community hall; land for a day-care centre, a school and a kindergarten; land for parks and playgrounds; money (through selling part of the land it owned to the City in a complicated deal) for the improvement of the estate's roads; and the improvement of the water system. Thus Tonan Shoji's capitulation owes as much to its perceptions of its own interests, as to the struggles and manoeuvering of the estate's residents and the city and prefectural administrations.

But things did not go entirely smoothly. One city official, in reviewing the variety of delaying tactics the developer used (for instance asking for repeated meetings in order to clear-up 'unclear' city directives), said the latter did everything lackadaisically (*shibu shibu*). A set of documents at the city office offers one such example. In 1974 Tonan Shoji undertook to build a small playground with slides and swings. But while the land was allocated, two years later there were still letters to the developer reminding him of his commitment to provide these apparatuses.

On the whole, however, the developer had satisfied the local authorities and received a go-ahead for the development of the third ward. This part, having been constructed under the guidelines of the new legal framework, differs from the neighbourhood's first two wards. Here while the size of the lots is even smaller (an average of 165 sq. m) than those in the second ward, the percentage of public land is much larger. Much space is allocated to wider streets, sidewalks, parks, a community hall, and citizens' centre. The rise in land values and the greater infrastructural investment by the developer has resulted in an increase from about 25,000 Yen per square metre in 1974 to about 80,000 Yen in 1983.

An interesting outgrowth of this was the addition of another element to the estate's advertising image. Real-estate ads began to stress not only the previous elements of 'environment' and 'accessibility', but also one of 'public amenities'. Tonan Shoji and other real-estate agents in the area have, since then, emphasized the existence of such facilities as the school, kindergarten, and day-care centre – those very facilities the developer had to be forced into providing.

From the developer's point of view it was very advantageous that no actual evidence or direct allegations were ever published about its illicit arrangements. For it made possible the continued operation of the company and the projection of an image of 'benefactor'. Thus at the beginning of fieldwork when I first interviewed the assistant head of Tonan Shoji Hieidaira branch, he emphasized a number of times that the granting of land to the residents was a *purezento* (present) the company president had decided to bestow on the residents.

While an examination of all the processes by which the school, kindergarten and day-care centre were turned into fully functioning institutions would take us much beyond the confines of this chapter, a few general comments may be instructive. In securing the operation of these institutions the procurement of land was only the first step. The allocation of local and national funds, the construction of the actual physical facilities, and the assignment of staff and other resources were also necessary. Towards securing these, the neighbourhood association, using its local communications and recruitment networks, launched a long flurry of petitions, appeals and meetings with the relevant City Office departments, the heads of the Board of Education, and the mayor. In these activities, the *jichikai* left the one-to-one relationship with the developer, and entered the realm of local government budgetary politics. It was at this point, in other words, that Hieidaira entered into competition with other communities, a competition for a share of the limited budgetary pie.

City officials who received the Hieidaira *jichikai*'s petitions, and who were present at these initial gatherings, were impressed with the force and style with which the demands were expressed. In relating to me the story of these initial contacts, these officials noted time and again the poise and confidence of the local leaders, the 'air' of knowledge and intelligence they exhibited, their verbal eloquence, but especially their tenacity and forcefulness. Hieidaira's *jichikai* began to be labelled (as some administrators told me privately) as 'troublesome' (*urusaii*) or a bit more mildly as 'enthusiastic' (*neshin ga aru*). This denoted not only the basis of their demands on the concept of 'rights entitled to', but also a new confrontational style instead of the more traditional accommodating one. Whatever the negative connotations of such a label, the citizens nevertheless achieved quite remarkable success in the next few years in securing local authority commitment to fund, build and run the school, kindergarten and day-care centre.

6 Concluding Considerations

This account of community action in Hieidaira underscores just how non-trivial locally effective resource mobilization and utilization can be. An understanding of the successes of the locals, however, involves not only an organizational focus, but also one on the models which guided the locals and the wider social and political circumstances within which they found themselves. In this chapter a treatment of the theoretical importance of these realizations is presented.

Organizational capabilities: resources and skills

Given the differential support and selective participation of the residents in community affairs, the achievements of the *jichikai* – like those of any local organization – depended in the first place on the local leadership, and on the organizational resources at its disposal. Put in a comparative perspective, Hieidaira seems fortunate in this respect. A persistent problem for neighbourhood associations of the new housing estates has been one of finding willing and capable officers (Nakamura, 1968:201). In the first few years, the Hieidaira *jichikai* lacked neither. Occupationally, the leadership differed from the local businessmen who dominated the ward associations studied by Dore (1958) in the early 1950s. In Hieidaira, the leadership included university teachers, civil servants, pensioners, white-collar employees, and some self-employed. While undoubtedly 'middle-class Japanese' (Kusaka, 1985), the composition of the leadership group was nevertheless varied. This social mix well reflected the cross-stratal nature of the problems the suburban estate faced, and assured (at least partially) that the traditional barriers between various social groups be broken. But it is in the organizational resources that these people provided that part of the reasons for the *jichikai*'s success can be found: political experience, intellectual capabilities, technical expertise, discretionary time schedules, communications and verbal skills.

A politically sophisticated group, most of the local leaders had had some kind of prior experience with political parties (progressives), the media, citizens' or students' movements, environmentalist and consumer groups, labour unions, or bureaucratic structures. Some even contributed regularly to newspapers and journals on matters involving citizens' activism and political affairs. Through participation in such groups they had been socialized into working towards the solution to their problems on the basis of a new kind of organized activity. First, they had become familiar with and learned to exercise the expertise needed in political strategizing, forging alliances and canvassing for support. Second, like people in other industrial democracies (Rochon, 1983:371) they acquired through participation in the multifarious post-war movements a readiness to use unconventional means to express their demands and pressure public officials.

Thus, included in their acquired expertise was not only the delicate sensitivity needed for judging the right political forces that would bring about political success. It also included the ability actively to monitor the environment, and to borrow successful 'innovations' in structure and conduct from other organizations. It is in this light that the borrowing by the new residential estates of a form akin to the *jichikai*, with its balance of ready communications and mobilization networks and direct links to local executives, should be seen. For this was an organizational form chosen by the locals as best capable of carrying their demands.

Political experience and proficiency were buttressed by the suburbanites' technical and knowledge skills, which were mostly acquired in the institutions within which the leaders worked. Assimilating ideas from books, researching an issue, analysing a problem, or drafting an official petition, were all familiar activities. They had already proved as much when they launched the ad-hoc committee to study the suburb's development (which involved knowledge of law, architecture, engineering, and development guidelines). Indeed one local intellectual published a short piece on the residents' success in a journal devoted to citizen activism (Watanabe, 1977).

This point is related to a decisive element in the success of citizens' movements in both America (McCarthy and Zald, 1977) and Japan (Krauss and Simcock, 1980:208; Tsurutani, 1977:196–8). This has been the technical advice and expertise provided by professionals. In this sense the intellectual capabilities and technical literacy of the *jichikai*'s leadership functioned as an inbuilt pool of professional resources, not unlike the expertise provided for Japanese labour unions by participating white-collar workers, or the advice given to the consumer movements by journalists and teachers (Maki, 1976:137). Thus, for example, the suburbanites did not need to secure the services of outside professionals like lawyers: services that are expensive, available for a short while (i.e. lack of continuity), and given by people without the dedication and commitment of a local inhabitant. In this way, in contrast to the situation of many lower-class groups (Downs, 1979:469; Lipsky and Levi, 1972), the existence of professional resources mitigated the need to trade internal organizational autonomy for the support of external sponsors and advisors, a trade which usually eventuates in the subordination of the local movement's ideals and aims.

Related to this point, again, was the presence of articulate university teachers and ex-civil servants who provided a pool of communications and verbal skills. These were used in the negotiations with the developer and the local officials in order to clarify and make explicit the aims and demands of the *jichikai*. But they were also used in a more emotive way, primarily through the network of *jichikai* notices and letters, in the process by which support from the rest of the community accumulated. Moreover, the high literacy rate of the local population ensured that few problems faced in this regard by movements in poor urban neighbourhoods would be encountered. The leadership could count on a highly literate resident population used to garnering information from printed sources.

The system of printed communications which the *jichikai* instituted seems to have fulfilled some of the functions the local press fulfills in other countries (Greer, 1972:108ff.; Janowitz, 1967). It was available to and supported by almost all of the residents of the area, and both reported on the ongoing negotiations with the area's external bodies, and interpreted the implications of wider events and decisions for the locality. Through the *jichikai*'s notices and dispatches not only did the suburbanites come to know and familiarize themselves with the local organizations and actors (the mayor, developer, city bureaucrats, community leaders), but through these communications 'Hieidaira' began to emerge as a social and political fact. For through the discussions and reports on the area's common problems, not only was a sense of identity conveyed to a diverse array of newcomers, but the residents could begin to define the suburban neighbourhood as a community which shared a common fate.

Related to this is the relatively low price of publishing a regular stream of newsletters and announcements as against a community newspaper. In the publication of the latter, economic considerations such as advertising space or staff salaries are quite central. In the issuing of the neighbourhood association's newsletters, by contrast, the only real cost apart from people's time were ink, paper and a low overhead. For the drafting of these announcements, their printing and their distribution were all done by unpaid volunteers.

The discretionary time schedules of the university teachers, self-employed and pensioners proved an added advantage. Not being restricted to the schedule or the work-related commitments of the *sarariiman*, few out-of-hours meetings with local government officials or the developer had to be held. Rather, the local leadership could pursue community matters within the regular working hours of these officials, without having to make special arrangements for 'time off' in their own working place for association matters.

Finally, take the participation of a significant number of housewives which itself is a new phenomenon in Japanese political culture (Tsurutani, 1977:195). These people with some free time, and again already predisposed through socialization and prior experience to political activity, facilitated the actual work of spreading petitions, or printing and circulating notices and leaflets. For most of these women – some of whom had participated in citizens' movements before moving to Hieidaira, some of whom had done so afterwards in the 'garbage' and consumer co-operative campaigns – taking up a *jichikai* function was not a matter of learning a completely new role.

Organizational capabilities: local images and reputations

In the Japanese context, the high educational level of the community's leaders carried with it a further advantage. In a society assigning high prestige to educational achievements, the presence of graduates of and teachers in the elite universities of the Kyoto area (mainly Kyoto and Doshisha universities), lent the organization an added measure of respectability and acceptance. As one astute restaurant owner in Hieidaira (who later served as one of the assistant heads of the *jichikai*) put it, for the officials of the City Office (and for many of Tonan Shoji's functionaries as well), having themselves advanced to the university level and then entered their career through a series of tests, the academic background of an elite university graduate is perceived as a measure of his success and intelligence. Thus when referring to Hieidaira's local leaders, city bureaucrats often call them *interi*: intellectuals or highly educated people. In fact so successful was one head of the neighbourhood association in presenting an intellectual image, that one Tonan Shoji official (now retired from the company) called him 'an expert in human engineering, a specialist in putting demands to local government officials and getting their co-operation.'

The locals at the same time are also keenly aware of this labelling and its political potential. A now retired Kyoto University professor who headed the *jichikai*'s environmental watchdog committee related how on a number of occasions when he called upon local officials, he would produce his *meishi* (name card). It has, he added,

'great name value, it makes a strong impression on local administrators, and predisposes them to take the matters I raise in a more serious way. That's probably one of the reasons why they recruited me into the *jichikai*' [he continued good-naturedly], 'so that every once in a while they could parade me in front of government officials (*matsuri ageru*).'

The labelling of the *jichikai*'s leadership as *interi* began, then, to be generalized into an image of the whole area. Hieidaira began to be called an *interi no chiiki* – an area of the highly educated, of the intellegentsia. This image included elements of both political

113

progressivism (confrontational posture, 'sticking' to one's rights), and a pervading emphasis on education and educational achievements. The emergence of this 'reputational content' (Suttles, 1972:14) for Hieidaira merits attention. First, as in other areas, small relative differences are amplified into what are then taken as 'fully fledged' representations. Hieidaira's significant minority of professionals and university teachers began to be taken as representatives of the whole area.[1] Second, the highlighting of the suburb's reputational content was not solely the outgrowth of 'natural' migratory patterns into the area. Rather it crystallized out of the management of the community's external relations: through both the activities of the *jichikai* and the labelling of outside bodies. Third, once the identity of a locality has emerged it may in itself have advantages (or disadvantages) as a resource. That is, the presence of 'intellectuals' in Hieidaira provided resources not only in the potential for expert advice, but on another level their very status was used as a resource itself.

Organizational contexts: models for action

At the same time, however, the activity of organized community groups is not dependent on organizational resources alone. This is best understood against an historical background in which such community-based organizations as village or neighbourhood associations, women's or youth groups, or fire-fighting units have existed in one form or another for hundreds of years in Japan. Moreover, such entities have not been limited only to rural localities, but could be found in central city or (in this century) suburban areas as well. Just as important for community action, then, are the historico-cultural models of associations and organizations. These models seem to be important in two respects.

First, such cultural forms provide rather concrete patterns and modes of organized action with which people are familiar: for example, ways of discussing, dividing labour, communicating, or making decisions in an organization. The jargon, the symbols which are used to speak about these things are already well known.[2] Dore's conclusions about the *jichikai* of new residential estates throughout the country could apply equally to the case of

Hieidaira. He says (in his introduction to Nakamura, 1986:190), 'if the organizations they form are likely to be remarkably similar to the old *choonaikai* in many respects it is for no other reason than that people naturally use the social techniques their culture bequeaths them.'

Second, such models are not inherently feudal or reactionary in nature. As Norbeck (1967:195; see also Braibanti, 1947; and Sakuta, 1978:239ff.) notes in regard to such local structures as neighbourhood associations, women's groups or agricultural co-operatives, 'as structural forms for organizing people into groups, they can be used for either democratic or totalitarian ends.' The uses to which community organizations are put seem to be related to trends in the nation's wider political culture. In the post-war period growing sentiments of the 'rights' of citizens (Dore, 1978:294–5; Ishida, 1986) have been coupled with a stress on confrontational politics (Bennett and Levine, 1976:483) to provide a background for new kinds of community action. The words of one of the leaders of Hieidaira's first *jichikai* well illustrate this. I had asked him about the basis for the neighbourhood association's demands when they approached the local government authorities, when he replied

'I want to be clear on this point. We came forward directly and said that as tax-paying citizens we have the right to expect the city and prefecture to provide us with public facilities. We have the right to tell them what to do.'

No less important than the concrete historico-cultural models of organized action, then, were the forms of political activity which were based on the pervading public moods and ideals at the time when the local neighbourhood association was active. Foremost in shaping these were the citizens' movements that swept Japan from the late 1960s. Their direct effect on localized action is best understood through their contrast to Western European movements (Rochon, 1983). While the European groups (for example, the ecology movements or the Campaign for Nuclear Disarmament) have tended to carry a countermodel to society, aimed at basic changes to the polity and economy (Parkin, 1968:38), the Japanese groups have stressed more limited goals. Here virtually no orientation towards basic changes to societal power relations is found, and the usual focus has been on locally specific issues. Thus while it is true that they have been hostile to the ruling Liberal-Democrats and much of the business community, they have not rejected the political system as a whole. Again, whereas the Western European movements have used tactics at the edge of legality, their Japanese counterparts have not. Rather, the non-institutional means used by the latter have been well within the bounds of legality. Finally, Japanese activists have been considerably more rooted in their communities, and used local organizations as bases for citizens' movements to a greater extent than have the Western Europeans (Rochon, 1983:356; McKean, 1981:chap. 7).

These features have, in turn, facilitated the ideological links between Japanese citizens' groups and local community-oriented efforts. From the point of view of individual participation, for example, an active part in community action did not explicitly or implicitly spell a posture of opposition to the basic arrangements of Japanese society. In Hieidaira this resulted in a willingness on the part of those not politically radical nevertheless to contribute actively to the *jichikai*'s efforts. Furthermore, the Japanese citizens' movements, through providing a vicarious sense of participation (Tsurutani, 1977:204), elicited a sense of potential political efficacy and competence on the part of those who did not participate. In regard to the suburbanites, this was especially crucial at those stages when they began to consider the effectiveness of a local organization.

Organizational contexts: ties with local government

This last point underscores the important historical element involved, for the point (mid-1970s) when the Hieidaira *jichikai* became active was that at which the citizens' movements had already had their greatest impact on local government and the neighbourhood associations of the new suburban estates. That is, not only were their ideals already politically established, but they had already had more concrete organizational consequences. In the late 1960s when they arose, citizens' movements filled a vacuum created by the lack of adaptability of the formal governmental machinery that processed citizen demands. But by the mid-1970s government (primarily local government) had already become more sensitive, more responsive in policy-making to citizen concerns.[3] Not only were local officials more willing to accept such demands, but they were also ready to accommodate the new guise of the neighbourhood associations. These associations, in turn, were not only permeated with the ideals of the citizens' movements, but had already entered into organizational links with local authorities within which some of these ideals were formalized. That is, by the mid-1970s consultation had become a more important means of influence than confrontation (Rochon, 1983:362). Hieidaira's *jichikai* could thus enter into the negotiations and relations with the Otsu City Office without having itself to lay down all of the 'confrontational' ground rules (rights entitled to, expression of demands).

In sum, then, what Hieidaira's residents succeeded in creating was a *jichikai* that combined the advantages of the more established neighbourhood associations – permanent ready communications and mobilization networks, procedures for recruiting activists, direct access to politicians and administrators – and the benefits of citizens' movements – legitimate and effective confrontational politics (within legally accepted limits), based on a high level of expectations and perceived 'rights' of citizens.

These are far from insignificant points. In both Hieidaira and Yamanaka the past fifteen years have been the scene of a number of highly oganized drives based on the new conceptions of confrontation and rights. Three years ago, for example, the estate's *jichikai* mounted a successful campaign against the movement through Hieidaira of trucks operated by a company quarrying sand from one of the nearby hills. As the citizens saw it, the tens of heavy trucks that passed along Hieidaira's main roads were causing a number of hazards: traffic safety dangers for children; noise pollution; and the worsening of the condition of the roads. The neighbourhood association and some of the officers of the PTA approached the police and city and prefectural authorities and requested that they direct the company to discontinue its use of the estate's main streets. After a rather prolonged struggle the company was ordered by the prefectural government to limit the daily number of trucks passing through Hieidaira to six, and to divert all of the other heavy traffic by a long and costly roundabout way.

In Yamanaka the construction of a bypass along which the

prefectural road which links Otsu and Kyoto now runs, was the outcome of similar activity by the villagers. The prefectural authorities originally declined to build the bypass despite the hazards and inconvenience posed by the traffic moving along the prefectural road that then passed through the village. The village *jichikai* in reaction mounted a number of 'strike actions' in which they stopped all traffic on the road for a number of hours each week. The prefectural officials capitulated and about fourteen years ago the bypass was completed.

That local associations have taken over many of the functions previously performed by movements outside the political establishment underscores the extent to which the new citizens–government relations have been regularized. City officials now not only accept the legitimacy of citizens raising demands and struggling for improvements to their everyday environment, but positively expect that such organizations as the *jichikai* take on such functions. These realizations are especially evident among the younger city bureaucrats, but they can also be found among some of the older administrators. One senior official now in his mid-50s told me the following:

'There is a big difference between the attitudes of citizens to the City Office before the war and after it. In the past the municipality was called the *Ooyakusho*. The use of the honorific "Oo" shows the kind of deference that was shown to us. People used to make a fuss if a city official came around to their neighbourhood. Today they just say *shiyakusho*, that is just plain City Office. That is, they see themselves as being on an equal footing with the people who work in the municipality. Many feel that the public services are "owed" to them.'

One such regular forum for cultivating citizens–City Office relations are the yearly meetings called the *gyoosei kondankai* (lit. friendly talks with the administration). These meetings – two of which I witnessed directly – are held in all 24 administrative districts of the city. They are held in the community meeting halls, and are attended by the heads of all the community organizations and by representatives of all the municipality's departments. These occasions – which can be very difficult for city officials – provide opportunities to review and question the municipality's progress in dealing with problems the community has raised, and to raise new problems. In pointing to the existence of such arrangements in Scandinavia and Japan, the American sociologist Suttles (1972:79), notes that

> The existence of national standards, big government, and big business need not be seen as antithetical or destructive to the local community as long as there is a thoroughly well-defined administrative framework within which consultation with local communities can be regularized and follow due process.

Such regular forums as the *gyoosei kondankaikai*, then, provide direct opportunities to hold officials accountable for the City Office's decisions, and to supervise their implementation of such decisions. Closer links to and greater dependence on government need not imply greater governmental control.

At the same time, however, one problematical aspect of these new arrangements has been brought out by Krauss and Simcock (1980:223). They point out that the solidification of direct citizens–administration links spells a further weakening of the role of the local legislature. In this way an important element of the representative democratic process becomes disemployed.

A further word of caution should be sounded in relation to the wider potential of community-based groups in Japan. Krauss and Simcock's (1980:224) conclusions in regard to the effect of new movements based on the sentiments of rights and confrontation should be kept in mind: while such organized efforts to 'serve a number of positive functions for democratic politics at the local level they are not likely to automatically usher in a grass-roots democratic or progressive millennium.' Thus Taira's (1978) assertions that community-based organizations and movements contain a base for changing Japan's central institutions, or Irokawa's (1978:282) views of these new type of community associations as the key to Japan's future seem to be too optimistic. Such views give relatively little recognition to the limits of local communities.

Some limiting conditions

The achievements of the locals in securing the establishment of the facilities they had lacked is still only partially explained by the community's internal organizational resources, by the astute strategies chosen by the *jichikai*'s leadership, or by the changed political moods in the country. For the success in organizing the citizens' local association is in part analytically distinct from the success of the association in achieving its aims. In the latter respect, the economic and political 'conditions' within which the association interacted with the developer and the local authorities are of prime importance.[4]

Two such conditions have been alluded to. First, the financial difficulties and uncertainty of the regional real-estate market (low demand, decline in investment, limited access to loans) were elements that did not enter directly into the negotiations with the developer, but that nevertheless proved central to Tonan Shoji's calculations and eventual capitulation. Likewise, the national changes in the Development Approval System, while of course not an outgrowth of the specific developer–local government relationship, still functioned as a structural condition that lent considerable strength to the local progressives' position.

Both points underscore a further realization: that the financial not only the political ability of local government to take effective action (given that it is motivated to do so) is itself a variable. For under different circumstances – say those of the early 1980s – the local *jichikai*'s efforts might have required much more time, or in the extreme case failed. The point is that the positive reaction of the Otsu and Shiga administrations cannot be understood apart from the country's general economic growth, and more specifically apart from the impact of this growth on government finances. The establishment of the facilities in Hieidaira, then, formed but a tiny portion of the massive outlays directed both at the system governing urban development (an enlarged bureaucracy, formation of new laws and regulations) and the actual subsidies and allocations for various infrastructural needs and public services, outlays which were themselves predicated on the questioning of the 'growth first' policy and the new political moods of Japan. Thus in this period that preceded the onset of a local government financial crisis (Katagiri, 1981), the local authorities could still afford to be generous in answering citizens' demands.[5]

In sum, an analysis of the successful achievements of Hieidaira's residents should be understood in dynamic and developmental terms. In other words, the elements stressed throughout this account – the resources at the disposal of the locals, the models and sensibilities which guided their actions, and the wider socio-political contexts – should be seen as unfolding circumstances which posed and counterposed possibilities and constraints for the citizens of the estate. Community autonomy and involvement, then, are matters best conceived of as evolving potentialities and their actualizations.

Part Four
MASS LONGEVITY AND COMMUNITY CARE

7 Introduction

Among the most conspicuous features of community activity in the Hieidaira–Yamanaka school district is the vast amount of organized effort that is directed towards social welfare. No less than seven local organizations and associations deal – whether directly or indirectly, on a district or on an individual community level – with welfare-related activities. These voluntary groups include the social welfare council (*shakai fukushi kyoogikai*), voluntary welfare workers (*minsei-iin*), old-folks clubs (*roojinkai*), neighbourhood associations (*jichikai*), women's associations (*fujinkai*), a fatherless families' group (*boshi no nozomikai*), and a new anti-delinquency organization (*seishoonen ikukai*). What is interesting, however, is that with the exception of the latter two, all the organizations are concerned to a very great extent with care for only one portion of the local population: the elderly.

Yet the provision of care for the elderly actually involves complementary approaches. The two most important and successful of the local welfare organizations well embody these. On the one hand, the *minsei-iin* (the voluntary welfare workers) are concerned with the variety of more formal services and programmes that provide aid and assistance to older individuals. On the other hand, the *roojinkai* (the old-folks clubs) are concerned with the more general aspects of the elderly's 'well-being': recreation, social contact and cultural pursuits.

The *minsei-iin* are non-professionals who are recruited from the area and serve a term of three years. Their designated role is to find and investigate families in need of assistance. But in practice they fulfil many other tasks such as aiding in filling out forms, facilitating contact with city welfare departments, visiting the elderly who are sick or living alone, informing the aged of city-level activities, and encouraging self- and neighbour-help. They are in constant contact with municipal officials, and attend regular meetings with *minsei-iin* from other areas. They are, then, concerned with that part of the older population that has problems and difficulties.

The old-folks clubs in the area carry out a range of activities: recreation clubs such as calligraphy, gardening or singing; trips; parties; meals; hikes and sports. They also function as a sort of political pressure group for the aged, for example in struggling for the initiation of a bus service to serve the needs of the elderly. Furthermore, they serve as a meeting ground for people, and as a framework for the emergence of informal networks of acquaintanceships and friendships. They maintain certain links with the City Office in such matters as the co-ordination of city-wide events or the receipt of subsidies. But the clubs are, on the whole, quite independent in regard to the running of their internal affairs. The *roojinkai* are oriented, then, towards that majority of old people who are still healthy and energetic enough to participate in activities and maintain social ties outside their family.

It seems, however, that the case of Hieidaira and Yamanaka is not unique in these respects. The growing concern with care for the aged by community-based groups like the welfare workers and old-folks clubs is apparent in a variety of localities, as central city neighbourhoods (Takayose, 1979a; Isomura and Sakata, 1981:3–4), suburban towns (Allinson, 1979:210), villages near urban centres (Hendry, 1981:72; Norbeck, 1977:55; Omori, 1976:438), or even in relatively isolated rural hamlets (Smith, 1978:197). Indeed the pervasiveness of voluntary welfare workers and old-folks clubs throughout Japan is striking. In 1982 there were over 170,000 such welfare workers, and about 120,000 clubs with a membership of nearly seven and a half million in the country (Koseisho, 1982:477, 491). To echo Linhart (1981:2) in this respect, it is no exaggeration to say that, taken as a whole, the old-folks clubs constitute one of the biggest organizations in Japan. I would furthermore suggest along these lines that *minsei-iin* provide the biggest single pool of social service personnel in Japan.

This huge involvement by community-based voluntary groups with providing care for the elderly all over the country is related to two major macro-sociological trends that have emerged in the last few decades. An understanding of the activity of local organizations like the voluntary welfare workers and the old-folks clubs must take into account both 'mass longevity' and 'community care'.

One of the corollaries of all societies that have achieved an advanced state of modernization is the rise of 'ageing' as a social problem (Lakoff, 1976). In these countries the proportion of older people out of the total population reaches such a size as to require the formulation of specific state policies aimed at them. Older people need help because the very process of ageing tends to make people dependent upon others for assistance: they are more prone to decline in physical and mental capacities, likely to suffer psychic depression, may suffer lowered incomes because of withdrawal from the labour force, or be stereotyped in a way that makes it difficult to find new employment. Thus it is not just the numbers of the elderly that pose problems of provision of aid, but the characteristics of this population. The need for government provision of assistance and special programmes arises, however, because of the weakening of the capacity of the family, the community and private institutions to provide. Yet while there is a broad convergence between industrialized democracies in terms of the emergence of 'ageing' as a social problem, the social 'solutions' and the state 'responses' to this difficulty are different.

Calling the country's major post-war demographic trend the emergence of 'mass longevity', Plath (1980:30) astutely observes that:

> since 1970 Japan has earned world acclaim for her 'miraculous' rate of growth. What is less widely known is that in these years Japan's rising rate of longevity has also set a world pace.

The rise of average life expectancy has been dramatic: the fifty-year mark was passed for women in 1946 and for men in 1947. By 1981, however, it was 79.1 years for females and 73.8 for males (Ministry of Health and Welfare, 1982:2). As a consequence, average life expectancy at birth is now higher in Japan than in the United States, and is comparable to that of the North European countries.

Towards the beginning of the 1970s these demographic trends began to pose serious problems for the nation. This was not only because of the growing number of elderly, but more importantly because of the very characteristics of this population: their greater potential and actual dependence on others for aid and assistance.

The problems and difficulties associated with this dependence straddle a variety of fields such as health and social security, employment and retirement, social contact and sense of worth, or the construction of special facilities for the aged. These problems were taken up by the mass media, and deliberated upon by Japan's central political institutions.

A major set of policies that emerged from these deliberations and that has been most explicitly formulated since the mid-1970s is that of community care for the aged.[1] These policies emerged out of three general considerations on the part of Japan's policy-makers: the changes the 'family' has undergone, and which have come to limit its capacity to provide aid and assistance for the aged; the search for a set of arrangements which would ease the budgetary burdens of maintaining huge welfare bureaucracies; and the awareness that parts of an increasingly affluent population could be mobilized for voluntary social welfare activities. In essence, then, community care policies implied, and still imply, the activation of community organizations and associations in order to aid the services run by government and public bodies.

An awareness of these demographic and political trends is important in an examination of community welfare activity in modern Japanese localities such as Hieidaira and Yamanaka. For such an awareness heightens one's analytical sensitivity to the way macro-sociological trends find their expression on the local community level. Yet a more specific exploration of the quality and potential of local voluntary organizations and of their implications for modern communities needs a more specific set of conceptual or analytic tools.

The literature on community care for the aged in Japan while offering a number of insights and underlining a few important analytical issues suffers from a number of weaknesses which have to do as much with the lack of any systematic theoretical approach to the field, as to the recency of the phenomenon. One type of literature seems to fall along a continuum between the disparaging and the laudatory. In its most depreciatory portrayal (Nihon Fujin Dantai Rengokai, 1980:196–7), community care is depicted as little more than a set of arrangements by which formal agencies 'sub-contract' certain welfare responsibilities and charges out to 'cheap' community groups. According to the proponents of this view, this set of organizational designs lends itself to the manipulation of government officials who act solely according to their aims and priorities. Volunteers, furthermore, are seen as political dupes who have no real say in regard to the services and programmes they aid in, no real independent ability to criticize welfare policies, and no potential for altering the existing set of priorities. While the importance of this approach lies in its highlighting the role of community welfare organizations as 'extensions' of the welfare bureaucracy, it pays almost no attention to two interrelated points: the qualitatively different kind of care that community groups are capable of contributing; and the potential volunteers do have for criticizing or at the very least providing a check on the priorities set by welfare decision-makers.

The 'official' or laudatory approach includes white papers of the ruling Liberal-Democratic Party or government publications (Ministry of Health and Welfare, 1974; Koseisho, 1982). One might also classify Vogel's (1979:199ff.) rather polemical stress on Japan's welfare arrangements as 'minimal bureaucracy, maximal impact' within this kind of literature. Here the view taken of community care is that of a highly successful system which provides crucial support to the formal services. Not only are community-based organizations necessary extensions of expensive services that are in difficulties due to a crisis in public finances, but they are an important administrative means by which information about the welfare needs of varied localities is gathered. But while this approach involves a positive evaluation of citizen participation in welfare programmes, this is seen as a limited kind of participation. Almost no leeway is given for any kind of critical appraisals by the citizenship of administratively initiated programmes. Needless to say, such 'official' examinations rarely deal with the problematic side of government intervention in local communities.

In between these two approaches are found much more careful and sophisticated commentaries by academics or leaders of national voluntary organizations. The problem is that these are not detailed studies of community welfare organizations, nor of community care programmes in particular cities or localities. Some of the studies focus on the state or national level. Thus, for example, Campbell's (1979) treatment of the evolution of welfare policy, Linhart's (1981) analysis of old-folks clubs, or Kitani's (1981) discussion of voluntarism, all concentrate on the country as a whole. When the focus is more ethnographic, say on a more regional or local level, the discussion of social welfare programmes and organizations tends to be incidental to the main thesis. Thus for instance Hendry's (1981:72) or Norbeck's (1977:55) observations about old-folks clubs, or Smith's (1978:30ff.) mention of voluntary welfare workers are rather peripheral parts of much wider examinations of village life and organizations. Allinson's (1978:206ff.) illustrations of municipal welfare policies in two Tokyo suburbs is but a small section in a wider analysis of city politics and development. This kind of literature presents difficulties not only in that it does not provide any kind of systematic conceptualization or analysis of present-day community care, but also in that it provides little in the way of a comparative perspective.

At the same time, however, some of the more general studies have been most perceptive in regard to a number of peculiar attributes and qualities of community-based welfare organizations. Linhart (1981:8), by portraying old-folks clubs as being at the same time both substitutes for professional social work, and important political vehicles for influence and participation (*ibid.*:14), underlines their duality. Essentially he seems to see these clubs as being at the same time potentially amenable to government control, and as capable of an independent stance on welfare issues. Isomura and Sakata, in a more conventional vein (1981:71), point to the delicate balance that needs to be achieved in the operation of such groups. On the one hand, according to their approach, some kind of administrative support and financial aid is crucial for the survival of such organizations. On the other hand, however, too much of this kind of guidance and help will lead to a breakdown of the informal aspect of voluntary activity. In a related way Fukutake (1982:217) cautions us that social welfare is not just a matter of building facilities or designing administrative systems. He stresses that at the heart of the discussions about community care is a quest for the recreation of human ties in the new types of communities that have developed. Kitani (1981:280–2) stresses that the activation of local voluntary organizations is a preventative measure that saves the nation heavier expenditures on welfare, but also that such an activation lends an added dimension to the formal services. In his view such community welfare groups add to the formal services a special sensitivity to the human circumstances of the locality.

Basic to these discussions, then, is an important realization that such local voluntary groups as the *minsei-iin* or *roojinkai* are characterized by an interstitial existence. These community organizations stand in between the more bureaucratized sphere of welfare provision dominated by statutory agencies on the one hand, and the more informal community networks of kin, friends and neighbours on the other.

While this realization of the 'interstitial existence' of local voluntary groups is crucial for their understanding, two further points must be underlined. First, the activation of community-based organizations within the policy of community care meant that they began to operate within an administrative context the scale and complexity of which were much beyond that of the community level. Community care for all its dependence on local volunteers and its close association with local organizations emerged at a time when the institutionalization of care in large and complex organizations was already an established fact. That is, it arose to a large measure out of the initiative of giant administrative bodies with their own ways of setting priorities and allocating resources. The challenge for my analysis, in this respect, becomes one of delineating the intricate web of co-operation, support and control between community organizations and the state apparatuses dealing with welfare.

On the other hand the activation of community-based welfare organizations is related to the emergent forms of Japan's modern residential communities. For the rise of 'communities of limited liability' has spelt not only the greater reliance of these localities on external agencies, but also the development of new types of more specialized and voluntaristic modes of provision of care. Here the aim of the present study is to explore how local organizations marshall the resources of the community in order to provide care.

In the following chapters I begin with an exploration of the administrative, financial and legal context within which community care and local voluntary organizations emerged. Next I deal with the voluntary welfare workers and old-folks clubs in the Hieidaira–Yamanaka school district. Finally, some of the analytical implications of the discussion are examined.

8 Community Care: Policies and Administration

The evolution of social welfare policies for the aged differs markedly from the way environmental and urban issues erupted in the late 1960s. While the latter issues arose out of activity outside the political establishment, social welfare policies developed within it. Not only were these policies the outcome of participation by parties, government bureaucracies and unions, but they were also rather quickly formalized into law, fixed budget allocations, and set programmes. Given the importance of this formal and institutional side of social welfare policies for the aged, it is essential to begin the examination of community care through its relation to policy-making and welfare administration.

The 'old people' boom: policies and programmes[1]

In the immediate post-war years two systems worked alongside the as yet undeveloped government schemes in aiding the 'family' in caring for the aged. The paternalistic view taken by many employers, and the patterns of mutual obligations fostered in close-knit communities, provided important sources of assistance (Dore, 1958:73ff.). But the destitution that affected almost all families, and the changes these institutions underwent – the 'depersonalizing' of employment relations in big firms and the loosening of community structures which had functioned to pressure junior household members to fulfil their filial obligations (Kitani, 1981:225; Lebra, 1979:339) – forced many to turn to the state for help.

Against this background, public assistance schemes were the first large government programme to be established after the war.

These were based on a conception of welfare rather than insurance (Dore, 1958:71; Taira, 1967:107), and were essentially designed to provide financial assistance for the indigent condition of a large section of the population. This was a time when a strong stigma was still attached to the receipt of public relief, and the wide perception that 'only failures needed government help' continued well into the late 1950s (Ernst, 1982:550; Vogel, 1963:16).

From this latter period, however, public assistance schemes began to diminish in importance as other systems began to be developed and improved. More importantly, a gradual shift in the assumptions at the base of welfare policies occurred. The change was from a welfare-oriented concept to one of universal right to a form of social insurance, and the guarantee of a minimum livelihood (Fukutake, 1982:chap. 23). Along these lines, a national health pension scheme was instituted in 1959, and two years later a national health insurance programme established.

Then, as some of the more immediate problems of material assistance and health care began to be settled, the national welfare bureaucracy began to turn its attention to other issues. The 1960s were the start of specific programmes aimed at providing care for the aged. This period saw the beginning of construction of homes and welfare centres for the elderly; the initiation of home-helpers and visiting nurses schemes; the start of subsidies for old-folks clubs; free health examinations for the elderly; and the establishment of 'Respect for the Aged Day' as a national holiday (Campbell, 1979:341ff.; Ministry of Health and Welfare, 1974, 12–17).

But the real 'old people boom' (Campbell, 1979) began only in the 1970s. At its inception, the 'boom' evolved out of a national debate about the problems of the elderly (Bennett and Levine, 1976:449; Lock, 1984:66). It was during this period that newspaper accounts and television programmes began to be devoted to such themes as the 'Greying of Japan', 'Fear of Retirement', or the 'Anxiety for an Ageing Society'. But the debate was found outside the media as well. Concern with the problems started to appear in government reports and surveys (Ministry of Health and Welfare, 1974), and in policy statements of various parties (Nihon Fujin Dantai Rengokai, 1980:196; Kitazawa, 1986).

More concretely, the central institutions of Japan embarked on a rethinking of the systems and schemes related to the elderly. Some of these that came under review were: employment policies for firms and government bodies, retirement rules, post-retirement employment opportunities (Tanaka, 1979), health and pension insurance systems (Ernst, 1982:542), the building of facilities for the aged (hospitals, social clubs), and the programmes aimed at elderly with special problems (Koseisho, 1982).

Although related to the new national emphasis on 'balanced growth' that emerged in the 1970s (Stockwin, 1982:77; Campbell, 1979:324), social welfare policies did not develop out of pressure exerted on different levels of government by citizens' groups. Rather, authorities took the initiative in regard to social welfare with little prodding from the public. There were already a number of established groups that had a built-in interest in the promotion of 'care for the aged': old-people's associations, labour unions, doctors' groups, welfare bureaucrats, academics, and small groups of social workers. In contrast to environmental and urban issues, there was much less of a need here for interest or pressure groups to organize, articulate their demands, and pursue them until policies were set.

As McKean (1981:227) puts it, it seems that the most important sources of policy

> were the natural competitive forces of partisan politics and bureaucratic initiative. . . . Politicians could integrate the idea of increased social services into their self-image as patrons and providers of pork-barrel rewards and government subsidies to their constituents. Similarly, policy planners in the relevant ministries readily accepted the importance of such programs as a professional responsibility and as a way to bring Japan's welfare policies into step with the new status as an affluent democracy.

In this way, despite the fact that public demand remained at a low level, a rapid but quiet growth in government provision for the elderly ensued. This complex process included the expansion of existing programmes, and the innovation of new schemes. Among the innovations introduced were free medical care, recreation areas for the elderly, free 'welfare' telephones for the needy, health education classes, or the promotion of sports. The previous programmes that were expanded included the construction of homes and welfare centres, the strengthening of the pension schemes, loans for the aged, and the allocation of subsidies for local clubs. In sum, then, while it hardly became a 'welfare super-power' (Nakagawa, 1979), Japan did nevertheless make considerable progress in providing care for its elderly.[2]

Welfare administration in Otsu: structure and policies

Far from being limited to national institutions, concern with social welfare policies and programmes also emerged as a major consideration for local authorities. In Otsu, serious attention began to be directed towards these policies with the election of the city's first progressive mayor in late 1972. It was under his direction that the City Office began – like local authorities throughout the country during that period (Krauss and Simcock, 1980:221–2) – to assign a high priority to matters associated with public provision for welfare. An energetic and determined man who has since then become a member of the national parliament, this mayor set about a wholesale reorganization of the related administrative structures and programmes. Although this reorganization included almost all of the fields of social welfare, for the sake of keeping the argument in the following text coherent I restrict myself to an examination of the specific measures aimed at the aged.

After moving into office, he quickly set up a study committee in order to investigate and put forward concrete recommendations related to the field. The committee was composed of local city officials, university teachers and social service professionals. With the publication of its report in 1973 (Yamada, n.d.), a whole series of measures were instituted. In the first place, a restructuring of the administrative units dealing with social welfare was effected. Instead of the existing welfare department (*minsei ka*), a new and enlarged welfare and health division (*fukushi hoken bu*) was set up, and within it a new department devoted solely to social welfare created (*shakai fukushi ka*). A few years later with the recognition of the growth of tasks and assignments related to the elderly, a new department dealing exclusively with this population was also established (*roojin fukushi ka*). Towards the end of the 1970s, two new old-people's homes were built – effectively doubling the city's capacity for residential institutionalization – and a project for promoting short-term employment for the elderly also started.

No less important is the fact that social welfare policies and programmes have become, since then, an integral part of the municipality's long-term planning. This includes the development of new
city tax and fiscal policies in order adequately to meet the future
needs of an ageing population.

An achievement which city bureaucrats and politicians point to
with great pride is the construction of the welfare centre for the
elderly. This is an institution that is open only during day-time
hours, but which draws to its activities old people from all over
Otsu. A three-storey concrete building with a floor space of over
1,800 sq. m, the centre was long in the planning and finally opened
in September 1980 (Otsu-shi, 1982:75). It has a permanent staff
of five people including one doctor. But for selected activities the
centre recruits part-time doctors, nurses, a few social workers,
and non-professional volunteers. In addition, some programmes
are carried out jointly with social service professionals from prefectural agencies. Among the activities it offers are the following:
daily health education and consultation classes with public nurses;
weekly gymnastics sessions; weekly medical examinations by doctors; twice weekly rehabilitation programmes; monthly consultations about livelihood; weekly consultations about work; daily
bath service; clubs (for example Chinese and Japanese chess and
checkers); and irregular lectures about general educational and
cultural topics.

Today the Welfare and Health Division has grown to encompass
seven departments, five of which deal with various aspects of
public welfare. Two departments deal with the aged. The elderly
welfare department comprises seven people: a department head,
his assistant, an officer responsible for old-people's homes, an
officer in charge of home visits, one responsible for the old-
folks clubs, and a secretary doing clerical work. Also within the
responsibility of the department is the newly built welfare centre
for the elderly. In addition the case workers who work within the
Social Welfare Department also meet and investigate the situation
of some of the old people applying for welfare benefits and other
types of assistance.

Yet one finds in the municipality – as in other local authorities
– a striking contrast to British (Walker, 1982b:322; Leonard,
1973:111) or American (Scott, 1969) local government. For a basic
feature that permeates the various welfare departments in the
municipality is a lack of any professional social work ethos or

orientation. This is related to the development, or rather lack of development of professional social work in Japan. Social work in this country has its origin in the Christian missionary work of the pre-war period, which was a charitable activity aimed at the indigent and those living alone (Fukutake, 1982:197). While there has been a slow recognition of social work as part of government-provided services in the post-war period (Taira, 1967), it still remains vastly underdeveloped by comparison with most Western countries.

Social work is taught at only about forty out of Japan's hundreds of universities and colleges. Where they are given, courses on social work include no practical training in institutions or agencies (Ministry of Health and Welfare, 1974:36–7). Few national associations of social workers exist, and there is very little contact between associations belonging to different governmental authorities and departments. Indeed in 1974 there were only 1,200 members in the Japanese Association of Social Workers. This figure is all the more striking when one takes into account that Japan has a population of over 100 million people. Moreover as the priority given to the promotion of social work is still low, salaries remain inferior and working conditions unfavourable (Fukutake, 1982:198).[3] The only two fields which do seem to be somewhat more developed are the rather specialized ones of medical social work (in hospitals and sanatoria), and psychiatric social work (treating 'deviants' and criminal offenders) (Ministry of Health and Welfare, 1974:37; De Vos and Mizushima, 1967:325).

In contrast to the United States and Britain, then, where social workers occupy a powerful position in defining needs, allocating resources, and initiating services (Walker, 1982b:31), Japanese social service professionals are well-nigh inconsequential.[4] In Otsu the few social workers that are found on the city level are employed either in health centres or hospitals, where they work alongside doctors, nurses and psychologists in teams, or in the welfare institutions for the elderly, where they participate in rehabilitation programmes. A few more hold positions in some of the prefectural government-run schemes and programmes, for instance as advisors for children with problems.

As a result of these circumstances, social welfare policies are determined and implemented primarily by politicians and administrators. Along these lines, the social welfare departments of the City Office are manned almost exclusively by bureaucrats. While such personnel can, no doubt, also be found in American or British agencies, in Otsu they even carry out case work. Thus all of the 11 case workers (one woman) and 2 supervisors (one woman) in the municipality are regular administrative staff. Not only are they recruited through the usual procedures common in Japanese local government – on the basis of educational achievements and entrance examinations to the municipal office – but there are no strict qualifications for becoming case workers.

According to one official from the Social Welfare Department, most – but not all – case workers have some kind of relevant background. They have either studied social welfare, social work, or a related field in university, or have served in a related capacity before – for example as heads of day-care centres. But this is by no means even an important criterion. According to other local officials, persons who have been judged by their superiors as capable of being sensitive and discreet towards welfare clients are seen as potential case workers. This is the case even though they may lack a sufficient background in welfare.

These case workers are bound like other City Office staff to the rules of personnel rotation (*jinji idoo*), and therefore come from and go to other administrative departments throughout the municipality. The actual position of a case worker or supervisor is undertaken – in ways similar to all administrative positions in Japanese local government – for a limited period of three or four years (Reed, 1982:148).[5] Like other tasks in the city administration, so too case work is seen as one that is learnt cumulatively through experience and through exchanges with superiors and co-workers. Finally, even within their jobs the criteria used for evaluation and advancement are administrative rather than professional.

In sum, then, unlike their Western counterparts (Scott, 1969:89) who do so through attending independent training centres and receiving the support of their 'expert' colleagues, Otsu's case workers have little opportunity to develop special norms or orientations to professional or welfare 'causes'. One cannot overstress the importance of these circumstances, for they colour every aspect and activity related to social welfare in the city.

Probably the most important consequence of politicians' and bureaucrats' prominence in the field of welfare is the centrality of political considerations and above all budgetary concerns in policy-making and implementation (see for example Isomura and

Sakata, 1981:47). Again such considerations often appear in welfare decision-making in Britain and the USA. But in Japan where there is a weak orientation to professional norms of conduct – or cynically, a weak pretence of deferring to such norms – it is considered more legitimate to use budgetary standards and considerations openly in decision-making. Thus a point reiterated by every local official interviewed was that any suggestion for a new programme, any proposal for the improvement of an existing service, is measured first and foremost in terms of its impact on the yearly departmental budget. This is not only in the rather simple sense of whether the requisite funds exist or not. On a more sophisticated level, such proposals are measured in terms of their potential in the political negotiations and bargaining that make up the budgetary process (Wildavsky, 1974). Thus, for example, even the small programme by which the city allocates funds for buses to be used for welfare purposes was preceded by a long line of action. In it, the heads of the welfare departments had to win the approval and support of their division head, the mayor, and finally the city assemblymen who vote on the yearly budget.

These considerations can undoubtedly also be found in regard to almost every initiative within the municipality. The distinctive financial arrangements of the welfare departments, however, pose further difficulties. In contrast to other local government charges (for example construction or environmental protection) welfare is one in which the municipality's leeway for manoeuvre is extremely limited. Under the formal designations of national law, the provision of social welfare services is a responsibility of the central government, which in turn entrusts its implementation to local authorities.

In more concrete terms this arrangement means that the financial discretion of local government in regard to social welfare programmes is severely circumscribed. This is not so much because the central government controls the purse strings of social welfare allocations, but rather because social welfare programmes are dominated by grants and allocations defined by very specific formulas written into law (Reed, 1982:156). That is, central and prefectural government revenues for social welfare are attached to specific and fixed programmes, and cannot be used according to priorities set by the local authority.

For example, the city receives the following subsidies from the national government according to the stated formulas: two-thirds of the funding for medical care for the aged, eight-tenths for welfare benefits, or eight-tenths for old-people's homes. The city also receives the following allocations from the prefecture: two-thirds of the funds for home-helpers, old-folks clubs, and health consultation classes, and three-fourths for exercise classes for the elderly (Otsu-shi, 1981:26–43).

Under these conditions, then, local governments like that in Otsu have little scope for initiating their own welfare-related schemes. What the Otsu City Office does, is to turn to other alternatives in order to boost its revenues and be able to offer a wider range of services. For example, it borrows, floats local bonds, or sets up city companies (public companies) that hopefully are profitable. But the Ministry of Home Affairs tends to put strict limits even on these options. Another alternative that is increasingly being relied upon, however, is community care.

Community care – assumptions and policies

Community care developed in Otsu at more or less the same time it did in other local authorities, and within the national welfare bureaucracy. This is not surprising, for welfare policies – as those of other fields – tend in Japan to vary within a very small range between local authorities (Reed, 1982:163; Isomura and Sakata, 1981:76; Samuels, 1983).[6] Underlying the similarity of specific policies is a more general consensus about the basic assumptions regarding social welfare. This is due as much to the direction and guidance provided by the central government, as to the dense communications between different city and prefectural administrations which is effected through such organizations as the National Association of Progressive Mayors. By way of introduction to community care in Otsu, a brief examination of this wider context within which the city administrators' views and programmes are anchored is essential in order to understand the mix of local and national elements that make up the implementation of community care.

Throughout the post-war period a number of interrelated premises have guided Japan's decision-makers in relation to social welfare policies. Since the early 1970s, however, certain demo-graphic, attitudinal and occupational changes have gradually forced these decision-makers to modify these assumptions some-what.

Probably the strongest premise held by the decision-makers is that of the need for, and existence of, a great degree of self-help or self-reliance on the part of the elderly. In the rather stark words of an official publication (Ministry of Health and Welfare, 1974:12; see also Naoi, 1980:122f.), the old 'are expected to pro-vide for themselves'. The concrete implication of this is that, like payments for insurance or the reception of relief, the provision of care for the elderly is never total: it is linked to an independent contribution by the individual (Ernst, 1982:550–1). As a number of scholars (Bennett and Levine, 1976:450; Stockwin, 1982:3) have observed, it is probably this situation of financial insecurity rather than inherent cultural traits of frugality or austerity that underlie the great Japanese propensity to save.

A second assumption – and this is a direct extension of pre-war attitudes – has been that in this self-reliance, the role of the family (immediate and extended) is central. That is, individuals are expected to turn to their kin as a primary source of aid and assistance (Taira, 1967:104; Plath, 1972:145). Based on these assumptions, a persistent effort has been made to establish social services that prop up rather than take over the role of the family (Palmore, 1975:50–1). One example of the concrete expression of this view has been the steady emphasis on providing home-help-ers. Indeed, according to the estimate of Palmore (*ibid.*:52), there are five times as many home-helpers in Japan, relative to the population, as there are in the United States.

A closer examination of developments since the late 1960s reveals, however, an emerging recognition on the part of the welfare policy-makers of changes in the capacity of the 'family' to provide care (for example see Ministry of Health and Welfare, 1982:17; Isomura and Sakata, 1981:48). While the drastic trans-formations – of a serious decline and breakup of families – which were envisaged by some post-war observers have not come about, steady changes have occurred in this respect.

With about 70 per cent of the aged over sixty living with a child, Japan still compares favourably with America (28 per cent), or Britain (42 per cent) (Tanaka, 1979:67; Ernst, 1982:545).[7] Yet other indices point to a decline in such arrangements. The number of aged households (i.e. an elderly couple or single person living alone), relative to the total number of households, has increased from 2.2 per cent in 1952, to 4 per cent in 1970, and to 7.4 per cent in 1982 (Ministry of Health and Welfare, 1983). Besides this, the few attitudinal studies and surveys that have been done (Palmore, 1975:40; Wagatsuma, 1977:186) all point to a slow but steady decrease in the number of those wishing to live with their children (or parents). Finally, as the average number of children per family has declined so have the number of potential care-givers for elderly parents. Here the change is marked: from 3.39 children in 1940, the average number of children has fallen to 1.92 in 1972, and 1.7 in 1981 (Ministry of Health and Welfare, 1982).

But it is in the growth of women's activity in the labour market that has in Japan – as in Britain (Walker, 1982a:7) – most seriously reduced the pool of care-givers to the elderly. As Garrick (1981:6–7) says, it is probably true that most Japanese women today have been socialized to fulfil domestic, supportive and nurt-urant roles, and a central aspect of these is providing care for the aged. But now other roles (Pharr, 1976), have begun to compete with the domestic one. Within the space of a few short years, the proportion of working women has increased dramatically: from 36.8 per cent in 1975, to 48.9 per cent by 1983 (Japan Foundation, 1983).[8] While women still do undertake the bulk of care for the elderly (Garrick, 1981:7), their capacity to do so is steadily declin-ing: not only are more of them working but other roles are putting ever greater demands on them in terms of time, effort and atten-tion.

It was only in the mid-1970s that the awareness by the local and national welfare bureaucracies of these changes began to be coupled with growing anxieties about the burdensome expendi-tures on welfare programmes. For it was during this period that the usual preoccupation of bureaucrats with budgetary affairs was made even more acute by the onset of a crisis in local government finances (Katagiri, 1981). Against a backdrop of a slowdown in Japan's economic growth a 're-examination of welfare' (*fukushi minaoshi ron*) was embarked upon (Yoshizawa, 1981:327). As part of this process administrators at all levels began an active search for new alternatives to social services.

What they looked for were options that essentially had two

advantages. On the one hand they would make it possible to increase the variety and quality of welfare programmes and schemes offered by official agencies. But on the other, because of the limit on raising revenues, they would do so without significant increases in expenditures. One major alternative, first explored (Campbell, 1979:344) and then slowly formulated into explicit policy, was that of community care.[9]

I encountered evidence for the way this search was carried out by the Otsu administration in both written material (Yamada, n.d.) and in the interviews held with officials from the welfare departments. Thus, for example, one such official who had been serving for about ten years in the City Office echoed many of the general themes and issues central to Japan's welfare systems. He began by explaining the continued emphasis on the family as the prime provider of care for the aged, but continued with a short analysis of the way the capacity of the 'family' to provide this care has declined. Finally, he noted the way in which a turning to various programmes associated with 'community care' and the utilization of community resources and volunteers had started as an augmentation of the services provided by the city's formal authorities.

An explicit statement linking the financial difficulties the Otsu City Office now faces with the need for an expansion of community care is found in the present mayor's introduction (Yamada, 1983) to an outline of the city's welfare services:

> There are signs that our country is gradually making a slow
> business recovery. The key to this, however, is, as always
> was, a low public expenditure. For that reason, the coming
> years will continue to be very difficult for local authority
> finances. . . . The city administration will, of course, make
> every effort to preserve the high quality of its varied welfare
> services. But as a foundation it is essential to think of the
> creation of a welfare community (*fukushi no machi tsukuri*).
> That is, there is a need to base welfare efforts on the family
> and the community (*chiiki shakai*). The city administration
> and the various voluntary organizations will, of course, take
> a major part in raising the consciousness of the citizens to this
> necessity of carrying the burden of social welfare.

The 'option' of community care, then, is consonant with the assumptions of self-reliance and the stress on the role of the family.[10]

The more concrete implications of community care, however, actually involve two complementary approaches. On the one hand, such a policy implies an emphasis on care *in* the community. Here, while the aid, assistance and guidance given to clients are still provided by formal and professional bodies, the clients continue to live in their own homes and localities. A prime consideration in this approach is to ease – at least during the day – the burden of care undertaken by the families of the elderly. This kind of arrangement makes possible close professional supervision and treatment without the costs incurred by institutionalization in residential centres.

Within this approach the city offers a plethora of services direct to old people's homes. Some of these have been instituted at the instigation of the national government (Koseisho, 1982:475–6). Aimed mainly at the bedridden and feeble elderly, these services include the supply of special equipment (baths, beds, wheelchairs or interphones); the activation of a visiting nurses scheme; the dispatch of long-term home-helpers who assist in everyday things like cooking, bathing, shopping or laundering; or the supply of short-term home visitors who carry out similar functions (Otsu-shi, 1983:17–20).

Other programmes have been established due to the initiative of the prefectural or city governments themselves. Thus, for example, the municipality encourages the building of small centres for the elderly in their own neighbourhoods. Since 1976 six 'houses of repose for the elderly' dotted around the city have been constructed. Next, the city runs rooms in 21 of its City Office branches in which special activities are held for the aged. And finally, since 1977 rest and recreation rooms for the elderly have been built through joint funding by the city and prefectural authorities. These are usually found in or next to the meeting halls of local neighbourhood associations, and are the site of recreation activities for the aged as well as city-run classes for such subjects as health education or gymnastics.

Budgetary concerns, however, are usually joined with more explicitly political ones. For example, Otsu's welfare centre for the aged was funded and constructed within a national programme (Koseisho, 1982:470). Here again, while a primary aim has been to provide professional care without institutionalization, there is an added political advantage. For as Campbell (1979:349) notes, despite the fact that there is no indication that such centres are in high demand:

Politicians are accustomed to think of the political benefits of public works projects, so when they became more sensitized to the problem of the aged, they almost automatically thought first of building local facilities that provide broad access.

It is no surprise, then, that Otsu's politicians and welfare administrators constantly offer the centre as a symbol of their commitment to the welfare of the city's senior citizens.

On the other hand, community care also implies care *by* the community. Here the stress is on recruiting local volunteers to man and run non-professional organizations that provide help and support within their neighbourhoods. This emphasis is related to the growing realization among welfare administrators that an increasingly affluent population with greater amounts of free time can be tapped for activity that supplements the more formal services (Koseisho, 1982:491). Voluntary activity is used in order to remedy shortages of personnel, or to raise the general standards of client care (Ministry of Health and Welfare, 1974:iv).

Some of these activities are carried out by extra-territorial voluntary organizations which include, for example, doctors' associations, lawyers' groups, the Japanese Red Cross, national youth and women's groups, Rotary or Lions. But the bulk of voluntary action is undertaken by local community organizations. These include such frameworks as social welfare councils, community chests, child welfare workers or goodwill banks (roughly similar to the British good-neighbour schemes). At the core of these activities, however, stand the voluntary welfare workers and the old-folks clubs.

Both organizations were already in existence in the late 1960s. The *minsei-iin* pre-date World War II when there were close to 15,000 such workers by 1930 (Taira, 1967:97–102), and the old-folks clubs began to be established in the 1950s. But it was only in the 1970s that their activation was joined with a new emphasis on care *by* the community. Thus organized care by the community has historical roots. In this sense, the propagation of such an approach by administrators and politicians was not totally innovat-

ory because community care involved to a great extent the utilization of existing schemes and organizations.

9 The Voluntary Welfare Workers

For a growing number of people – the elderly themselves, their families, friends and neighbours – mass longevity has brought with it a multitude of new problems and made existing ones more acute. Personal apprehensions about such issues as post-retirement employment, the adequacy of savings and pensions, or the availability of health care, are compounded by worries about more mundane but no less real difficulties. For, to paraphrase Wicks (1982:97), old age is about increasing problems of loneliness and isolation; illness and incontinence; support at times of stress and distress; doubts about self-determination and self-worth; help with climbing stairs and bathing; aid in preparing meals and housework; and access to welfare officials and services. Of all the neighbourhood-level organizations operating in the city of Otsu, the group that undertakes the bulk of care for older people with these varied difficulties are the voluntary welfare workers (the *minsei-iin*).[1]

Recruitment and work

There are 344 such workers in the city (1982) and the area assigned to each is determined by a combination of population, topography and administrative borders. *Minsei-iin* are usually recruited for a term of three years, although more than 70 per cent serve more than one term in their capacity (Otsu-shi, 1983:46). The general tasks and concerns of the *minsei-iin* are summarized in a government manual on social services in Japan (Ministry of Health and Welfare, 1974:34):

In accordance with the Law Concerning Volunteer Workers in Welfare Services, a *minsei-iin* is assigned to an area of a city, town, or village to investigate the social conditions of his district. A *minsei-iin* is to find out families in his district who are in need of public assistance . . . [and] to help the recipients of public assistance to rehabilitate and support themselves. He co-operates with public assistance workers in the operation of public assistance services. He is usually active in various community projects, is an influential member of the voluntary social services, and is interested in developing the social programme of the community. He is generally a member and leader of the Council of Social Welfare. . . .[2] Upon the recommendation of the prefectural governor the Minister of Health and Welfare appoints the *minsei-iin* for his term of service.

In the Hieidaira–Yamanaka school district there are three such welfare workers. One is assigned to the village and is in charge of 62 households. The other two work in the suburban estate and oversee 363 and 280 households each. Although all three are women, this seems an exception, for on the city level only 38 per cent of the *minsei-iin* are women (Otsu-shi, 1983:45).

Although now in charge of only a limited number of households (the city average is 210), in terms of both age – she is 67 – and experience, Yamanaka's *minsei-iin* is the senior of the three. Having married into the village from a nearby hamlet at the outbreak of World War II, she soon became a war widow and brought up her only son virtually single-handedly. Two years ago she retired from Otsu's municipal office where she had worked in the welfare departments for over two decades. But she is still highly active and vigorous in daily life. Now completing her fourth term as welfare worker, she was first asked to undertake this position in 1970 by the head of the village's *jichikai*. Until 1978, when the population of the suburban neighbourhood topped 400 households, she also doubled as Hieidaira's *minsei-iin*. That year she and the head of the estate's neighbourhood association turned to the city authorities for the creation of independent *minsei-iin* positions there as well. They succeeded, and two such positions were created.

In addition to her present role in Yamanaka, she continues to be active on the city and school district levels as well. She still serves as a city guidance officer for widows, as chief organizer of the Hieidaira–Yamanaka association for fatherless families, and as a member of the local social welfare council. It is not surprising, then, with her experience and familiarity with social welfare problems and procedures, that the younger and newer *minsei-iin* of the estate turn to her for advice and guidance.

Hieidaira's two welfare workers are 50-year-old housewives, one of whom took on her position in 1978 and the other in 1981. They differ markedly, however, in terms of their personality and approach. The *minsei-iin* who began in 1978 is married to a white-collar worker employed in a Kyoto manufacturing firm, and is an outgoing type who is active in many other community affairs. She is an energetic participant in the neighbourhood association, junior high school PTA, children's sports club, and coaches the women's volleyball team (*mamasan bare*). In addition, she runs gymnastics and recreation circles for the handicapped at the nearby City Office branch. Being a *minsei-iin* for her, then, is part of an array of functions she participates in but is an important one. Thus, for example, she related that when the priorities of the welfare worker role conflicted with those of the PTA a few years ago, it was the former that took precedence.

Hieidaira's other *minsei-iin* is married to a Kyoto University professor. She is a much more reserved type, who also teaches flower arrangement (*ikebana*) to a few of the estate's women. As a young girl she was raised in a small country Buddhist temple that after the war began to undertake welfare activity.[3] There, she says, she learnt much from her mother about the discretion and demeanour this kind of work entails.

Both were asked by the head of the neighbourhood association to become *minsei-iin*. It was he who used the formal network of the association in order to find and then draft them into their roles. One was recruited through the recommendation of her neighbour who was then serving as the deputy head of the *jichikai*. The second was encountered when she participated in the association's drive to set up a voluntary fire brigade in Hieidaira. Each was approached separately by the head of the *jichikai*. He explained the importance of and sensitivity and tact needed in welfare work, and invited them to take on the job for a term of three years. Thus while they are appointed by an authority from above, in reality this is no more than a formal authorization. This is because, in effect, the prefectural governor (and by extension the Minister of Health and Welfare) accepts the recommendations of neighbourhood-level leaders who are most attuned to their areas' special needs and problems.

At the same time it must be stressed that although people are officially nominated for and accepted into the *minsei-iin* role by local officials, at base the act of becoming a welfare worker is a voluntary one. People can and do refuse to take on this kind of community role. This is not to deny that a certain measure of public pressure may be gently put on people to become a welfare worker, or that some people are more susceptible to such pressure. But it must be understood – and again this is much clearer in the estate – that people feel they have a positive right not to undertake public posts in the community.

Along these lines the reasons for assuming the *minsei-iin* role should be seen less in terms of answering public expectations, and more in terms of self-fulfilment through community activity. Thus among all of the three voluntary welfare workers, I encountered a dignified pride in what they are doing. But, this was not coupled with the sentiments of either a 'do-gooder', nor of pompous self-importance. The feeling was rather one of a realization on the part of these people that they are doing important and responsible work.

Duties and tasks

Although they do occasionally deal with problems of fatherless families or children, according to all three welfare workers the bulk of their work is centred on the aged. This is borne out in city statistics (Otsu-shi, 1983:48–9) about the hours devoted by *minsei-iin* throughout the city to different welfare populations. The share devoted to care for the elderly takes up more than 50 per cent of the time *minsei-iin* devote to voluntary activity, and amounts to more than all of the other eight given categories combined (handicapped, children, fatherless families, etc.).

Measured by the ebb and flow of urban systems, Hieidaira is new-born. Gauged, however, in terms of the personal biographies of its residents, the suburban estate is, as one local lady noted, old enough for people to have aged and died in. In the decade or so of its existence, the proportion of those over the age of sixty has grown to 9.8 per cent (in 1982), or 217 people. Some have migrated into the estate with their children and now live with them or close by. Most of the elderly, however, have moved to Hieidaira as a couple just before or in the early years of their retirement. Some were 'forced out' of their previous residences when they had to vacate the company housing they had lived in for twenty or thirty years. Others came out of a desire to own their own house, or because they sought a calm, restful place in which to spend their last few years. In this respect Hieidaira has come to resemble most areas in and around the large cities where there is a lower proportion of elderly living with their children (Maeda, 1978:55).

In Yamanaka the elderly over the age of sixty-five number 34 people or 14.8 per cent of the village's population (in 1982). This is significantly higher than the comparable share of the elderly in the city (12.2 per cent), prefecture (13.9 per cent), or throughout the country (12.9 per cent) (Otsu-shi, 1983:15; Asahi Shinbunsha, 1983). But the figure for the village is still lower than that of other villages more distant from the urban centres (Maeda, 1978:52; Smith, 1978:39). Almost all of the older villagers were born in Yamanaka, or in one of the nearby hamlets of Otsu or north Kyoto (Kitashirakawa). About two-thirds live with their children, grandchildren, and to an increasing degree great-grandchildren. The rest live alone or with their spouse, their children having left the village in search of jobs, never to return.

Compared with the elderly of other areas in Otsu, the older population in the Hieidaira–Yamanaka school district is well off. Securing welfare pensions seems to be a rather limited task for the local welfare workers. The district has the lowest number of old-age welfare recipients in both relative and absolute terms. As almost all of the elderly who moved to the suburban estate did so with their own resources, few families are in financial difficulty. In Hieidaira thus only nineteen individuals receive an old-age welfare pension (*roorei fukushi nenkin*) which is granted to households with incomes falling below the national minimum.[4] In Yamanaka there are three such households (Otsu-shi 1982:199–200), as here even those who do not live with their children may receive some assistance from them or have independent sources of income. The only other households receiving financial assistance are 9 fatherless families and 4 families with a handicapped person.

Hence the situation in the district is similar to that found in the village studied by Smith (1978:31), where the most common variety of family on welfare consisted of elderly pensioners.

Yet even though the individuals receiving a welfare pension may only be a small proportion of the elderly in the district, the estate's welfare workers have considerable difficulties in reaching them. This is related to a more general point. For from the *minsei-iin*'s point of view probably the most representative contrast between the two communities lies in the differing degrees of difficulty in finding those elderly people who are in need of some kind of care, attention or financial assistance. This is a representative contrast in that, although a practical difficulty, it directs attention to the contrasting social milieux within which the voluntary welfare workers have to operate.

In Yamanaka, the small size of the village, and the intertwining of kith and kin networks, make almost any change in family circumstances part of 'public knowledge'. Accordingly, when an elderly couple or single person are left alone, encounter sudden illness or are in need of other kinds of care, this is immediately relayed to the *minsei-iin*. This is done directly by the person in need – or more frequently by members of his or her extended family, friends or neighbours. Moreover, because there is no problem in knowing who she is, the period of time it takes for the *minsei-iin* to become informed is quite short. The obverse consequence of this is that any sign of deterioration in mental, social or material conditions is very quickly fed into the gossip of the village, with little regard to privacy.

By contrast, in Hieidaira which is growing yearly by 40 to 50 households – almost the size of the whole village – changes in family conditions are less noticeable and finding aged people with problems is therefore more problematical. Not only are neighbouring relations not yet solidified in many parts of the estate, but the pervading urban sentiments of 'minding one's business' limit the effectiveness of such informal relaying of information as is found in Yamanaka. Moreover, while I have no statistical data on this question, my impression from interviews held is that Hieidaira is the site of problems that are found – according to city officials – in new residential areas throughout the city. Thus my feeling is that there are quite a few families who do not know who the *minsei-iin* are. This is despite the fact that the neighbourhood association regularly publishes their names and phone numbers.

The organization by the Hieidaira–Yamanaka social welfare council of the annual Memorial Service for the War Dead (*Ireisai*) in 1983 is an example of these difficulties. While the welfare worker from the village could provide a detailed list of all the families interested in participating, the *minsei-iin* from the suburban estate could give only general estimates. They explained that an effort had been made to publish an announcement about the service in the neighbourhood association's newsletter, but that there were still problems in reaching those who did not belong to the *jichikai* or who were still new in the area.

The suburban workers do however use other strategies in order to overcome these obstacles. First, they use the more formal network of the neighbourhood associations. This is done primarily by asking the heads of the association's base groups (*kumi-choo*) to inform them of any old people they think may have problems. Second, they are informed by the owners of the two most popular establishments of the area, the rice shop and *sake* store. These shop-keepers come into contact with the majority of the suburban neighbourhood's residents and from time to time drop a discreet hint to the *minsei-iin* that some elderly person may need looking into. In this capacity, the *minsei-iin* function as an active 'outreach service' for the city. In this role they serve to overcome some of the difficulties encountered by social services for the aged, in reaching what have come to be called the 'invisible' elderly (Beattie, 1976:626).

In all cases, however, the approach and preliminary probe is done by the welfare workers themselves. Great care is taken in these first meetings, which are held in the elderly person's house. The atmosphere is one of a neighbourly visit rather than that of a therapeutic session or of a bureaucratic interview. Instead of being isolated from familiar surroundings, the people the *minsei-iin* approach are on their own 'home turf'. In this situation, where the elderly person plays host, all can join in the Japanese social ritual of tea-drinking (*ocha*). Thus through this equivalent of the American 'dropping in for a cup of coffee' (and not the highly formalized tea ceremony), they can enter into a general conversation. The *minsei-iin* for their part are not bound by the tight schedules of formal agencies and so can join in these encounters at a leisurely pace.

Direct questions are avoided, and as far as possible the older individual is encouraged to raise and discuss problems at her or his own pace. Once these arise, however, talk is usually not limited only to financial matters. They also speak about other issues such as health and illness, social contact, or everyday things like shopping. Nor are these relationships limited to the initial encounter. Provided the older person is interested, and almost all are, the *minsei-iin* usually drops in for a chat at least once a month. On these occasions little pressure is felt on either side to talk about 'welfare' difficulties, although if any new matters arise they are discussed.

Once the welfare workers have learnt about an elderly individual's problems and difficulties they basically help either by linking them to the plethora of services that exist on the city level, or by providing them or their families with the pertinent information. In Hieidaira and Yamanaka the *minsei-iin* have given assistance in the following areas: arrangement of home-helpers and visitors, attendance at day centres, commitment to homes for the chronically ill (and providing for the elderly spouse left at home), finding employment, filling out difficult application forms, and securing welfare annuities and grants for such expenses as gas and electricity. On rare occasions they have also been the ones who notify kin in cases of sudden illness or death. In this sense the *minsei-iin* function as extensions of city information and referral services. This is achieved not only by multiplying the City Office's capacity to make the elderly aware of the services and programmes that exist, but also in explaining and facilitating their use.

Related to this function is the role of the *minsei-iin* as 'communicators' for city-level services. Thus, for example, they remind some of the elderly people of the free medical examinations the city provides every year for the over 60s, or of the periodic visits of the motorized X-ray unit operated by the municipality. Here the provision of information is to the elderly population as a whole, rather than to specific individuals in need of a specific service.

In contrast to the period spanning the immediate pre-war and post-war eras, there now exist multiple access routes to the information, services and resources of the city's welfare departments. This point merits emphasis, because it underscores the significant change that the voluntary welfare worker role has undergone in post-war Japan. Gone are the days documented by Dore (1958:70; see also Braibanti, 1947:146–7) in the early 50s, of the all-powerful *minsei-iin* who functioned much like the bosses of American political machines. At that time, local welfare commissioners, as the term was then usually translated, had a monopoly of access to city agencies and could give or withhold allocations as personal favours. Through that they incurred an indebtedness on the part of the welfare clients that was repaid at times of local elections.

Now, it is no longer mandatory to pass through the neighbourhood *minsei-iin*. In those cases, then, when an older person does not want to meet or talk to the welfare worker, they are free to go directly to the City Office. Indeed, according to the estimates of one city welfare official interviewed, about 60 per cent of applicants approach the city directly, 30 per cent come through the *minsei-iin* channels, and the other 10 per cent are directed by such functionaries as city assemblymen or heads of neighbourhood associations.

When I asked Yamanaka's welfare worker about the *minsei-iin* role in relation to these varied channels, she astutely observed that the present system is a flexible one. On the one hand, the *minsei-iin* facilitates access to social services of just those people who have difficulties in applying for help. Thus, for example, they may help those people who are illiterate, shy or simply apprehensive at approaching government bureaucracies. On the other hand, because the voluntary workers reside in the same area, some persons may be reluctant to raise what they take to be very delicate problems with neighbours. In these cases they can approach the City Office directly.

Another aspect of the *minsei-iin* role in Hieidaira can best be understood in the light of the contrasting social circumstances of the suburban estate and the village. Health, medical care, and facilities seem to be major concerns that the welfare workers encounter among the residents of both communities. These are concerns that appear not only among the old who are sick or feeble, but also among the majority who are still healthy and sprightly.[5] But in Hieidaira these apprehensions seem to be associated with other problems as well. The following words of a doctor who operates the small clinic in the estate illuminate this point:

'People over the age of 70 are exempt by law from paying medical expenses. As a consequence they tend to come and visit me even when there is no real reason to. For example, while this population of over 70s makes up about 30 per cent of my patients, they account for over 60 per cent of the visits.

155

This is not just a matter of them being more ill. Rather, I sort of feel that they sometimes like being sick. It's as though they're looking for some kind of contact. At times I feel as if the clinic on Friday afternoons has become a salon for the aged. One gets the impression that it's as if some of the oldsters have been pushed away by their children. Their kids have cast them away (*ubasute*) up here into the mountains into Hieidaira.'

Indeed, when I visited the clinic, I almost invariably met a group of elderly people chatting with the doctor's wife (who is also the receptionist), or talking among themselves in the waiting room. These people represent, no doubt, only a minority of the elderly in the suburban estate, but underline a difference from the village. For in Hieidaira, the problems of separation from family that some old people undergo are compounded by the general difficulties of striking up relationships in a new residential area. In Yamanaka, while a sizeable group of older residents have suffered a similar separation from their children, they have not been left in new and insecure surroundings. For while their children have left, these people still have the network of local friends and groups to which they have belonged since childhood or marriage.

Along these lines, the *minsei-iin* of Hieidaira see it as part of their role to encourage those elderly people living alone to develop friendships or acquaintanceships with other older citizens in the estate. This is usually done through suggesting that the older person join some of the activities of the old-folks club. The ultimate aim, according to one of the welfare workers, is to reach a situation where that person joins a network of friends who visit each other when someone is sick, can call a doctor in times of need, or help with everyday things.

Unlike the links that develop in most voluntary organizations that have a high personnel turnover, the relationships between *minsei-iin* and the elderly people they deal with are not a short-term matter. Because they serve a term of three years or more, welfare workers can develop a long-standing rapport, as well as a sensitivity to changes in the circumstances of the elderly in the area. Conversely, they are given ample time within which to familiarize themselves with the various welfare agencies, pro-grammes and procedures. It is probably for this reason that an official in the City Office stressed the value of *minsei-iin* continuing more than one term in their position, and the accumulated experience this implies.

While the position of *minsei-iin* is not coveted by 'budding local politicians' (Dore, 1958:70) seeking an electoral base or by people who regard their position 'as more an honor than as a responsibility' (Braibanti, 1947:147) any more, it still does carry with it a measure of prestige, as well as some political import. In Hieidaira and Yamanaka the voluntary welfare workers are invariably invited to community functions. For example, they are invited to the school entry and graduation ceremonies or the annual sports field-day. On these occasions they are formally and publicly introduced, and sometimes asked to say a few words.

Moreover, in their capacity, *minsei-iin* are regularly asked to participate in the meetings of the local neighbourhood associations and the social welfare council, as well as in the meetings of these organizations with the mayor and other city officials. On these occasions, the welfare workers are not only consulted as 'experts' on social welfare issues, but take on a more explicit political role as well: political in the sense that they become a kind of proxy representative of the aged and their interests.[6] Thus, in a number of meetings I attended, the *minsei-iin* – usually in concert with the representatives of the old-folks clubs – urged the improvement of the bus service to the welfare centre for the aged, and the quick repair of potholes which posed a danger for elderly people walking the estate's streets. In addition, according to one of Hieidaira's welfare workers, she and her colleagues were instrumental a few years ago in a successful struggle against the raising of the price of bus tickets. This price rise, they thought, would make it difficult for elderly people living on a welfare pension to travel.

City links

Once a month, all three voluntary welfare workers attend a meeting of the District Council of *Minsei-iin*. As there are only three *minsei-iin* in the school district of Hieidaira–Yamanaka, an independent council has not been established there yet. Consequently they join the welfare workers of a neighbouring district in a group

157

totalling about twenty people. The meetings are attended and run by official representatives from the municipal welfare departments, and are held in a branch of the City Office a few kilometres from the suburban estate.

These monthly meetings are but the more formalized and regularized of the city–*minsei-iin* contacts, which also include personal appearances at the City Office, or communication by telephone. The monthly engagements do however show quite clearly how the *minsei-iin* are taught about their role. First it is primarily on these occasions that city staff introduce and explain the structure and activities of the city-level social services. So too they regularly bring welfare workers up to date on any new welfare 'rights', procedures or programmes.

Second, city bureaucrats use the monthly meetings as forums within which to gather information about the welfare needs of the different neighbourhoods, and the level and quality of the city-run programmes. The *minsei-iin* are encouraged not only to provide 'statistical' information (for example the number of clients reached), but to advise city officials about the weaknesses of and possible improvements to existing arrangements. According to one of Hieidaira's welfare workers the atmosphere is constructive and the *minsei-iin* are often explicitly critical of city programmes and schemes.

Third, these are occasions for the *minsei-iin* to raise cases or problems they have encountered. These are analysed and related back to the policy lines, rules and programmes of the municipal office. In this sense – rather like the efforts directed at the American 'friendly visitors' (Beattie, 1976:623) – the meetings provide opportunities for developing the *minsei-iin*'s capacity to recognize potentially problematic conditions which they report to the city officials.

Seen against the background of the city departments' 'administrative' rather than 'professional' orientation to social work, the activation of these volunteers on the basis of written rules and directives has certain advantages.[7] It is much easier to teach the proper application of rules to a specific case than to impart the knowledge that will make for good treatment. The welfare worker can be useful, from the city administration's point of view, in just those areas where no great amounts of training are needed, i.e. in those tasks where few decisions need to be taken. Moreover, like certain lower staff participants in American or British welfare agencies (Scott, 1969:131) they can in this way be introduced rather easily to the workings of city welfare programmes and administration.

The administrative orientation of the city officials has another advantage. One finds none of the criticisms and derogatory remarks that are so characteristic of the way social workers view volunteers in Western countries, i.e. as indiscreet, interfering and unreliable versions of existing services (Hill, 1980:57). Thus the skills of recognizing and referring problems that city officials try to inculcate in the welfare workers are based upon these officials' accumulated experience rather than on a more abstract concept of professional behaviour.

From the *minsei-iin*'s point of view, such meetings, by bringing them together, provide good opportunities for mutual support and the pooling of relevant experience. In this respect some of the problems of isolation and lack of contact between volunteers in more individualized services (Abrams *et al.*, 1981:114; Isomura and Sakata, 1981:70) are overcome. Yamanaka's welfare worker mentioned that in addition to these regular opportunities she also met with Hieidaira's *minsei-iin* on less formal occasions, where similar discussion of welfare-related matters ensued.

The cost for the municipality of having the formidable array of tasks carried out by the *minsei-iin* is extremely low. An analysis of data provided by the City Office (Otsu-shi, 1981:81) illustrates this. The cost of activating all of the 344 *minsei-iin* in Otsu represents only 12 per cent (23 million Yen in 1982) of the Social Welfare Department's yearly budget. This sum includes not only the personal expenses paid to the welfare worker, but also expenditures for such things as printing announcements, circulation of questionnaires, or for meetings. In fact, the personal expenses for the *minsei-iin* represent only 3.3 per cent of the department's yearly budget. This means that the welfare workers each receive as direct compensation for their work only about 1,500 Yen a month, a sum that does not even suffice for the telephone and travel expenses they are supposed to cover.

The contribution of these volunteers to the city's welfare efforts is even more pronounced when other figures – for man-days worked – are examined (Otsu-shi, 1983:48–9). On the average each welfare worker contributes a staggering 101 working days a year in her or his capacity: in 1982 the 344 welfare workers contributed 36,897 days. If one converts this figure into comparable working days of fully paid city staff, the result is no less striking. It seems that these voluntary workers carry out work that would take about 140 paid officials to do. It is no surprise, then, that government officials refer to the *minsei-iin* as the core of voluntary welfare work.

10 The Old-Folks Clubs

It is easy to overstress the pains and difficulties of the aged. Indeed, despite popular stereotypes, the general view emerging in the literature on the elderly in Japan (Linhart, 1981:14; Palmore, 1975:6, 32; Office of the Aged, 1981) offers a contrasting picture. The vast majority of the country's older citizens – like the elderly in other advanced-industrial democracies (Tornstam, 1982:188; Maddox and Wiley, 1976:14, 38) – are on the whole healthy, well integrated socially, and have good relations with their families. A prime reason for this situation seems to be the existence, throughout the country, of a host of organizations and associations for old people. These provide for many individuals frameworks for initiating social contact, pursuing sport and leisure activities, and creating networks of self-care and mutual help. These organized groups are formed, for example, by trade unions, large firms, political parties, universities, or religious movements (Linhart, 1981:12–13). But by far the most numerous and important of these organizations are the old-folks clubs. Among the hundreds of such clubs in Otsu City are the two *roojinkai* of Hieidaira and Yamanaka.

Local sentiments and organizational assumptions

While the suburban and village clubs are similar in some respects – for instance in receiving city subsidies or designating club officers – in many ways they differ markedly. One cannot understand their differences, however, only through a study of their dissimilar organizational dynamics, for the clubs operate in social milieux with contrasting assumptions and sentiments.

161

An image that still pervades much of the Japanese literature on the problems of today's aged is a strongly negative one. One critic, for example (Tanaka, 1979), sees the problem as a basic shift in social valuation. Traditionally, according to his argument, it was the elderly who were seen as the prime contributors to society. Now with the growing importance attached to the young's contribution to the 'economic miracle', the old are shunted aside. While he concedes that many elderly still live with their children, in his view they are all the same, 'spiritually living apart, existing physically in the midst of the family, or society, but tormented by an incurable sense of exclusion' (*ibid*.:67).

From my observations in Hieidaira and Yamanaka and from the remarks found in the literature (Palmore, 1975:108) this portrayal seems extreme. This is not to deny the negative impact of Japanese modernization on the life of the elderly, but rather to argue that the picture is much more complex. Thus I agree with Smith (1978:198) when he says that 'all in all, the new Japan has dealt its elder citizens a very mixed bag of blessings and keen disappointments'. But I would go beyond him, and suggest that this 'mix' takes on different expressions in varied localities.

In Yamanaka, a combination of elements is used by the elderly in order to evaluate and interpret present circumstances. On the one hand, they juxtapose certain parts of the Confucian model of family relations, and especially respect for the aged and the fulfilment of filial duty, with present practices.[1] On the other hand, current customs are placed within the context of long-standing village traditions. Thus, for example, towards the end of an interview with a Yamanaka widow now over eighty, she made the following observations:

'I suppose that, all in all, we're lucky here in countryside
villages, a little of the way things used to be remains. We do
get some attention from the youngsters. Mind you, they don't
make a fuss over us but at least they treat us like ordinary
human beings. I know, because I watch all those television
programmes about how badly the old are treated in other
parts of the country, especially in the cities. Still, there's a
lack of courtesy and respect (*giri to ninjoo*) here in
Yamanaka, which used to be taken for granted. I'll give you
an example. The other week I attended a function at my
granddaughter's nursery. What happened was that there

weren't enough slippers to go around. It turned out that the young brides had all taken them, and there weren't any left for us old folks. It used to be that the older people were first every time, but now no one pays attention to this any more. It's the same on buses and so on. Just the same, however, here in the countryside we do get treated better. . . .

'In fact we also have an active old-folks club. We play gateball, eat together and so on. And once a year in June the whole village turns out to treat all of us over 60 to a feast (*gochisoo*). It's a very big meal and the custom has been going on since I was a child. In fact I think it's been going on for hundreds of years.'

Combined with the strong dose of complaint here, there is still an appreciation that the lot of the old in the village is not one of total exclusion, and more than a hint of pride at the continuation of long-standing customs.

In Hieidaira not only are the suggestions of annoyance and discontent with the way the elderly are now treated more muted, but there is an additional conception that stands in marked contrast to that in the village. In the suburban estate there is a rather distinct perception that effective organized activity can be undertaken on the part of the aged in order to ameliorate their difficulties. An illuminating example was provided by the head of the suburb's old-folks club in regard to the adult activities that completed the annual children's festival (*Jizoobon*).

From about 1975 this summer festival has been organized by the neighbourhood and children's associations in two parts. During the day the children had various games and competitions for their entertainment, while in the evening a *Bon* dance was arranged for the adults. This was carried out in the traditional way with singers, platforms, decorations, drums and flutes. In 1982, however, a change was suggested, and as a result the adult activity chosen was the latest in public entertainment: a *Karaoke*[2] tournament. Organized by professionals from outside the area who included MCs, comedians and technicians, the tournament involved singing popular songs to the accompaniment of a pre-recorded tape with no vocals on it. It was very popular with the older children who had stayed up, and with most of the younger adults. But that was exactly the problem. The head of the *roojin-kai* said to me the next day:

'I've talked to some of my friends about the *Karaoke* tournament. It seems that they were not too enthusiastic about this public singing of modern popular songs. We'd much rather have had another *Bon* dance, or something traditional like that. Trouble is, however, that it's very boring for the youngsters. Although I know it's difficult to find something for everybody, we should I think make an effort to find a programme that has something for both young and old. In the next meeting of the neighbourhood association that is being held to consider and conclude this year's activities, I'll raise the matter. So in this way we can begin to plan just such an activity for next year.'

Coupled with an awareness here that the tastes and preferences of the young should not be rejected, is a sentiment that an accommodation between the groups should be actively sought. The concept, then, is that things are remediable through collective and organized activity.

In sum, then, there are contrasting sentiments and assumptions at the base of the actions of the two clubs. If the activities of the *roojinkai* in Yamanaka are seen to be dictated by long-standing patterns of tradition, in Hieidaira they are felt to be very much the result of organized collective action on the part of the old.

Establishment and affiliation

Yamanaka's old-folks club is called the *Jurakukai* (meaning roughly 'enjoyable old age association') and was formally established in April 1969. It includes *all* the individuals in the village who have passed the age of sixty-five, and in 1982 these numbered 34 people. In one respect, the present *Jurakukai* is no different from the old people's association that existed before it.[3] For it functions, like the older association, as the last step in the progression of the locals through age-grade organizations. In other respects, however, its establishment represents the formalization and the beginnings of a certain administrative intervention in an intra-village group. This can be understood as part of the government promotion of old-folks clubs.

In the late 1950s and throughout the 1960s, old-folks clubs were established locally either by community organizers or by groups of old people themselves. These were organizations whose primary aims were recreation and diversion. From the mid–1960s, however, bureaucrats at the Ministry of Health and Welfare seem to have realized their potential, and 'decided to take advantage of them' (Linhart, 1981:14). The ministry, through local authorities, began an active subsidization programme, the results of which were twofold. On the one hand, the country experienced a tremendous growth in the number of clubs: the level of participation of old people over the age of sixty rose from 12.8 per cent in 1962, to 47.2 per cent by 1973 (Linhart, 1981:4). On the other hand, clubs began more and more to comply with government directives and guidance. From purely recreational frameworks, old-folks clubs had, in order to receive official subsidies, to turn into organizations that facilitated activities like health and education classes, or participation in community affairs.

In Otsu, the municipal office began to offer subsidies and other assistance in the mid-1960s. The formal establishment of Yamanaka's old-folks club arose, according to the club's head, out of a decision within the village to take advantage of this aid. Thus, the City Office's recognition was secured, and the old people's association given the more ceremonious name of *Jurakukai*. Today the club is subject to the same rules and regulations, and receives the same financial allocations that other clubs throughout the city do.

When Hieidaira's club was established in June 1978, the whole governmental apparatus dealing with old-folks clubs was already in existence. The suburban neighbourhood's club is simply named *roojinkai*, and is open to anyone over the age of sixty. In 1982 it had 92 members or about 50 per cent of the people of that age. Before the club opened, old people in Hieidaira had no organized activity, and according to local people very little intra-age group social contact as well. In the words of one club member, the contact was limited to about as much as 'saying hello' (*Konichiwa gurai*).

The opening of the club owes much to the initiative of the locals. In 1977 a small group of older citizens, led by a very energetic retired man who had moved from Kyoto, enlisted the aid of the neighbourhood association and *minsei-iin*. These approached the City Office and asked for assistance in establishing

165

an old-folks club. Within a few months this was arranged, and aid and assistance were granted. The estate's elderly citizens were gathered one day in the neighbourhood association's meeting hall, and given an explanation by city officials about the aims and operation of the club.

Parallel to the opening of Hieidaira's club, a new Hieidaira–Yamanaka alliance of old-folks clubs was also formed (*roojinkai rengookai*). This was done primarily in order to receive further city subsidies (Otsu-shi, 1983:17), and to facilitate the participation of the clubs in city-wide events. The chief officers of this alliance are the two heads of the village and estate clubs.

Today, the 244 such clubs throughout the city are organized into 24 area alliances. The 12,600 people who are members of these old-folks clubs make up 45 per cent of those over sixty and 63 per cent of those over sixty-five in Otsu (Otsu-shi, 1983:17). According to the city officer in charge of liaison with the clubs, Hieidaira and Yamanaka's participation rates are representative. In the older areas which were or still are predominantly agricultural, the rate varies between 80 and 100 per cent. In the newer residential areas the rate hovers around 50 per cent. The average size of a club is around 50 members, although this varies considerably according to local conditions. Thus while the suburban estate's *roojinkai* is rather big, as Hieidaira continues to grow it will probably divide into separate clubs for each ward.

Similar to the pattern found throughout the city, women outnumber men both in Hieidaira's and Yamanaka's *roojinkai*. In both areas the club ratio is about two to one. This is no doubt a reflection of the fact that some men work into their seventies.[4] But it is also related to the longer life expectancy of women. For as Plath (1980:30) notes, older age in Japan has come to be a matter of 'older womanhood, of widowhood' (see also Woss, 1982). Indeed, among the general population in the district the proportion of women grows in the higher age categories. Thus, for example, while the ratio for the over-60s is three women (119) for every two men (84), for the over-70s it is two (43) to one (24).

The participation of the entire group of over-65s in Yamanaka reflects an underlying premise that is found with regard to organizational membership throughout rural Japan (Fukutake, 1982:38; Hendry, 1981:72), i.e. that affiliation with the old-folks club is automatic or semi-automatic. Indeed, the villagers constantly speak of a 'natural' (*shizen*) or 'traditional' (*dentoo*) progression from one age-grade organization to the next. As youngsters they belonged to the elementary school, then the youth group (*seinen-kai*) and when married split into a women's association (*fujinkai*) and men's association (*seiikukai*). Upon reaching the age of sixty-five it is taken for granted that they leave these last two groups and join the old-folks club. Even if someone does continue to work, they make an attempt to join at least some of the club's activities. In this way, the continuity of membership in age-groups reinforces the orientation of the oldsters – almost all of whom were born in Yamanaka or lived there since marriage – to the village as a collective unit. Proud of the participation of everyone over sixty-five, the villagers often contrast their club with that of Hieidaira, where many of the elderly seem not to want to, or not to be able to join.

A number of interrelated reasons seem to account for this. One, cited by the head of Hieidaira's club, is that many are afraid to join because they see in this act an admission or acceptance of the label 'old'. Affiliation with the club becomes for these people, then, a formal validation of their new status as elderly people.[5] I encountered this attitude a number of times when talking to the suburbanites. Once, when I inquired of a young couple why his mother, then living with them, does not join the club, the son replied,

> 'She doesn't like to be around old fogies, it makes her feel old and useless. She'd much rather be around young people, or even sit at home and just watch television. Besides, she says she just doesn't have the energy to go and try any of the club's activities. She just won't.'

A further reason is related to the general difficulties of initiating contacts and recruiting individuals into community groups in new residential areas like Hieidaira. Some who move to the suburb may know about and want to join the activities of the club, but just haven't had the opportunity to do so. They may wait for an invitation from one of the club's officers or members. Or, if they are still working, they may wait for final retirement before joining. Many, however, seem to suffer from the 'social inertia' that poses obstacles in joining any group. Because there is no general expectation that affiliation is automatic, taking that crucial first step is tough. As one club member put it in regard to some of the older individuals who do not join, 'it's like saying you don't like some food without trying it' (*kuwazu girai*).

Still others do not join because they have alternatives. A few seem to maintain links with their previous localities. Thus an old lady who moved to Hieidaira with her daughter still maintains strong ties with the old-folks club in the area where she used to live, and travels there to Kyoto three or four times a week.

Besides these categories of people, however, there is another one whose size is difficult to measure. For persons belonging to this category, old age seems to be a time of gradual liberation from social intercourse and its constraints, and a time to cultivate more personal, more private pursuits. Again, during an interview with a couple who work together in an independent business, I was provided with an example of this pattern of ageing. When I mentioned that the man's father might enjoy the activities of the old-folks club, the daughter-in-law replied that the old man wouldn't go. He seems, she said, to be perfectly happy to tend his little garden, watch television, and content to limit his contacts only to the family living in the house.[6]

The existence of this category of people underscores another more general difference between the suburban estate and the village. This point is related, according to many of the estates' adult citizens, to a social advantage Hieidaira has. People often remarked that here they felt much less constrained by the general social expectations of participating in community activities and organizations. These kinds of comments were often put forward as a contrast to more traditional areas like Yamanaka where such participation is not only automatic, but where sanctions can be applied in cases of lack of participation. The advantage of Hieidaira, then, from the point of view of many of the residents is that here there is a freedom not to join.

Management and finances

The two clubs also contrast in the way things are run. The activities of Hieidaira's *roojinkai* are based on publicly published rules and regulations that are revised periodically. These open with a preamble-like statement reminiscent of official government publications regarding old-folks clubs. This statement includes the general aims of the organization: the furthering of mutual help between the elderly; providing an enjoyable and congenial atmosphere; and facilitating engagement in different hobbies. The rules further specify such matters as criteria for membership, club officer roles and functions, meetings, reports and financial procedures.

Once a year, at the beginning of April, a general meeting attended by about half of the members (45–50 people) is held. This meeting is run by an election committee, and includes the selection of the coming year's officers, as well as a discussion of future plans and programmes. Throughout the year, however, it is the executive body which is in charge of the actual implementation of the plans and programmes. This body includes the following members: the club's head, his three assistants, accountant, inspectors and thirteen leaders of territorial groups whose function it is to convey messages and recruit members to activities. The executive is usually convened once a month or before major activities. A number of the club's members told me that in all meetings the atmosphere is lively, and different opinions are voiced and argued about. Moreover these occasions are opportunities for socializing as much as they are for actual 'work'.

In contrast to other clubs (Linhart, 1981:5–6), where men usually predominate, two out of every three officers in the estate's club are women. Thus, for example, two of the three assistants to the head of the club are women. While the head of the club – an energetic former civil servant with the Kyoto prefectural government – that was mentioned before has remained in his post since the club's establishment, a positive effort is nevertheless made to recruit at least some new club officers every year.

Linhart (1981:5) observes that the proliferation of club officer roles has an adaptive function. Especially for the older men who have left their jobs in companies or other institutions these roles seem to provide a substitute status satisfaction. The relish with which these are taken, and the importance attached to them by their incumbents in Hieidaira lead me to concur with his findings. I would add, however, two points in regard to the estate. First, this is a satisfaction that is not limited to men, but is found among the women officers as well. Second, this is not just a matter of status satisfaction, for these roles also provide an important outlet for those people who like 'organizing' affairs, or 'dealing' with people.

In the village, on the other hand, there are no written rules or regulations. There is a general feeling that the programmes and affairs of the club are 'fixed' or 'known' (*Kimatte-iru*) and that there is no need for the elaborate set of discussions and gatherings found in the estate. The main club officers, too, tend to retain their positions for many years. For example, the club's head – a former rice merchant in Otsu – completed his fourteenth year in this position in 1983.

Once a month, or once every two months, the village club's members congregate on a chosen morning at the village shrine. After sweeping and cleaning the grounds, they assemble at the shrine office for a meal and drinks. During lunch various announcements about forthcoming events are made and some discussion carried out. When the need for special announcements arises, these are conveyed personally by the club's head, his wife and his assistants, or, more and more, by phone.

The yearly membership fees for the clubs are 1,200 Yen for Hieidaira and 2,000 Yen for Yamanaka. Both fall well within the wide variation found in Otsu's clubs. Yearly fees in the city fall anywhere between 600 and 2,400 Yen. These fees are paid in one lump sum at the beginning of the year, and are held in an account in the Post Office Bank. The money goes towards partial financing of the club's activities, and towards covering the cost of food and drink procured. Sometimes the members are asked to supplement these regular fees with one-off payments for outstanding events: for example towards paying the guide, bus and hotels on a club trip. Together these sums make up about 50 per cent of the club's revenues. A further 20 per cent is received from the local neighbourhood associations. Another 10 per cent is made up of contributions from well-to-do members, and may total 20 or 30 thousand Yen a year.

The final 20 per cent of the yearly budget is given to the clubs as a subsidy from the Ministry of Health and Welfare and the prefectural government, although the money is directly administered by the city. The sum includes subsidies paid directly to the clubs, and a grant allocated to the Hieidaira–Yamanaka alliance. In addition, from time to time further allocations are given by the city. For example, during the period of fieldwork Hieidaira's club received a special sum in order to set up a flower garden. All of these sums for all of Otsu's old-folks clubs, however, total only just over one per cent of the yearly budget of the Elderly Welfare Department (Otsu-shi, 1981:84–5).

Over and above these financial links, both clubs are tied to the City Office in other ways. The officer in charge of co-ordinating the activities of all the city's clubs is a full-time member of the Elderly Welfare Department. The heads of the clubs maintain close association with him through the phone, visits and news-letters. In addition, bi-monthly meetings of the heads of the school district alliances of old folks clubs are held at the City Office. As the head of Hieidaira's club serves conjointly as head of the school district alliance, it is he who usually attends. In such meetings, city-level events, functions and services are reported and dis-cussed, and the yearly subsidies announced. In addition these meetings provide opportunities for the bestowal of certificates of commendation (*hyooshoo*) to club officers who have served 5 years or more. The head of Yamanaka's club proudly showed me how he already has a certain number of these.

Furthermore, these meetings function as arenas for officers of the old-folks clubs to take on – like the *minsei-iin* – the active political role of pressure groups. But in contrast to the welfare workers who tend to limit their demands to specific problems in programmes serving the aged, representatives of the *roojinkai* put forward demands related to the whole range of schemes and services connected with the welfare of the elderly. A good exam-ple of this wide spectrum of claims is found in a meeting held between the citizens of Hieidaira and the mayor of Otsu and some of his senior administrators. The meeting was designed to give an opportunity for the residents of the suburban estate to discuss the problems facing Hieidaira. But although representatives of all the local organizations and associations participated, the meeting came to be dominated by issues related to Hieidaira's elderly. The problems raised by members of Hieidaira's old-folks club included: the lengthening of the bus route connecting the estate with the Welfare Centre for the Aged in the heart of Otsu; multi-plication of daytime buses linking Hieidaira with Otsu, so that daily concerns like shopping would be easier to carry out; the mending of potholes in the streets; the construction of a cemetery on some of Hieidaira's land; and the inclusion of facilities for the elderly in the planned citizens' centre – for example a bath and recreation and games rooms. In other meetings the construction

171

Changing Japanese Suburbia

of a medical clinic to serve the needs of the elderly was also raised.[7]

Activities and events

The long list of activities carried out in Hieidaira's old-folks club attests not only to the energy and initiative of its main organizers, but to the diversity of interests and concerns among the local residents as well. Among the regular features offered are: calligraphy, taught by a local Hieidaira teacher for free – 10 people; recitation of Chinese poems – 12 people; singing of Noh songs – 10 people; cultivation of miniature trees – 10 people; walks and hiking to such places as Daimonji or the Kyoto Botanical Gardens; and two or three times a year *sake*-drinking parties.

A leading activity that has been popular since the club's establishment, and also seems to be popular all over the country (Linhart, 1981:12), has been the cultivation of a small vegetable garden. Compared with clubs in the centre of the city the suburban *roojinkai* seems rather fortunate in having a field at the edge of the estate. Here, tomatoes, eggplant, sweet potatoes and other vegetables are grown. This activity seems especially rewarding for those older suburbanites who have never had the opportunity to do agricultural work.

In October, the children from the kindergarten and day-care centre are invited to come out and dig for sweet potatoes. Some of these are taken home, and some taken to the educational institution to be cooked collectively. During this time the children are told about cultivation and the annual agricultural cycles. But, more importantly, both the teachers and the representatives of the *roojinkai* that are on hand stress such themes as co-operation in work, regard for grandparents, and gratitude to the older people who have grown the sweet potatoes. The children for their part sing the oldsters special songs, and present them with handmade tokens of appreciation (usually badges or ornaments).

In addition, representatives of the old-folks clubs are invariably invited to the commencement and graduation ceremonies of the school, kindergarten and day-care centres. Especially in the last two establishments they are asked to give a short talk in which

172

they speak about the importance of family relations, or the significance of respect for the elderly.

In Yamanaka everyone knows and interacts with each other in extra-club contexts. Not only do they meet as kin, as neighbours or as participants in village events, but their relationships usually have a long history stretching back decades to childhood or marriage. As a consequence, club functions are not merely one of a set of alternatives for social intercourse, but have further implications. They promise very little flavour in terms of meeting varied and interesting people. Thus, the activities that are seen by the villagers as most 'fun' are those in which the club comes into contact with other old-folks clubs rather than the internally organized events.

Indeed, compared with the estate's club, here the *roojinkai* seems dull. Thus, for example, while it is the old who cultivate vegetables and fruits this is done invariably on personally owned land, rather than as a joint club venture. The main regular activity is the previously mentioned bi-monthly morning on which the local shrine is cleaned communally. The lunch in which everybody participates afterwards is an occasion for some socializing and discussion of the club's participation in events with other *roojinkai*.

Once a year in June the village pays its formal respects to the aged. The women's and village associations prepare a festive meal which is served at Yamanaka's citizens' hall (*kaikan*). There, new members who turned sixty-five during the year are formally welcomed to the club. Villagers emphasize that this is a custom that predates the club's existence, and is related to an ancient agricultural holiday when the local farmers paid their regards to the elderly on a special day of rest. As one man nearing his eightieth year explained, despite the fact that there is no agricultural season in Yamanaka any more, the custom remains.

Village and estate: joint activities and links

Although their relationships are tinged with a good deal of good-natured competitiveness and rivalry, the elderly of Hieidaira and Yamanaka seem to get along very well together. Nowhere is this more apparent than in what has become one of the favourite topics of conversation in the clubs: the regular competitions of gate-ball. Roughly similar to croquet, the game is played by two teams of five members each, and lasts about twenty minutes. It is a sport that is officially encouraged by the city authorities (Otsu-shi, 1983:178) who help in procuring equipment and organizing tournaments, and is also popular throughout the country, being featured in some television programmes and newspapers.

Weather permitting, the game is practised or played almost every day: in Hieidaira in an open lot destined one day (funds forthcoming) to become a local park. In Yamanaka it is played in the small public grounds next to the kindergarten. The club's members play on a number of levels: among themselves, between the village and the suburban estate, against other school districts in north Otsu, and once a year in a city-wide tournament. On these last two kinds of occasion, a joint team made up of players from Hieidaira and Yamanaka represents the district alliance of old-folks clubs.

In October 1982 the game was introduced as part of the annual Hieidaira–Yamanaka sports day (see Part Five). The aim, according to the chief organizer from Hieidaira, was three-fold: first, to put forward an 'introductory offer', as it were, to those older citizens who did not know the game. Second, to let people outside the old-folks clubs know about the existence of such activities. And third, to make gate-ball a regular feature of the field-day and therefore add another event the elderly can participate in.

Much is made of who won or lost through mild kidding and banter between the two localities. But it seems that these results are especially significant for the Yamanakaites. Whether at the bi-monthly club lunches, or when slightly drunk at village festivals, the good results of the village gate-ball team are paraded and discussed. Underlying these remarks one can often feel the assertion of village pride in identity and achievements.

A problem that crops up in relation to the gate-ball competitions as well as other activities is the precarious health of some club members. Because their state of health changes from day to day, more than in other organizations, there are instances of cancellations and people not turning up.

Other occasions for pleasurable outings together are the day and overnight trips to various parts of Japan. These once- or twice-yearly outings that are organized by the clubs usually go to famous Buddhist pilgrimage centres or hot springs. They are partially financed by the city – which also sends an accompanying nurse – but are bona-fide tours run by commercial companies. These firms are usually the ones who make all the arrangements for transport, hotels, meals and guides. In 1982 the old-folks clubs went on a one-day tour to Fukui Prefecture and an overnight trip to Shimane Prefecture.

According to members, there is (compared with such organizations as the neighbourhood associations or women's groups) much less of a we–them feeling between the *roojinkai*. Not only do the elderly of the village and suburban neighbourhood have similar preferences for traditional clothes, mannerisms and entertainment, but they share something deeper. It is the feeling of shared historical experiences and attitudes that makes for their easy intermingling. For example, older members from both clubs often referred to themselves as Meiji-men. That is, they referred to their affiliation in the elite group of people who were born during the Emperor Meiji's reign (1868–1912), and who have accompanied Japan during her turbulent modern history.

Although I have no direct data in relation to this problem, it seems (from various allusions some of the older people made) that in the meetings and outings of the club, the shared sentiments and experiences provided something else. They provided a common stock of symbols and feelings which the older people use in order to help each other come to terms with old age, and create what Lebra (1979:349) calls a sense of intimacy and emotional interdependency.

The party held on 'Respect for the Aged Day' (*Keiroo no hi*) is the principal occcasion in which the whole of the Hieidaira–Yamanaka school district pays its respects to the elderly. Declared a national holiday in 1966, the festivities that are carried out every 15 September are very similar to those performed throughout the country (see for example Brown, 1979:25; Lebra, 1979:349; Smith, 1978:197–8). Under the supervision of the social welfare council – a district organization – preparations begin near the end of August and involve a number of matters. As the party is held in the school's gymnasium, the principal is formally asked for permission to use the premises as well as other equipment like tables, mats and rugs. The women's associations of the estate and village take on the preparation of box lunches as well as the decoration and cleaning of the hall.

Formal invitations are sent to the mayor (who can rarely attend), city assemblymen, City Office welfare officials, the principals of the school, kindergarten, day-care centre and the middle school the children attend, heads of the PTAs, heads of the neighbourhood associations, and the *minsei-iin*. Next, through the neighbourhood association's newsletters and announcements of the old-folks clubs, all of the people over the age of sixty-five are invited. Only about half of these – nearly 90 individuals – actually attend.

Entertainment used to be provided by professional singers and comedians. But, as the head of the social Welfare Council explained, there are few funds for this now and an attempt is made to rely on the communities' own resources. The chorus group that has been organized in Hieidaira is asked to perform some older songs from its repertoire, and the children of the kindergarten and day-care centre are asked to prepare short programmes.

On the day itself, the organizers come early so that by half past ten when everyone starts arriving all is ready. Guests are asked to register by eleven when the programme begins. From eleven, for about an hour, the invited guests are asked to give short speeches. The municipal officials, for example, talk about the city's older population and social welfare programmes, while the heads of the neighbourhood associations speak about the links between the communities and their elderly. Other invited officials are merely presented by name. Food and drink are usually served from noon, and at one o'clock the entertainment begins. The songs and presentations by the children and chorus group usually take about an hour, and for the next sixty or so minutes the elderly usually sing and dance by themselves. The day's festivities are formally closed at three in the afternoon.

In some instances the clubs are asked to send a number of representatives to help with the operation of activities run by other local organizations. For example, the Hieidaira–Yamanaka sports committee regularly asks for help in the registration and recording involved in the annual sports field-day. The children's association secures the help of about six elderly individuals in listing the contributions received during the annual children's festivals. Yet again, during elections to city and prefectural offices, members of the *roojinkai* act as observers at polling booths. In all such cases, the oganizational networks of the old-folks clubs are used in order to mobilize members towards activities not directly related to the elderly.

The variety and range of activities and functions carried out by old-folks clubs in the village and the estate are not only the outcome of the resources and support given by their communities and local government. On another level, the activities of the *roojinkai* are related to a basic valuational change that has emerged in post-war Japan. While we shall return to this in Part Five of the book, suffice it to say here that whereas in the former Japanese version of the Puritan ethic leisure was seen as a kind of evil, it is now considered as essential for recreation and personal development (Linhart, 1975:206). From a practical point of view, however, it is primarily the elderly who can, in terms of time and relative lack of obligations, most make use of the new right to leisure.[8]

City encouragement and self-reliance

A number of health-related programmes provided by the city are extremely popular among the older residents. Twice a month a free medical massage is given to the over-65s in a small room adjoining the Hieidaira neighbourhood association's meeting hall. Sometimes specialists in acupuncture (*hari*) or acupressure (*shiatsu*) join these sessions and provide some treatment as well. Three times a year a public health nurse (a city employee) holds health classes for the elderly. These are occasions when special exercises and elementary medical practices such as measuring blood pressure are taught. The aim of these, according to the public nurse, is to achieve a measure of self-reliance among the older people. They are encouraged to carry out regular exercise programmes, and to learn to judge by themselves when there is a need to call a doctor.

Many acquaintanceships and some close friendships have been initiated through participation in club activities. As one retired university teacher told me, for some men these are relationships that are sustained through groups of 'old cronies'. These groups regularly assemble three or four times a year at the house of one of the members for drinks and a chat. For many women, however,

177

these contacts are a daily occurrence and involve mutual visiting, shopping or the occasional excursion together into the nearby cities.

Such new-found relationships are most apparent, however, when someone becomes ill. In such cases friends from the neighbourhood sometimes call on the sick person where he is hospitalized, or on his spouse at home. They may bring with them small gifts (flowers, fruit, sweets) and report about the goings-on in Hieidaira and the *roojinkai*. By the same token, a return to the club after a long absence – as one member who has frequently been hospitalized commented – feels at times like a return to friends.

Closely related to these kinds of relationships is the effect that affiliation with the old-folks club has on three-generational families. I had an opportunity to question household members in regard to this point in three of the suburban estate's families. My impression is that the participation of the grandparents in the *roojinkai* makes – in ways resembling other parts of the country (Linhart, 1981:14) – for smoother relationships with their children and grandchildren. This is effected through the sheer physical removal of the older individuals from the house for a number of hours a day, as well as helping the elderly to create focuses of interest and social contact outside the family.

While Palmore (1975:116) observes that such patterns of mutual support emerge throughout the country, she does not seem to appreciate to what extent they reflect – albeit a partial reflection of – an active administrative interest. This was brought home to me most clearly in an interview held with the official in the municipality who is in charge of liaison with the city's old-folks clubs. He stressed a number of times that although it is an important one, providing recreation and diversion was not the primary aim of *roojinkai*. From the city administration's point of view, the main aim is to foster (*ikusei*) what he termed communication (*komyunikeishun*) between the elderly residents of an area. That is, to encourage the creation of mutual visits and social calls through which a network of self-reliance emerges. Concretely, this implies, he said, city help in establishing facilities and frameworks that help the development of these acquaintanceships and friendships. It is in this light that the governmental promotion of old-folks clubs should be seen. For like health education and exercise classes, so the provision of official support for the old-folks clubs (subsidies, holding city-wide events) is oriented towards helping the aged take care of themselves.[9]

11 Concluding Considerations

The emergence and activities of present-day *minsei-iin* and *roojin-kai* point I believe, to the development of what Fukutake (1982:217) terms new community 'solutions' for the aged. The beginnings, in place of the aid and assistance given by traditional communities, of a new kind of 'organized co-operative care': care based on administration-by-dialogue, co-operative help, and recreational pleasure. Yet the establishment of this new kind of care has not been without certain difficulties. In this concluding chapter some of the analytical implications – advantages as well as perils – of the account given in the previous chapters are presented.

Local voluntary organizations: potentialities

At first sight the characterization of local voluntary organizations as little more than cheap administrative sub-contractors or political dupes seems to fit the case of *minsei-iin* and *roojinkai* well. The city secures the discharge of many of its assigned welfare responsibilities for a very small outlay. Moreover, it achieves this through organizations that are subject to its administrative control mechanisms such as financial review, liability to rules, or the more subtle creation of a consensus about shared aims. It is no surprise, then, that officials – politicians and administrators – constantly stress the need for more and more volunteers in the city of Otsu.[1]

Looked at more closely, however, the depiction of voluntary welfare workers and old-folks clubs as mere tools in the hands of local government is too simple. For in effect, built into their very existence as interstitial organizations between the formal and informal spheres of provision of care is a potential for other kinds

180

of action. That is, inherent in their 'situation' are possibilities for an independent assessment of statutory services, an active articulation of political demands, and a special sensitivity to local conditions and circumstances.

This potential is predicated on the fact that the *minsei-iin*, and even more so the *roojinkai*, are not totally dependent on the city officials for guidance, financial help or job evaluation. Moreover, in ways no different from the case of voluntary welfare groups in other post-industrial societies, the welfare workers and members of the old-folks clubs are not ultimately accountable to government representatives (Townsend, 1983:182). For if the accountability of the local authority worker is primarily to his employer for public money spent, for the volunteer it is ultimately to no one but the people he works with and his or her own conscience.

This is not of course to suggest that the *roojinkai* and *minsei-iin* are wholly independent of the city welfare departments. Nor is this to deny that they are in many respects highly successful and effective extensions of the city's agencies and services. For in fact both local organizations do receive much tangible assistance and guidance from such formal entities, and do share with them many of the overriding goals of provision of care. What the argument does imply is that these community organizations have both a critical facility, and a potential for providing different kinds of care than that provided by the more formal organizations.

Organizational responsiveness

The municipal welfare departments have constant problems in adequately coping with the diversity of indvidualized needs and local conditions that mark the groups and communities they serve. In rather abstract terms, these difficulties arise because their 'organizational environment' is never fully known or controlled. The problems seem especially acute among agencies that provide care for one of the most territorially bound of local groups – the aged. This, as Beattie (1976:625) observes, is because 'no life stage categorizes as similar so many persons with different needs and identities.'

The *minsei-iin* – and to a lesser degree officers of the *roojinkai*

– by providing alternative channels of access to and outreach from the City Office, enhance the capacity of these municipal services to cope with their environment. On one level, this is achieved through a simple quantitative multiplication of the official services. In this sense local voluntary organizations extend the municipal office's capacity to provide and gather information, and process feedback. This seems an especially important set of functions within the context of the last decade and a half. For it is primarily during this period that multitudinous programmes and schemes have been created for the aged. In contrast to the *minsei-iin* of the 1950s who dealt almost exclusively with monetary 'benefits', today's workers have to be aware of a whole range of new services that have been established such as medical massages, home-helper schemes, or even the operation of chess and checkers clubs in the city's welfare centre for the aged.

On another level, however, the voluntary welfare workers and old-folks clubs provide a qualitative addition to the formal services.[2] The *minsei-iin*, unlike the city officials, share with the elderly of the area the experiences of locality. This has important advantages in terms of the work they do. The first is a point touched upon by an older resident of Hieidaira who had served before coming to the estate for two terms as the *minsei-iin* of another area in the city. According to him, someone from outside the area may be more likely to miss the more subtle cuing and non-verbal signals that are often indices of problems and worries. A sensitive official can often become aware of these in relation to an elderly individual. But the advantage of the welfare workers is in being able to spot such signals from the behaviour of people around the elderly person.

Second, shared local experiences mean – as the *minsei-iin* in Hieidaira and Yamanaka emphasized – that it is considerably easier to link people to the groups and activities of the community. Thus, for example, in Hieidaira the welfare workers inform any older resident who is alone about the old-folks club and its various functions and circles. In Yamanaka the elderly may be reminded by the *minsei-iin* of certain ceremonies and rites at the village shrine.

Third, the voluntary welfare workers appear to help many clients who perceive the welfare bureaucracy as 'abstract' (Berger *et al.*, 1973:165), i.e. as a formal and remote entity. The workers thus not only 'humanize' a process prone to technicalities and impersonalism. They also help give concrete meaning to the variety of administrative definitions, categories and allocations.

Yet in some communities such as the suburban estate even a shared experience of the locality does not guarantee full coverage of all the potential 'clients' in the area. The fourth point is thus related to those places where there are difficulties in searching for such people. In these cases the voluntary welfare workers can – much more than representatives of the formal agencies – use their knowledge of the informal networks of the locality in order to find just those elderly in need of help or aid. The case of the information provided to the estate's *minsei-iin* by the rice-store or *sake* shop owners is one illustration of this.

One danger that lies at the heart of such arrangements, however, is that of the potential infringement on people's privacy. There is no real guarantee from the prying of an overzealous *minsei-iin*. While there is no guarantee against such prying by a social service official either, the integration of the welfare workers into the neighbourhood's informal social circles makes for a potentially more damaging effect. This is because the worker can leak information to those people the 'client' has to live with on a day-to-day basis.

Three points should be made in regard to this. The first was made by one of the city officials interviewed. He explained that every effort is made to recruit individuals who in the judgment of local leaders or previous *minsei-iin* have a certain measure of maturity and discretion, and thereby minimize the risks of such a danger. The second point lies at the heart of much of the struggle in Europe and America for the establishment of community care. The assertion is that despite the potential violation of privacy, it becomes much more difficult for cases to be overlooked or ignored when there are permanent volunteers with a heightened awareness in the locality. The third point is that while the informal provision of care that characterized the traditional community also ensured that no cases were overlooked, the link to formal agencies in modern-day communities ensures that the quality of care given remains high.

Organization and local peculiarities

Despite the apparent bureaucratic uniformity of the *roojinkai*, both clubs seem somehow to 'fit' their respective communities. That is, compared to the *minsei-iin* which tend to be more administratively regulated, the old-folks clubs have much more leeway to show initiative or place different emphases upon varied local customs and practices. Yet this peculiar 'openness' to local social and cultural influences is more than just an expression of some kind of organizational susceptibility or shortcoming, although city officials may at times insist that this is so. Rather, this peculiar 'openness' is a central factor in the success of such local clubs, despite formalization and city links.

Central to an understanding of the organizational strength of the *roojinkai* is an awareness of the way their activities and structures are arranged. Essentially the clubs are organized in such a way that the activities within each, or within the city departments, are only weakly connected to, or only weakly influence the structure and activities of other clubs.[3] This means that while the old-folks clubs are sensitive or responsive to the city's directives and guidance, in important respects they maintain their own separateness, identity and capability of reacting to their immediate environments – the local communities.

The responsiveness of the clubs to, the way they retain strong links with, and the support given to them by the two communities are underscored by many examples. Just as in Hieidaira the general behavioural premise of the right not to join is evident in club affiliation, so in Yamanaka the automatic nature of membership is clear. In the village the 'natural' culmination of age organizations in the *roojinkai* is contrasted to the much more volitional – and problematic – mode of joining in the estate. Again, the centrality of the shrine – the symbol of the village as a collectivity – as a meeting place and focus of activities in Yamanaka, is paralleled in Hieidaira by the lack of any similar focal point. Finally, the stress on achievement in sports in the village must be set against the diversity of interests in the suburban neighbourhood.

Advocacy

The independent posture of the *minsei-iin* and *roojinkai* is probably most evident in their role as political pressure groups. In this
capacity they function not only as a form of 'quality control' for
the organizational output of city services, but also as groups that
can suggest new welfare arrangements and designs. Moreover, in
this role the representatives of the old-folks clubs and the welfare
workers provide the clearest and strongest links between community care and community action. Whether through their own
independent action, or in concert with local organizations like
the neighbourhood associations, these welfare groups enter into
struggles for community resources. That is, they begin to contend
not only for facilities and resources for the aged *per se*, but for
these to be allocated to their own community.

The outcome of all this is rather ironic. For, as it turns out,
from the city's point of view the activation of voluntary groups
'on the cheap' does not always turn out to be a 'bargain'. The
situation is much like that in other advanced industrial societies
where formal agencies come to subsidize their own pressure
groups (Hill, 1980:157). A good example is the struggle waged by
Hieidaira's welfare workers and heads of the old-folks club for a
bus route linking the neighbourhood to the newly built welfare
centre for the aged. A prime concern for the city when it built
the centre was to forgo the costs of institutionalization. But once
it was built, other groups which the city promotes and supports
began to urge the provision of access to the centre. For the city
again, this spelt further expenditures – negotiation time with the
bus company, help with the placement of bus stations or the
improvement of roads.[4]

Furthermore, this kind of voluntary activity provides in itself a
model for further development of advocacy roles, as well as griev-
ance procedures. This was especially apparent in the interviews
held with the heads of the suburban estate's old-folks club. Thus
one man stressed how the growing importance of old people's
associations nationally has had implications for the relations
between local government and specific *roojinkai* as well. His
impression of the municipality's attitudes was that local officials
now accept the legitimacy of the political activity and demands
put to them by alliances of old-folks clubs in the city.

The separateness and close identity with the local community that were alluded to in the previous section may admittedly be a source of weakness. For under certain circumstances this inter-club segregation may stand in the way of united political action. The organizational machinery provided by the alliance of old-folks clubs, however, serves to forestall most such difficulties. Thus the struggle by the alliance for providing facilities for the aged in the planned citizens' centre is a struggle on behalf of all the district's elderly. Moreover, the fact that in those struggles it is the estate's officers who take the initiative and the lead may compensate for the lack of confrontational attitudes among the village's elderly.

A word of warning must, however, be sounded in relation to these remarks. It is all too tempting to overestimate the power and political influence of these voluntary welfare organizations. The *minsei-iin* and *roojinkai* should be seen not so much as powerful political lobbies struggling for major resources, but rather as 'watchdogs'. That is, they make certain that whenever pertinent decisions are made, the interests of the aged are taken into account. This is a point made by political scientists in regard to such groups advocating the 'cause' of the aged throughout the world. As Hudson and Binstock (1976:389) note, if anything is clear it is that:

> these organizations have at least some power, enough power to ensure that elected officials, legislative staffs and bureaucrats will not totally ignore their existence and aspirations.

Organization and community: resources, models and attitudes

Community care, like community action, is dependent foremost on the resources and skills found within the locality. Thus, for example, the recruitment of volunteers like the welfare workers presupposes the existence of mature and experienced individuals who will have the commitment, understanding and requisite time to invest in their work. As is evident especially from the case of

Hieidaira's *roojinkai*, club activity is also predicated on the existence of older individuals with time, leadership skills, and a predisposition to become involved in community groups and organizations.

A related point involves the peculiar way in which the voluntary oganizations of modern communities can concentrate their limited resources in order to achieve an impact. For it is against a background in which women – the prime care-givers in modern Japanese society – are entering the job market, that the hundreds of hours the *minsei-iin* contribute should be seen. Although I have no way to quantify this assertion, it does seem that the district's three welfare workers substitute for a significant amount of effort that would have to be undertaken by the families of certain aged people, did the *minsei-iin* not exist. For this is the new type of organized, co-operative care that is emerging: the use by the district's communities of the time and skills of only three women in order to provide not only information and referral but, as importantly, social visits, advice and an introduction to the activities going on in the locality.

Indeed, in another sense the success of the *minsei-iin* and *roojinkai* is related to the fact that they are so dependent on community resources. Because there are no real or pretended aspirations for achieving 'professional' treatment, or basic reform of the structural arrangements of city politics, such groups accomplish their rather limited aims very well. To reiterate, local volunteers are most successful in providing information, referring to proper services when it is crucial, and in building networks of mutual help.[5]

On another level, however, the provision of aid and assistance on the basis of voluntary community groups is predicated on the existence of a 'model' for such organized action. This implies more than the establishment of formal guidelines for setting up old-folks clubs or activating voluntary workers. For these organizations must be seen against a background of the historical and cultural legacy of territorially based organizations in Japan. Thus when the old-folks clubs were established and the voluntary welfare workers' role changed after the war, they took their place alongside a host of other community organizations, such as village and neighbourhood associations or women's and youth groups. This situation not only facilitated their recognition and acceptance as valid means by which to further the good of the community, but also for people who were already either directly or vicariously familiar with the routine of local organizations, the complex processes of recruitment, management and support of these local welfare groups were made easier.

Related to this point again is a realization of how the *roojinkai* fulfils welfare connected functions while being at the same time ostensibly oriented to social recreation and educational goals. The point is that for the older members participation in the club is seen as participation in a 'regular' community association and not as participation in an organization of welfare 'clients', or of the needy. The point is not so much that the oldsters are inattentive to the welfare functions that the club fulfils, as that the model of a community organization facilitates a general perception that one is engaged in communal concerns, leisure activities and socializing.

Finally, the success of community care and local voluntary organizations dealing with welfare is related to the controversy about what Fukutake (1982:205–6) calls a 'Japanese-type welfare society'. I agree with Townsend (1983:182) when he concludes that 'it would be foolish . . . to think that a greater proportion of work done by volunteers will solve many of the problems of large-scale authorities'. But it does seem that the advantages of voluntary groups – their potential for extending formal services, as well as for autonomous critical and political postures and their special sensitivity to local circumstances – have been more easily and quickly institutionalized in Japan.

Part Five
THE SPORTS FIELD-DAY: LEISURE AND COMMUNITY SENTIMENTS

12 Introduction

The annual event which draws to it the greatest number of local residents and officers of community organizations is the *undookai*: the sports field-day. Over 600 residents of Hieidaira and Yamanaka congregate on this day in the school's sports grounds, and participate in a series of events which include public exercises, tugs-of-war, individual runs, relay races and humorous competitions. The organization of these festivities and activities provides the inhabitants of the two communities with an atmosphere well suited for indulging in a variety of games and contests, and with opportunities to break down social barriers and become familiar with each other. Many take lunch or drinks together, while others find themselves co-operating in team sports or as fans encouraging their own ward representatives. Throughout the day, local and city officials stress such themes as community unity, good sportsmanship, friendly participation, or the fostering of local ties.

The *undookai* is organized by over 40 volunteers from the school district's sports promotion committee (*taiiku shinkoo kai*), neighbourhood associations, youth sports teams, women's groups, children's committee, old-folks clubs, and the primary school's PTA. Under the direction of the sports committee, these volunteers take charge of a complex set of preparations and responsibilities that begin weeks before the sports field-day. These include, for example, the invitation and reception of municipal dignitaries, mobilization of participants, liaison with community organizations, management of events, preparation of equipment, recording of results, allocation of prizes, and the cleaning and preparation of the grounds.

Throughout the autumn months such sports field-days take place in local communities all over Japan (Brown, 1979:25; Hendry, 1981:70). Yet they can also be found within the framework of manufacturing firms (Dore, 1973:205), commercial enterprises (Rohlen, 1974:110–11) or educational establishments (Dore, 1978:179; Hendry, 1986:142–3). Indeed, in the Hieidaira–Yamanaka district, *undookai* were held in the week preceding the community sports field-day in the school, kindergarten and day-care centres.

An understanding of the Hieidaira–Yamanaka *undookai* necessitates placing it within the wider context of the emerging patterns of leisure activities in the country. For the efforts at organizing the field-day represent not only the quantitative growth of free time that can be devoted to such affairs. They also represent what is perhaps a subtler but no less important shift in the emphasis placed on the workplace and its relation to the family and to the local residential community.

In this respect, a number of features which characterize Japan in the past few decades seem especially relevant. The post-war period has been one marked by the growth of leisure and leisure activities in all of the advanced industrial societies (Kumar, 1978:284ff.). Despite the widespread stereotype of Japan as a work-a-holic nation, these trends are evident in the country as well. Indeed, although the Japanese on the average still work more than Americans or Europeans, since the mid-1960s Japan has shown the steepest decline in hours worked (Economic Planning Agency, 1972:82–3; Cole, 1979:230). While there is as yet no full two-day weekend, the general pattern has been towards the establishment of regular and fixed periods for time off (Yamazaki, 1984:12). The trend towards this regimen is most clearly typified by the six-day work week of the salaried employee and the emergence of Sunday as the day of rest. Indeed, so pervasive is this pattern that one commentator has been led to quip of Japan as the land of the rising Sun-day (Plath, 1969:107).

Yet despite the growth and regularization of time off, for some Japanese leisure activities remain in effect an extension of work. This is especially true for the minority of workers – blue- as well as white-collar – who are employed in the larger firms and institutions. Many of the activities such workers participate in are carried out within official frameworks of the enterprise: for example, in company-sponsored hobby clubs, sports teams, or trips and outings. Moreover, for these kinds of employees much 'unofficial' socializing is also carried out with workmates (Atsumi, 1979; Norbeck, 1977). In other words, for these people, 'the work

relationship tends to carry over into the utilization of leisure time'
(Cole, 1979:231).

Since the 1960s, however, things have begun to change in this
respect. As part of the questioning of the 'growth first' policy and
its implications for the structuring and content of work, doubts
have begun to arise. Like workers all over the 'first' world
(Kumar, 1978:318) the Japanese have begun to challenge the
values of hard work and the encroachment of work-related considerations into their time-off (Linhart, 1975:199).

Surveys, opinion polls, as well as detailed studies of specific
companies all point to the emergence of a sense – especially
among the younger workers and among women employees – that
more flexibility and importance be given to free time, and that
the enjoyment of leisure become one of the prime purposes of
life (Passin, 1975a; Fukutake, 1982; Economic Planning Agency,
1972; Rohlen, 1975:203). Thus for example, Clark (1979:213ff.)
in his ethnography of a Japanese company finds that the rejection
of leisure periods as occasions for getting to know one's workmates better has been accompanied by a much more active pursuit
of private interests. He goes on to conclude that there 'are signs
that companies are having to compete with wives, families, and
hobbies for the time and energy of even their older workers.'
What seems to be emerging, then, is 'a picture of a society where
the attitudes towards work and leisure are slowly changing from
a very one-sided over-emphasis on work to a more balanced outlook on work and leisure, seeing both as necessary' (Linhart,
1975:206).

The rapid expansion of the post-war 'leisure industries' well
mirrors these trends, as well as their relation to the rise of the
nation's economic prosperity. Today's Japanese have a staggering
array of leisure options from which to choose. For example, even
a partial list of these options would include the following: the
media (radio, television, newspapers and journals); travel (both
within and outside the country); family outings (the Sunday drive,
bowling, shopping, picnics, or amusement parks); spectator sports
such as baseball or sumo; traditional clubs and hobbies (calligraphy, singing, painting); or gambling (*pachinko* and mah-jong par-
lours, and boat, bicycle, horse, or motorbike races).

At the same time, however, the expansion of such leisure-
oriented concerns has been accompanied by a related development on the local community level. Since the mid-1960s the host

of local groups established throughout the country includes not only voluntary welfare organizations or citizens' political movements. Since that period residents of local neighbourhoods have begun to set up a whole range of what are sometimes called 'cultural organizations' (Yamazaki, 1984), which include, for example: civic choirs, arts and crafts groups, environmental beautification associations, community colleges, doll-making or pottery clubs, reading and self-study circles, local history societies, traditional song, dance and theatre clubs, poetry-reading groups, or softball and volleyball teams (for examples see Plath, 1969:148 and Dore, 1978:224).

Some of these seem to have been established with the aim of 'regenerating' or conserving traditional mores and customs such as folk songs or crafts (Brown, 1979). Others seem to have been set up in order to enjoy more modern pursuits. Yet others stress the building of a more pleasant and 'live-able' residential environment. Whatever the initial impetus to their establishment, their significance seems to lie, as Yamazaki (1984:17) emphasizes, in their serving as 'nuclei to encourage residents to identify more closely with their community.'

It is, I think, as part of this trend that the holding of the Hieidaira–Yamanaka *undookai* should be seen. The interpretations offered by a number of scholars who have discussed *undookai* in a variety of frameworks well underline the special potential of such public events. Hendry (1981:70), for example, stresses that such activities can contribute to the fostering of local identities. Brown (1979:30) in a complementary way talks of the way individuals are integrated into their communities by participating in the sports days. Dore (1978:179), for his part, discusses the co-operation of local oganizations that is involved in these events, and the sharing of the participants in a joint activity of fun and entertainment. Finally, Rohlen (1974:111) highlights the positive functions that are accomplished through the inversion of social hierarchy, strengthening of solidarity, and relaxation of social relations on such days.

Yet the creation of 'integration', a 'common identity' or a 'sense of sharing' seems to be especially problematical in modern artificially created territorial units such as the Hieidaira–Yamanaka administrative district. In contrast to rural villages, such communities are marked by the fact that they encompass people with a multitude of diverging interests, orientations and external social ties. In this sense, communal *undookai* share many of the problematic features of other modern secular rituals. For it is in such public events that an attempt is made to create a sense of commonality among a combination of strangers (Moore and Meyerhoff, 1977.

To an extent these are problems shared by artificially created territorial units all over the world. What I argue here is that the Hieidaira–Yamanaka sports day represents a Japanese attempt at meeting these problems. An examination of the Hieidaira–Yamanaka sports field-day, then, involves addressing the issues at the heart of this 'urban' theme of strangers and commonality. On the one hand the internal construction and organization of the *undookai* must be related to its potential for inculcating the messages of unity and sharing, and for facilitating the breakdown of social barriers between local residents. On the other hand, there is a need to examine the wider context within which people are brought into participation in the sports field-day, and the implications of this participation for the identity of and identification with new communities.

13 Preparations and Expectations

The sports promotion committee

The sports promotion committee (henceforth referred to as the sports committee) is a school district level organization. It is comprised of an equal number of representatives from the village and each of the estate's wards. Being a school district level organization means that these representatives do not carry out any independent activities on the ward or village level. Thus in contrast to some of the activities of the neighbourhood associations and the old-folks clubs, all the events and meets organized by this committee are open to the participation of all of the district's residents.

The twenty members who make up the committee are on the whole quite young (there is only one man over the age of forty-five). The head or chairman – an electrical subcontractor for a North Kyoto firm – is in his early forties. His two assistants – an owner of a car agency, and a manager of a stationery store in Kyoto – are both in their late thirties. The occupations of the other members – most of whom are in their twenties and thirties – are varied and include the following: students, municipal employees, a carpenter, the local rice shop owner, a university lecturer, a kimono designer, a truck driver, a blue-collar technician for a national company, and a number of white-collar workers employed throughout the Osaka and Kyoto areas.

Most members serve a term of two years, although about half continue for a longer period. They are recruited into the organization in a number of ways. A few are asked by the heads of the neighbourhood association to join. Others, whether by intermediary or through personal acquaintanceships, are approached by people already in the sports committee. Thus, for example, two members were recruited by their high-school friend who was already active in the committee, while another man was approached by one of the committee's assistant chairmen whom he had met when their children played in the same school volleyball club.

The reasons cited for joining the committee include a desire to contribute something to the local neighbourhoods, or the enjoyment of sports. More often than not, however, one finds that combined with these is a wish related to the opportunities such an association offers for striking up new acquaintanceships. The words of one member – an industrious carpenter who works in Otsu – well illustrate this:

'All in all I have very few opportunities to get to know anyone here in Hieidaira except maybe my immediate neighbours. I usually leave the house at around seven or eight in the morning and rarely come home before eight in the evening. So you see joining the sports committee has been a good way for me to get acquainted with other people in the estate and with the villagers.'

Indeed, a good part of the time the committee members spend together is devoted to socializing. Thus for example the final hour or so of every committee is spent in 'idle' talk over a few glasses of beer or *sake*. In addition three or four times a year the committee goes out as a group to a nearby restaurant or tavern for an evening's outing. The 1982 year-end party (*boonenkai*) was spent at a hot spring resort just to the west of Yamanaka.

Given that all of the members are men, it is not surprising that the atmosphere at the committee's meetings is very much an all-male one. The general deportment is marked by relaxation and informality. The language adopted is the rather rough and direct one used in all male situations. Some of the men sit with their slacks open at the top, while others lie back with their feet on the low tables and sofas of the estate's meeting hall where the committee assembles. Yet others openly pick their nose or groin. The conversation in keeping with this general climate is managed with a minimum of fuss or ceremony, although it is kept on a serious track with matters being considered and deliberated upon in a clear and purposeful way. Most of the talking is done by the committee's chairman and by his two deputies, although other members participate freely with remarks and recommendations.

The annual programme of the sports committee includes a crowded array of activities which are held both within and between school districts. The events which are regularly held within the Hieidaira–Yamanaka district include softball tourneys, swimming meets, volleyball and table-tennis matches, and a yearly ski outing. In addition the committee members take turns in opening the school gym every Saturday night for the benefit of the adults and middle and high school pupils who wish to participate in the games held there. On the inter-district level Hieidaira and Yamanaka invariably send teams to participate in softball and volleyball tourneys and to the Otsu City Citizens Sports Field Day (*Otsu Shimin Undookai*) in which representatives from all over the city take part. For those people who participate in *all* of these events – and there are a few such mild fanatics – participation may take up close to 18 of the year's Sundays.

The head of the sports committee is also a member of the city's sports association (*Otsu-shi Taiiku Kyookai*), which is a body comprised of representatives from all of Otsu's administrative districts. This association, which is directly linked to the Board of Education's sports department (*taiiku-ka*), is involved in discussions and planning related to city-level sports activities and budgets. These activities include over and above the events already mentioned a yearly marathon, sports clubs for the handicapped and outcaste groups, and the activation youth teams (Otsu-shi 1982:188).

Since 1970 the sports facilities (grounds and gyms) of all the city's primary schools have been made accessible to the residents of each of their respective school districts (Otsu-shi Kyoiku Iinkai, 1982:96). Based on a number of city ordinances promulgated since that time, an arrangement by which the sports committee of each district takes on the responsibility for these facilities during off-school hours has now been reached. These same voluntary committees are also in charge of liaison with the local school principal, the care and cleanliness of the grounds and gym, the protection of school equipment, and the safety of the competitors and participants.

The residents of the Hieidaira–Yamanaka district are rather fortunate in terms of the local sports facilities. The gym, which was completed in 1980, is large and has a good high-quality wooden floor. The grounds are a spacious 9,700 sq. m and include a baseball field, pool, slides and swings, sand-box, exercise bars and storerooms.[1]

As mentioned, the Hieidaira–Yamanaka sports field-day is the high point of the district's sports calendar. Not only does it involve the greatest number of participating residents, but also a highly complex set of tasks and responsibilities that the committee must undertake. For this reason much attention and effort is devoted to the prior arrangements and preparations.

In the rest of this chapter and in the one following it, the preparations for and execution of the *undookai* that took place on 26 September 1982 are described. Consequently, the transition is from a present to a past tense.

The programme

The establishment of the programme of events, the allocation of specific duties and tasks to the committee members, and the monitoring of those tasks already accomplished, were all carried out in a series of meetings that began weeks before the sports day itself.

The programme that was decided upon was based on the one carried out the previous year. Essentially, the broad division of the sports field-day into five main parts would remain unchanged (see Appendix B for an outline of the programme). The opening ceremony would include greetings and short speeches from city officials and community functionaries, an introduction of guests and warm-up exercies in which everyone would be asked to participate. At around ten the first part of the competitions would begin, and be followed around midday by lunch. Next the second part of the sports events would commence, and end at around three. The final part of the *undookai* – the closing ceremony – would include the announcement of the results of the inter-ward competitions, the presentation of victory cups, and some words of thanks from the honorary head of the sports day.

Also left unchanged was the choice of Sunday as the day on which to hold the *undookai*. This seems to be part of a general trend in Yamanaka and Hieidaira and indeed throughout the country. Now, almost all community-related activities and events have begun to be held on Sundays. This applies to such secular events as the drills of the fire brigades or the PTA bazaars, as well as to the more 'religious' activities such as the summer children's festival (*Jizoobon*) or the village's main communal fête (*Oomatsuri*).

A few alterations were suggested in regard to the *undookai*. These were put forward either at the initiative of some of the committee's members, or by the committee's head. He constantly referred to the recommendations of a meeting convened the previous year to review the sports day, and to programmes of *undookai* in other places in the city. In every case, however, the suggestions put forward were of an incremental nature. That is, they were restricted to relatively minor changes and not to a basic restructuring of the sports day.

Two types of considerations seem to have guided the deliberations about introducing new events into the programme. On the one hand a constant emphasis was put on bringing about the maximal participation of different groups in the two communities. On the other hand, this was coupled with a regard to what the committee saw as the physical limitations of people from these groups.

Along these lines each of the three new events that were introduced was designed to bring about the participation of a different group or organization from the village and the estate. The first event – a short exhibition game of gate-ball – would be directed chiefly towards the district's elderly population (see also chapter 10). Next an event designed exclusively for women was adopted. This game of *tama-ire* ('chuck-the-ball') would consist of throwing balls full of cotton wool into a basket tied to a bamboo pole. The game would be held as an inter-ward competition with teams of 20 women representing each ward competing for the greatest number of balls thrown into a basket in a set time period. The final event to be agreed upon involved the three youth sports teams which had been set up the previous April (*Supootsu Shoonendan*). These new teams were to be asked to present a number of demonstration drills displaying team co-ordination and a spirit of working together.

At the same time, in the discussion of these and other events, the relative physical difficulty for the participants was also brought out. Thus, for example, it was decided to limit the egg-and-spoon race the elderly were to participate in to 40 metres. By the same token again, after one man remarked that placing the baskets in the chuck-the-ball competition at the height of four metres would be too difficult for the participants, the committee resolved to fix them at about two and a half metres. The idea, as one of the deputy chairmen told me, was to fix a height that would not be too easy to reach and thereby provide no real challenge, but that at the same time would not be too difficult and bring about the disappointment of total failure.

The committee then decided on the five inter-ward competitions that were to be interspersed among the 'individual' events held throughout the day. These included not only the chuck-the-ball contest, but also a tug-of-war and three types of relay races. As the estate's second ward had a very big population it was decided to continue last year's arrangement by which the ward was divided into two parts each of which would field a whole team of contestants. Yamanaka, despite its relatively small size, was to be a competitor on an equal standing with the estate's teams.

In order to facilitate the easy identification of the five teams fielded, the committee also resolved to allot each one its own team colour: the first ward – blue; the first team of the second ward – red; the second team from the second ward – green; the third ward – yellow; and the village – white.

Budgets and contributions

Much of the discussion was devoted to finances, for the organization of the sports field-day involves not only the time and effort contributed by volunteers, but also a number of substantial expenses. By far the biggest of these was the outlay for the prizes, which in the previous year amounted to just a little over 170,000 Yen. Next came the expenditure on lunch boxes (*obentoo*) which were ordered from the estate's local *sushi* eatery. These lunches included a rather fancy version served in lacquer boxes for the invited dignitaries, and a simpler one in hard plastic containers for members of the sports committee. Another item was the publication of the *undookai*'s programme. Printed at a Kyoto press, this was to include a schedule of the events and ceremonies, map of the sports grounds and tents, a small scoreboard for team events, the names of the organizing volunteers, safety rules, and a list of businesses contributing money to the sports day. Other expenditures included payments for the equipment needed on the day – for instance hats, balls or flags.

The most important source of funds for the *undookai* were the contributions (*kyoosankin*) solicited from local shops and businesses. Nine committee members took it upon themselves to approach those establishments and request their donations. Six of these people had prior experience in such solicitation or were acquainted with some of the owners or managers of local businesses. The head of the sports committee said that he would approach the chairman of the estate's shop-owners' association (*shootenkai*) and ask for their collective presentation. But as this association included only about a third of the local business establishments, there was a need to go out to the rest of the commercial concerns in the two communities. Accordingly, people soon began to offer to go to some of these concerns. One young university student who frequented one of the estate's coffee shops said he would approach its manager. Another agreed to ask his father who ran a real-estate agency in Hieidaira. Yet another man who was friendly with the local newspaper agents took it upon himself to talk to them.

A number of queries raised at this point bring out some of the issues and assumptions involved. The first question, which was about the new businesses that had been set up in the estate in the preceding year, well underlines Hieidaira's continuing growth. The owner of the rice store who was also serving as the committee's accountant was asked about these new establishments and their location. People seemed to assume – rightly, I think – that in his capacity as 'deliverer' of rice to all parts of the estate he should know of such things. And, indeed, he suggested two such possibilities: a new hobby store and a gas merchandising outlet.

Perhaps more interesting were the questions of those who had no prior experience in the solicitation of such monies. They began by asking about the amounts of money involved. The chairman replied by reading out some of the sums given the year before: Don Taro's Steakhouse – 5,000 Yen; Iruujan (Illusion) tea Room – 3,000 Yen; Toorei Haujingu Reality" – 10,000 Yen; Lilac Hill Art Works – 5,000 Yen; Koozan's Noodle Shop – 3,000 Yen; and the local outlet of a national drug company (Otsuka Seiyaku) – cartons of soft drinks.

The slight anxiety of the newer members further appeared in their questions regarding the attitude of the local businessmen towards community activities. One of the deputy chairmen seemed to sense their unease. He suggested that they take programmes printed in previous years and show them during the overture. 'Show them,' he continued,

> 'the way the names of all the contributing shops and businesses are clearly printed on the back of the programme. . . . But in the approach itself maybe try and do what I do. When I ask for a contribution from shop owners, it's as a humble request, as an entreaty (*onegai*). I tell them that the shop is part of the neighbourhood, and that they the owners are members of the community. The *undookai* is an opportunity to provide enjoyment for the residents, and so I ask for their contribution towards that end. . . . I also ask them – especially the newer shops – to come and actually participate on the day itself.'

In subsequent conversations with local shopkeepers these as well as other considerations were brought out. Thus, for example, on one occasion the proprietor of a food shop attributed his contribution to a wish to give in some small way towards a community event which will strengthen local sentiments. Another time, the manageress of the *sake* and liquor store stressed – more forthrightly – that such contributions are part of the shop's advertising budget.

At the same time, however, in comparison with other – usually older – areas in Japan, there seems to be much less of a 'compulsory' attitude associated with these contributions. It is possible to refuse to give any kind of donation, monetary or other. Indeed, as it turned out, three of the estate's business establishments baulked at contributing anything. When I inquired of the man who had approached one of these places as to the reasons given, he replied that they alluded to their precarious economic situation. In any case – whether justified or not from the committee's point of view – the withholding of such contributions serves to underline the essentially voluntary nature of such communal activities in modern localities like Hieidaira.

When members had secured the contributions of the local establishments they were asked to notify the committee's head. He had the responsibility of recording the names of the contributors on the programme and of having it published. The money itself was handed over to the accountant who kept it in his safe in the rice shop. It was also he who handed out any sums needed for expenditures.

From a later conversation with this accountant, it appears that a total of about 260,000 Yen was collected from contributions. This sum was supplemented by 20,000 Yen received from the district's alliance of neighbourhood associations, 80,000 Yen secured as a subsidy from the city's association, [2] and 50,000 Yen brought by the dignitaries invited to the *undookai*.

Prizes and equipment

The next set of items to be discussed were the prizes to be awarded for each event. Here again, one of the assistant heads of the committee produced the lists of prizes awarded the preceding year. The four men who volunteered to go to one of Otsu's department stores in order to buy these prizes were instructed to buy items at more or less the same value as those of prior years. Thus, for example, the prizes for the races the school children had participated in were pencils and small notebooks worth between 100 and 300 Yen. The pre-schoolers who took part in the previous year's 'tiny tots' race received candies worth between 20 and 40 Yen.

Some of the other prizes which these four men eventually bought include, for example, the following: tissue packets (120 Yen) for the tug-of-war participants, aluminium foil (130 Yen) and cellophane wrapping paper (170 Yen) for those taking part in chuck-the-ball competitions, shampoo (130 Yen) for the relay racers or packets of disposable chopsticks (100 Yen) for the 100 metre dash contestants.

These same people also continued on to a special sports equipment shop to buy a further number of articles. These included balls for the dribbling competitions, a starting gun and caps for the races, coloured flags and banners the 'fans' of each ward would use to show their support, and coloured head towels (*hachi-maki*) to be worn by each ward team.

Another six men from the sports committee were asked to form an equipment sub-committee (*yoogu kakari*). A young man in his late twenties who had some past experience in this capacity volunteered to become the head of the sub-committee. The responsibility of this group of people lay in making sure that the equipment needed for each event be ready while the prior event was going on, and in laying out the equipment at the beginning of each race or competition. Towards that end, members of this sub-committee prepared a set of maps and diagrams for each event. Based on similar maps from the previous year, these included both a list of the equipment required and its exact place-ment on the grounds. Thus, for example, the map for the obstacle course included precise details regarding the arrangement of nets, mats and beams around the running track.

This sub-committee also undertook to prepare a number of posters and placards. These included the following: a large score-board on which the results of the inter-ward competitions would be recorded; signs to be placed next to each of the ward's tents; and a large banner proclaiming this the district's fourth *undookai*, which was to be hung outside the main tent. Someone suggested that they ask one of the estate's calligraphy teachers to help them with the actual lettering.

Finally this group proceeded to check that all of the equipment was clean and intact. Thus, for instance, all the tents were inspected for holes or missing pieces. In the same way, they went over the flags destined to be hung up as decorations all over the fields. These plastic banners consisted of recurring series of United Nations, Scandinavian, American, Soviet, and pre- and post-war Japanese flags.

Contact with other organizations

Contact between the sports committee and other local and city groups included the exchange of invitations as well as liaison for more practical purposes. The invitations, which were accompanied by a formal letter and a copy of the day's programme, were sent both to city-level officials and associations, and to most of the community-level functionaries and voluntary groups. The following people were invited from the city: the mayor and his deputy, prefectural and city assemblymen, heads of the Board of Education, chairman of the city alliance of neighbourhood associations, and the head of the city's sports promotion committee. Those invitees associated more closely with Hieidaira and Yamanaka were the principals of the primary school, kindergarten and nurseries in the two communities, the principal of the middle school the children of the area attend, the heads of the respective PTAs of these educational institutions, the chairmen of the two local old-folks clubs, the chief of the voluntary fire brigade, the voluntary welfare workers, heads of the children's committee, and the chairwomen of the women's associations of the village and the estate.

In addition to this, the sports committee entered into contacts with a number of other local bodies. The appeal to the shop-owners' association has already been mentioned. In addition the school was also turned to for the use of its playing field and toilets and for the use of the following equipment: tents, tables, chairs, benches, amplifier, microphone, loudspeakers, washstand, baskets, bamboo poles, ropes and flag poles. The chairman of the committee also asked the fire brigades and neighbourhood associations for the use of their tents.

Next, the neighbourhood associations, PTA, children's committee, women's associations, and old-folks clubs were approached and asked to provide a number of volunteers to help during the sports meet itself. This included such things as the clearing and preparation of the playing field, cleaning up once the events were finished, and aid in a number of sub-committees set up especially for the *undookai*. These special groups – like the equipment sub-committee set up earlier – were to be comprised of between three and eight people and cover the following assignments: management, starting of races, recording of results, recruitment of participants, prizes, first aid, and reception of guests.

Finally, the women's associations of the village and the estate were invited to perform a traditional dance as they had done last year. The heads of these groups readily agreed and practice sessions began in Yamanaka's sports hall about two weeks before the *undookai*.

Mobilization of participants

It is, as one member of the sports committee noted, much easier to mobilize people who hold an organizational role, or are affiliated with one of the local associations, than it is to recruit participants from the communities' 'public at large'. Consequently, a large part of the discussions held in the committee's meetings was devoted to exploring ways of getting as many people as possible to participate. These discussions revealed the great importance that is attached to the maximal participation of the locals, as well as the problematic nature of this participation in the estate.

The words of one committee member illustrate the weight attached to the mobilization of local residents:

'The *undookai* is *the* opportunity for people to get to know each other. So the most important thing is to facilitate the participation of as many adults and children as we can. Even though hundreds came last year it wasn't enough. We have to make an even greater effort this year with posters, notices and other kinds of publicity.'

Another committee member related this to the very process by which communities are created:

'One of the most important ways in which neighbourhoods are formed is the process by which people become acquainted and familiar with each other. And the importance of the sports day lies in the possibilities it provides for such things.'

At the same time in Hieidaira such participation takes place in a social context in which sharing in communal affairs is far from being 'a taken for granted' matter. This was brought home to me by the head of the district's alliance of neighbourhood associations. One summer evening we began to discuss the sports day when he said:

'The *undookai* is the festival (*matsuri*) of the whole area. There are plenty of people who want to take part in the whole affair with its lively and enjoyable atmosphere. Others, none the less, feel that taking part in such events poses a restriction on their free time. The *undookai* is always held on a Sunday, which is everyone's day of rest, and I guess these people want to go elsewhere. Then you get some university professors or doctors who are snobbish about the whole thing. They think they're, well, kind of superior (*erai*), and don't like to come to such gatherings. But isn't it like that everywhere?'

To a certain extent this seems to be a true assessment of some people's attitudes. Thus for instance, one highly educated woman who is employed in the prefectural government said,

'Listen, I'm all for sports field-days and other such occasions when people who live here can get together. But personally, I'm too busy. We always go somewhere else on Sundays.'

While this woman still sees communal events as having an essentially 'positive' character, others are not even willing to grant it this much. The observations of a 30-year-old man who is employed in a Kyoto research institute well exemplify this kind of attitude:

'I never go to *undookai*. There are lots of activities like that here in Hieidaira but they don't really interest me. In truth they're a bit of a bother after a while. Of course if it's things that have to do with the kids – say the school bazaar – then I go along for a while. But apart from that I never really feel like participating.'

Many 'educated folks' – doctors, university teachers or other professionals – do, however, take part in such local festivities as the *undookai*. But the existence of the non-participants serves to underline again the conditional and voluntaristic nature of participation in the estate. Those who do not join may be labelled as snobbish or as egoistical, but more serious kinds of moral censure or social sanctions are not invoked against them.

Against this background it may be understood why much effort is directed at recruiting non-joiners through affirmative methods rather than by the use of 'negative' sanctions. Take, for instance, the following measures which were instituted by the sports committee: posters announcing the *undookai* – place and schedule – were hung up on all of the estate's notice boards and in public places like the supermarket; the printed programme was sent to all the households belonging to the neighbourhood association through its organizational network; and the children belonging to the youth sports teams were instructed to 'bring their parents'. Finally the leaders of the *jichikai*'s base groups (*kumi-choo*) were instructed to approach individuals in their groups and get them to join one of the competitions. I was approached in this way in order to lend my (then) hefty 117 kilograms to the first ward's tug-of-war team.

In Yamanaka, by contrast, the mobilization of contestants as well as 'fans' and supporters poses no real problem. Not only are people 'expected' to participate in such communal events, but the tight networks of kith and kin that cover the whole village ensure that information about the *undookai* reaches everyone. Moreover the long familiarity villagers have with each other makes for a much easier recruitment of individuals to events suited to their athletic capabilities.

Saturday afternoon

From about one o'clock on the Saturday afternoon before the *undookai* about 40 volunteers began to converge on the school grounds in order to help with the preparations. These volunteers included all the sports committee's members except for three who were still working; the committee chairman's wife and four other women from Yamanaka; the head and two members of the estate's old-folks club; about 10 officials from the neighbourhood associations; the chairman of the children's committee; 12 coaches and activists from the youth sports teams; the owner of Hieidaira's supermarket who came in his capacity as head of the voluntary fire brigade; and the assistant manager of the Hieidaira branch of the development company. Except for this last person who arrived still wearing a business suit, everyone turned up either in a track suit and sneakers or in working clothes.

Almost no instructions or directives were given. Members of the sports committee who seemed to know what had to be done took the initiative with others soon quietly joining them. From time to time someone would ask the head of the committee for more specific instructions, but on the whole very little exchange of orders took place. The work itself was divided among a number of groups who worked simultaneously. Once a task was finished people quickly moved on to help another group with its assignment.

One group began to rake and smooth the grounds and to throw away any small stones or bits of hard clay that could potentially be dangerous to run on. Once finished these people used tape measures to mark out the running tracks, location of tents and points for arrangement of equipment. These were then clearly outlined with whitewash and raked smooth again. The head of the old-folks club and his friends marked out the boundaries and points for the gate-ball competitions in the middle of the grounds.

Another party began the erection of four flag poles (each about 4 metres high) in the corners of the grounds, and then moved on to the erection of the tents. These were actually cover tents which consisted of a canvas top attached to metal frames, and built to provide a modicum of shelter from the sun. The eleven tents which were erected necessitated the concerted efforts of about 20 people. These people first connected the metal pipes making up the frame, then spread the canvas top and attached it to the frame. Because there was a possibility of bad weather overnight, the tents were left with their legs folded so that they would be less likely to be toppled by strong winds.

Another five individuals including one of the assistant heads of the committee went to the meeting hall located in another part of the estate. There they prepared the prizes for the next day. Each batch was carefully divided up and clearly marked.

A wide plastic sheet was unrolled at the entrance to the school's sports hall. This was done, it was explained to me, in order to protect the hall's floor from the traffic of people expected to go to and from the inside toilets. On this canvas another group gathered together all of the equipment lent by the school such as tables and benches, the public address system or the first aid bag. These people also laid out and cleaned the poles and baskets for the chuck-the-ball event, and the long ropes for the tug-of-war.

At this point the coaches and some parents of the children participating in the youth sports teams began preparations for something they thought of introducing for the first time in this year's *undookai*. In the best of entrepreneurial traditions these people decided to set up a number of food stands the proceeds of which would go towards equipping the children's volleyball, baseball and soccer teams. To that end they entered the classroom used by the school for cooking lessons and began to prepare the giant pots and kettles and foodstuffs for the stands. The plan was to provide during lunch and throughout the day the following dishes: curried rice, frankfurters, *oden* (boiled vegetable roots and bean curd in sauce), and tea and coffee. The money received from the sale of these, one energetic mother explained to me, would help cover the cost of equipment (hats, bats, bases, first aid kit) and transport to and from 'away' games.[3]

At about half past three the supermarket owner disappeared for a few minutes to return later with small bottles of Coca-Cola and Fanta. He probably felt, one man commented, that all the people there were co-operating for the sake of the communities and wanted to show his thanks. As most of the work had already been done everyone gathered round and drank together. At about four the head of the sports committee thanked everyone and asked that only the committee members remain. After completing a few minor tasks still left, we were told to be at the school the next day at half past eight in the morning and wearing dark blue slacks and white T-shirts.

14 The Sports Field-Day

Last preparations

Some apprehensions about the weather were voiced by the volunteers who started to gather soon after eight on a cold and blustery
Sunday morning. The strong winds and occasional drizzle soon
began to die down, and by ten the school grounds were bathed
in sunshine.

The last preparations were carried out in a flurry of activity. The
sports committee and a few representatives of the neighbourhood
associations unrolled the long lines of flags and attached them to
the four flag poles. Next they took out the benches, chairs and
tables which were in the sports hall and arranged them in the
main tent and in the tent designated for the elderly. Then the
amplifier, microphone and loudspeakers were assembled and
connected to the school's electricity supply by means of a long
extension cord someone had brought from home. Next the signs
prepared for each ward were placed next to their respective tents.

At the same time, the women in charge of the reception sub-
committee filled a large electric kettle with barley tea, and prepared three trayfuls of empty cups. They then began – with the
help of women from other sub-committees – to hand out yellow
ribbons to all of the volunteers organizing the *undookai*. Small
ribbons were given to the sports committee and to all of the
members of the sub-committees. Bigger ones were handed to the
heads of the neighbourhood associations, and to the chairman of
the sports committee. The ribbons were attached either to the
lapels, or – especially by the younger men – next to the right-
hand pocket of the sports slacks.

One of the assistant heads of the sports committee handed out
to the committee's members blue baseball hats with a big letter

'H' (in English) at the front. He explained that these 'Hieidaira' hats were bought in order to make it easier for various participants to identify the organizers. He asked that they be returned to him at the end of the day.

At around nine the head of the youth sports teams – a highly energetic and eloquent professor of Chinese history – attached a tape recorder to the public address system. This man – who as it later turned out was the master-of-ceremonies during the day – began to play Western marches at a rather high volume. With the exception of an occasional speech by an official or this man's running commentary on what was happening in the *undookai*, this music was to accompany the festivities for the rest of the day.

People began to drift into the grounds just after nine. The Yamanakaites came first. They stood their tent on its legs, and spread out under and around it. By the time the Hieidairaites started to arrive a few minutes later, groups of organizers had already prepared their tents.

The crowd was dressed for the most part in track suits, T-shirts and sports shoes. Almost all of the school children wore that institution's sports costume.

Most people arrived with their families, although some of the teenagers and members of the old-folks clubs came with their friends in groups of twos or threes. At the tents people tended to sit next to or nearby friends or people they already knew. Once in a while one could see men or women who had met before introduce their respective spouses and children.

At the same time the invited guests and dignitaries began to appear. The assistant head of the Hieidaira–Yamanaka alliance of neighbourhood associations, who functioned as the honorary head of the *undookai*, welcomed each of these officials personally. Dressed immaculately in a white track suit with matching tennis shoes and baseball hat, this honorary personage gave each guest a bow, showed him to the chairs reserved for dignitaries, accepted the envelope bearing the guest's gift for the sports day, and after exchanging a few pleasantries left him to the mercy of the reception committee. The guests – dressed in dark business suits and ties – were quickly served some tea and rice crackers, and invited to watch the day's events. Each guest brought about 3,000 Yen as a contribution.

Most of these officials stayed between twenty minutes and two hours. When I inquired of one city employee as to the reason for this limited time period, he replied that the elected officials as well as administrators had to attend a number of *undookai* that day. They thus had to arrange a well orchestrated round of visits to different districts so that the municipality's representatives would be present in as many places as possible.

The expectations of the local organizers seemed to fit this. Guests were not, at any time, urged to stay on, but politely seen out of the grounds when they had to leave. Indeed, one white-collar member of the sports committee commented – perhaps half seriously – that as the city and prefectural elections were only half a year away such events as the *undookai* presented good opportunities for local politicians to display themselves (*kao o dasu*).

Shortly before the opening ceremony, members of the sub-committee in charge of recruitment began to make their rounds in the tents. These organizers notified individuals who had already agreed to take part in a specific event of its scheduled time and location, and canvassed others for the remaining open slots. That the sports day went by smoothly can be attributed in no small measure to the constant activity of this sub-committee throughout the day.

At nine-thirty the MC caused a small commotion when he couldn't find the tape of music for the public exercises among the tens of cassettes recorded with marches. Soon, however, the tape was found and he announced that he was ready. A metal podium about one-and-a-half metres high was brought to the centre of the field just in front of the main tent.

The MC then invited all the participants to form five columns according to the division into ward teams and to face the central podium. Within each column people stood in the following order. At the front were the kindergarten and primary-school children, which were followed by the middle- and high-school pupils. At the end stood the adults with the smaller children at their side or in their arms. A few elderly people and mothers with babies stayed in the tents, but they all stood up during the opening ceremony itself.

The invited guests from the city and from the two communities arranged themselves in a line to the left of the central podium, while the sports committee stood in a line to its right. Both lines faced the five ward columns with the main tent at their backs.

The crowd quietened down with no prompting from the MC. All was ready.

The opening ceremony

At forty minutes past nine, one of the assistant heads of the sports committee ascended the podium. In one short sentence he declared the sports field-day officially open.

The honorary head of the *undookai* went up after him. The children in the crowd returned his short bow and 'good morning' with their own greeting uttered in unison. This man's short welcome included a thanks to the organizers for their efforts on behalf of Hieidaira and Yamanaka; an acknowledgment to the guests and residents who had come to participate; a hope for good weather to accompany the activities; and a stress on the themes of good sportsmanship, the enjoyment of participation and the importance of such public occasions as the *undookai* when the people of the local communities join together.

Next came the turn of the chairman of Otsu's Board of Education. After repeating much the same things as the man before him, he went on to relate the activities taking place in the district to wider city and national affairs. Last year, he reminded everyone, the national sports meet (*kokutai*) had taken place in the city. He would like, he said, to thank again all of Otsu's citizens for their efforts on that occasion when participants and athletes from all over Japan came to the city for a week-long series of competitions. This year, he continued, the meet is held in Shimane prefecture and he would like to wish the citizens of that area, as indeed everyone in the country taking part in sports activities, to 'put up a good show' (*ganbatte*).

The next speaker, the master-of-ceremonies, left his place next to the microphone and quickly mounted the podium himself. His role consisted of introducing the invited guests and dignitaries. The following people were introduced in their official capacity: city and prefectural assemblymen, municipal officials, school and kindergarten principals, PTA functionaries, head of the fire brigade, chairman of the old-folks club, and the voluntary welfare workers.

The last speaker was a member of the sports committee. He first asked that as the clay on the field was still soft from the rain that people not wear any spiked shoes or football boots. He continued and stressed the general need to keep to the safety rules published in the programme, and then finished by asking everyone to spread out and get ready for the next activity.

The public exercises – *rajiyo taisoo* (lit. radio gymnastics exercises) – were the last activity to be held before the beginning of the competitions. Everyone appeared to be familiar with these warm-up calisthenics. One young woman later explained that this set of drills – timed to music and accompanied by a male voice recorded on a tape – was used since her childhood in schools or community sports meets. About 95 per cent of those present – including the city officials who came in business suits – participated in this three-minute set of exercises which included neck and body twists, jumps, running in place, and different bends and bows. There appeared to be little of the self-conscious feeling that often accompanies such activities in many Western countries. The general expectation was that anyone not too old or occupied with small children should participate.

Morning events

The first two events – both 50 metre races for children from the primary school – began immediately at the end of the public exercises. In each event about 20 heats of 6 youths each – boys and girls – raced each other half-way around the track. The first event was open to children from grades one to three of the primary school and consisted simply of running. The second, which consisted of dribbling a ball over the same distance, included youths from grades four to six.

Each heat was started by members of the 'starting' sub-committee who allocated the running tracks and operated the starting gun. At the finishing line three women picked out the children who had come in the first three places, and sat them down in columns in the middle of the grounds.

No further races between these 'finalists' were held. The three children who had not succeeded in reaching one of the first places were given pencils as consolation prizes (*sankashoo*) for their participation.

The next two events were again races. Here, however, the degree of difficulty was greater. Boys and girls from middle or high school in the first, and men beyond the high-school age in the second race had to run over an obstacle course. Thus, they had to crawl under a net held to the ground by four people; do a head roll over a mat; walk along a wooden beam; shoot a ball into a basket; and run to the finishing line.

After the first two or three races, the crowd's attention seemed to vary in accordance with the participation of someone familiar to them: kin, friend or neighbour. Thus while many cheers or cries of support could be heard during these and other 'individual' competitions, they were, for the most part, directed towards specific competitors by their friends and relatives.

Quite a few people came to the *undookai* toting their cameras. But they almost invariably took only pictures of their children or children of their friends. One man took more 'general' pictures of the proceedings on his video camera. But this seemed less out of a wish to record for memory's sake the public event taking place, than out of the fun he was finding in fiddling around with a new toy and its accompanying zoom lens, sound equipment, light filters, shoulder rest, and leather carrying case.

The next activity marked the beginning of the inter-ward competitions. In this event – a relay race – each team fielded six participants: one from each (primary) school year. Within each team, however, the younger children (grades one through three) ran 50 metres, while the older ones (grades four through six) ran a full 100 metres. In this race, as in all of the inter-ward contests, the team colours were displayed. This was done with narrow towels (*hachimaki*) tied around the heads of the participants, and with coloured squares pinned to each runner's chest and back.

This event caused much excitement. Not only was the crowd's attention now fully focused on the race, but people now began actively to cheer their own ward teams. In addition, a few ward officials and volunteers handed out flags matching the team colours, and exhorted the supporters – adults and children – to applaud and shout. Some children and two elderly men even ran to the finishing point just in front of the main tent and shouted their encouragement from inside the track itself.

At eleven Otsu's mayor arrived. All of the activities were stop-

ped and the MC invited the crowd to listen to this elected representative's speech. People listened to his short address attentively. Sporting a wide Jimmy Carter-like smile, the mayor
apologized for his intrusion in the middle of things. He talked of
the sports field-days going on in other school districts throughout
the city, and expressed his hope that these games be carried out
in the best of sportsmanlike spirit, and to the full enjoyment of
the participants. He concluded by noting that the Hieidaira–Yamanaka school district was a young one, and by expressing his hope
that the large number of children in these localities continue to
participate in *undookai* in the future. Then, giving three short
bows – to the crowd, to the other invited guests, and to the sports
committee – the mayor went off to the next stop on his one-day
round of sports events.

The activities were renewed immediately after the mayor's
departure with two events involving the oldest and the youngest
members of the two communities. Both events took place in the
middle of sports grounds over a track about 30 metres long. In
the first one, the over-60s had to run 10 metres, pick up a cloth
ball, put it on a large soup ladle, and run another 20 metres to
the finish. The prizes these 50 or so oldsters received had no
relation to their placement in the race. Everyone received a box
of tissues and a metal umbrella stand. The old people appeared
to be enjoying themselves immensely. Although a good deal of
self-conscious talking and laughing was carried out before and
during the race itself, all of these older individuals ran as though
the completion of the 30 metres was in itself a challenge to be
met seriously.

The 80 or 90 pre-schoolers who followed them in groups of
twenty were started by the gun. Most ran alone, but the younger
infants were often carried by their mothers. Upon reaching the
finishing line, twelve adults handed them each a sweet and a small
plastic doll representing a character from a popular television
series (*ararechan*). Although the prizes were again all of comparable value, size and taste the children appeared to take the race
in earnest, and to make every effort to come in one of the first
places.

In a characteristic Japanese use of English words the next event
was named *Kaado de deeto* (lit. dates through the use of cards).
This 'cards and dates' race proved to be one of the most popular
competitions among the adults. The race itself was simple. Equal

numbers of men and women lined up at opposite sides of the running track. At the sound of the starting gun groups of six males and females would run to the edge of the track and pick up numbered cards which were placed there before the heat. They would then seek the person of the opposite sex with the same number, stand side by side and tie one of their legs together (leaving the other free), and run as fast as possible to the finishing line about 25 metres away.

This was the only part of the *undookai* where physical contact between adult men and women was allowed. Some couples hugged each other closely slipping a hand around each other's shoulders or hips. Others, feeling more awkward perhaps, held each other's hands or elbows rather stiffly while holding their bodies apart. The crowd's reactions ranged from good-natured laughing and chuckling at the stumbling and at times inelegant style of the contestants, through to hooting and cheering directed at those couples who bravely embraced each other and ran at top speed to the finish. The prizes for those who came in first place were rather expensive in relation to the prizes for other events – shampoo and cooking foil.

One man in his late thirties who stood next to me during this event couldn't stop smiling and giggling. At one point when a couple who were embracing each other particularly avidly passed us, he turned to me and remarked: 'Sports field-days in Japan are amusing (*omoshiroi*) aren't they?' This as though to refer to the enjoyment that can be had when certain rules of social decorum are broken down for a short period of time.

The primary school pupils had their turn again in the following event. Here the children, in heats of six, had to run about 30 metres to a point where two adults stood. This pair held between them a thin rope to which lollipops were attached by means of clothes pegs. The children had to pull these lollipops off the line without using their hands, and then race on to the finishing line.

The organization of this contest provides a good illustration of the way each event was contingent on a range of prior and ongoing organizational efforts. No less than 20 adults were involved in organizing different aspects of this competition: recruiting the children, allocating running tracks, starting the gun, holding the rope with lollipops and replacing those that had been pulled off, meeting the runners at the finishing line, and allocating the prizes. In addition, while this was going on the MC not only announced the next set of events, but when not enough contestants turned up for the races, he urged others to come forward.

My big turn came in the event that followed: the tug-of-war. At the beginning the teams representing each ward – twenty men and a team leader – were assembled at the side of the field. Then two teams at a time were invited to the centre of the grounds for the tug itself. Loud cries of *ganbatte* ('put up a good fight') and clapping accompanied each team as it entered the arena. Little children – many with plastic fans matching their team colours – gathered near the competitors.

After the blowing of a starting whistle by one of the referees, the tug began. Team leaders – often with the help of the supporters who had gathered nearby – tried to give a steady beat by which to pull the rope. In this respect, however, the Yamanaka team had an advantage. In contrast to the different estate teams, for many of whom this was one of the first occasions for acquaint-anceship let alone co-ordinated rope-pulling, the village team had pulled together for years. One villager later told me that this was a team that had participated in many past *undookai* when Yamanaka had taken part in another larger district's sports day.

I was asked to take up the 'pin' position – at the end of the rope – for the first ward's team. While I wrapped the rope around me to give a good fit, a number of hecklers from other wards began to make some sarcastic remarks. Some commented about the awe-inspiring proportions of the anthropologist. Others went even further and remarked about the unfair advantage of having a team member the weight and height of a medium-sized sumo wrestler. I don't know whether it was my actual size, or just the psychological advantage it gave the team, or both, but we won our two preliminary matches. In the finals we thus found ourselves pitted against the well co-ordinated village team who had also won their preliminaries. I like to think that we gave them a good fight, but after a few minutes we succumbed to the Yamanakaites.

After the match we were thanked by our team leader for our participation and efforts, and acknowledged our thanks to the other teams by bowing or nodding our heads. Members of the village team won a box of tissues each.

The chuck-the-ball competition which closed the morning set of activities was again an inter-ward contest, but one open only to women. The bamboo poles with the baskets attached to them were held in the middle area of the grounds by members of the sports committee. Around each pole the equipment sub-committee scattered about 40 cloth balls. The twenty-member teams from each ward then had two tries of a full minute each to throw in as many balls as possible. The sum total of balls from the two tries determined the overall placement of the teams. Yamanaka's women won this competition once more. They were closely followed by a team from the second ward and then by the third ward.

At this stage the MC announced that the time was ten minutes past twelve and that the competitive activities would be started again at one. He reminded everyone of the youth sports teams' food stands and wished the crowd *bon appetit*.

Lunch break

Although a few of the Hieidairaites returned home for a quick lunch, most of the people ate their midday meal at the grounds. Just about everyone had brought some kind of food or drink in lunch boxes and flasks. Quite a few, however, supplemented the refreshments they had brought with them with portions of *oden*, curried rice or popcorn and cups of black coffee prepared by the people from the youth sports teams. The few families who hadn't brought any liquor with them went, during this interim period, to the estate's *sake* store and brought back jugs and cans of beer and *sake*.

While a small number of people – mainly older folks and the invited guests – sat on the chairs and benches brought from the school, just about everyone else sat on thatch or plastic mats laid on the ground. As is usually done in such situations, people took off their shoes before sitting on the mats.

Talk usually revolved around the 'happenings' of the *undookai*, and around life in the local neighbourhoods. A little later as the food and drink began to have their effect people began to relax. They then exchanged cans or glasses of drinks, and offered each other a taste of the dishes brought from home.

A number of lunch boxes (*obentoo*) bought earlier from the local *sushi* eatery were served to the invited guests and to the members of the sports committee. These were brought to the

221

school grounds by one of the committee members in his (delivery) van. Each of these people also received a cold cupful of barley tea.

During lunch the head of Hieidaira's old-folks club, his wife and 15 other oldsters played an exhibition match of gate-ball in the middle of the grounds. The game was accompanied by a running commentary about its rules, suitability for older individuals, and the different club frameworks within which it is played. At the same time some of the younger children began to spread around the grounds and play on the swings, slides and sand-boxes behind the main tent and in the kindergarten adjoining the school.

At half-past twelve a public raffle was held. It appears that the owners of the gas station situated at the edge of the estate had suggested a special arrangement as their contribution to the sports day. They had agreed to sell the sports committee twenty jerry-cans of oil (for house heating) for a reduced price, and proposed that these be raffled out during the *undookai*'s lunch break. Accordingly every family participating in the sports day filled out one of the corners of the programme with their name and address and placed these in a box next to the main tent. During the raffle itself one of the dignitaries from the municipality pulled out the winning tickets, and the master-of-ceremonies announced their names on the loudspeaker system.

The march music which was being played during the midday break was periodically interrupted by different announcements. The head of the sports committee came on a few times, and reminded people of his request that they take their garbage with them when they leave at the end of the day. Then, when a shortage of plates for the curried rice had developed, people who had already finished their portions were asked to return them. A few minutes later, when it became clear that a large amount of food was still left, the MC began pleading with the crowd to *ganbatte* – to give of its best efforts – in order to finish the leftovers. His efforts were buttressed by the campaigns the coaches of the youth sports teams began to mount among the crowd. Thus, for example, the head volleyball coach approached me and began informing me of the special dishes and atmosphere that could be experienced at the food stands.

At about five to one the head of the youth sports teams came on and asked the children participating in the exercise exhibition to assemble next to the sports hall. The teams, dressed in baseball, soccer and volleyball uniforms respectively, took up their positions dutifully. All was ready for the continuation of the sports field-day.

Afternoon events

The teams entered and arrayed themselves around the field with their coaches. The MC explained that the sports teams were a new organization that had been set up during the previous April, and that they practised twice a week on Wednesday and Saturday afternoons. He then introduced each of the coaches by name, and said that the children would present a short set of exhibition drills. These consisted of a number of rather simple exercises executed with bamboo poles.

The next event – a relay race between the voluntary fire brigades of Hieidaira and Yamanaka – began as soon as the youngsters cleared the field. In this competition, which pitted twelve representatives from each community against each other, it was the villagers again who had the upper hand. But despite the fact that both brigades received equal prizes – two giant bottles of *sake* each – the Yamanakaites found a happy way to express their victory. They immediately opened their bottles and began to offer drinks not only to the village people, but to any man standing or sitting in the vicinity of their tent.

As they had done after most events that took place on the field, a number of people now quickly moved in to remark the running tracks with whitewash. Interestingly, the sport committee was aided in this by individuals who came out from the crowd at their own initiative. Indeed such spontaneous help was extended to other tasks such as carrying equipment, fastening lollipops or starting heats of runners. Some of the people who came out to help had been members of the sports committee in previous years. Most, however, were simply bystanders who felt that there was a need for some assistance.

At about ten minutes before two, fifty women from the *fujinkai* (women's associations) of both Hieidaira and Yamanaka came out of the sports hall and arranged themselves in a large circle

223

around the field. All were dressed in informal summer *kimono* (*yukata*) in shades and patterns of blue, and had red sashes tied around their midriff. The traditional dance they performed consisted of a slow clockwise movement around the field which was accompanied by a recurrent rhythmical waving and clapping of the hands, and an intricate sequence of steps.

Despite a few hitches with the accompanying taped music the crowd looked on attentively and in relative quiet. From time to time, however, as a woman passed her children she would wink or smile an acknowledgment to their cries of *okaasan* (Mummy). A few people later said to me that the performance of such a dance in the context of the sports day was a bit out of place. Thus, the following day the head of the first ward's neighbourhood association gave me his impressions of this performance:

> 'It's great when people from the communities make a strong effort to organize and participate in such sports days. But it does have its funny side when people try to mix the old and the new. For example, I felt a queer sort of, an uncomfortable feeling (*hen na kimochi*) when they put on that traditional dance in the middle of the *undookai*.'

The 'Catch a Fish' competition which followed was open to primary-school children and to the over-60s. Essentially, the competition consisted of running a few metres, picking up a fishing rod, latching a wooden fish onto it, and running to the finishing line. A few of the elderly who had problems in bending down to pick up the fishing rods were aided by spectators standing nearby or by other oldsters. In the same way some of the over-60s who were still agile and sprightly accompanied individuals who were having difficulties all the way to the finishing line without trying to overtake them. In this way they seemed to be underlining the contrast between the 'participatory' involvement of the elderly, and the 'competitive' involvement of the children. By the same token, while the children received prizes according to their placement in each heat, the elderly all received the same gifts, regardless of how they had done in the race itself.

The humorous competition which followed had men running with lit cigarettes in their mouths, lighting a joss (incense) stick without the use of their hands and finishing around the track. This was quickly followed by open races for middle- and high-school pupils and the afternoon 'tiny tots' race which took the same form as the morning one.

Such events underscored the somewhat different demeanour displayed by the children and adults who competed. The children competed in utmost seriousness with almost no self-consciousness and little apprehension at opening themselves up to contentions of over-involvement. The pre-race excitement, the large number of false (early) starts, or anguish of deep concentration on the faces of the runners well attested to this.

By contrast, many of the adults smiled and joked when they participated. Whether this was out of a mild but genuine embarrassment on the part of first-time participants, or out of a feeling that they could and should not show that they are totally caught up in things, this behaviour seemed to underline a certain distancing from the activities. This was especially apparent at the beginning of the day. But by the time people had begun to be tired not only did social barriers between groups begin to melt down, but the efforts at keeping up a public face began to weaken as well. Thus throughout the afternoon events the adults seemed more and more to enter the 'spirit' of the contests without paying heed to 'external' considerations of social proprieties.

A relay race which pitted the ward representatives of local organizations against each other came next. This race included both women and men. While the women had to run around the track and shoot a cloth ball into one of the *tama-ire* baskets, the men had to dribble a ball around the track. As this event once again included people who were at least potentially limited in terms of physical activity – for example some of the late middle-agers who were heads of the neighbourhood associations – it was decided to award all of the teams an equal number of points.

By half past two many of the younger children were getting tired, and a small number of families began to leave. Others split up, with the mother going with the younger children and the father staying on with the older ones. As they passed one of the organizers of the *undookai* on their way out, people stopped and expressed their gratitude. Giving a shot bow or a nod of the head, many used the customary expression: 'Thank you for your efforts and troubles' (*gokuroosama desu*).

During this last half hour or so the MC's announcements about the food remaining in the youth sports teams' tents turned from notification to supplication. Almost begging people for their last efforts at the curried rice still left, this man explained time and again the important aims to be achieved through the sale of the food.

The penultimate event was again a humorous one. After running about two-thirds of a lap, heats of six people – women and men – ran up to and picked up a card out of a heap at the edge of the track. Each card had instructions about finishing the race in a certain running style – for example, rabbit hops, frog leaps, skipping, or running backwards. Some men picked up a number of cards and chose the easiest running style with which to finish. But after one of the organizers on the spot saw this, only as many cards as there were runners were placed in the heap. The winners received toilet odorizers. The losers happily accepted cans of a health drink called '*pocari sweat*'.

The final event was again an inter-ward relay race, although this one was based on the participation of people from different age brackets. Each ward sent a five-member team consisting of a middle-school student, a person up to the age of nineteen, one up to twenty-nine, one up to thirty-nine, and one over forty years of age. The first ward's team came in first, and was followed by the team from the third ward.

The head and one of the members of the sports committee went over to the scoreboard and began to tally up the results of the inter-ward competitions. The overall winner was the Yamanaka team. It was followed 'closely' by the first and then the third wards. In the next-to-last and last places were the two teams from the estate's second ward.

Before the closing ceremony everyone was asked to help in cleaning up the grounds. With the members of the sports committee taking the initiative all the bits and scraps of garbage in and around the tents were collected in large plastic bags. While this was going on, a table and the microphone were placed in front of the main tent, and the crowd was again asked to form columns by wards in the middle of the grounds.

The closing ceremony

As they had done in the opening ceremony the five ward columns stood facing the two lines of guests and officials and the sports committee who arranged themselves by the main tent. Although some of the spectators and participants had already left, close to 500 people stayed on for the closing ceremony and the bestowal of the victory cups.

The head of the sports committee took his place next to the microphone and began his announcements with the declaration that Yamanaka's team had won the inter-ward competition with a total of 16 points. A great din of shouting and clapping punctuated by cries of *banzai* (hurrah) accompanied this announcement. Then, when this initial hubbub had died down, the chairman announced the achievements of the other teams. Here again each announcement was accompanied by applause, but every consecutive one elicited a definite drop in the loudness of clapping. When talking of the team (from the second ward) which had placed last, he referred to it as the team which achieved fifth rather than last place. The head of the sports committee continued and thanked all of the people who had helped organize the *undookai*. His final words played on the theme of friendship:

'The sports field-day is one of the most important functions that is carried out in our school district. This is an occasion for everyone to meet and become friendly with each other. This is especially important for an area like Hieidaira which hardly has any kind of communal festivals or functions. Let's all make an effort and continue to hold the *undookai* in the future with the same enthusiasm as shown here today.'

When he had concluded the honorary head of the *undookai* was invited to award the victory cups and to give a short concluding address. Two children – one from Yamanaka and one from the first ward – were called forward to accept the cups for first and second places. After receiving the cup each boy bowed to the honorary head, turned to the crowd and raised it above his head. Then, after another round of applause each took his place at the head of his column.

In his short concluding address the *undookai* honorary head touched upon a number of points. He began customarily by refer-ring to the weather, and how in spite of a rather turbulent start, the day had turned into a warm and sunny one.

He went on and said that he hoped everyone had enjoyed themselves to the full, and that in the future there would be many more opportunities to re-enact such festivities. Especial thanks, he continued, must go to the many people and organizations who had worked hard for the success of the *undookai*: the sports committee, PTA, children's association, women's groups, old-folks clubs, youth sports teams, and neighbourhood associations. He concluded by noting the amity produced by the *undookai* through stressing how such events as the sports day provide oppor-tunities for people from different areas to become familiar and friendly with each other.

One of the deputy chairmen of the sports committee was the final person to approach the microphone. He quickly asked that people who had not yet returned equipment – flags, hats, etc. – to do so, and announced that there would be a need for help in the clearing and cleaning of the grounds after the ceremony. He then proceeded in one short sentence to proclaim the sports field-day formally closed.

Close to a hundred people helped in the variety of things involved in winding-up the *undookai*: cleaning and folding up the tents and then returning them to their storehouses; returning the equipment borrowed from the school and other local organiza-tions; taking the empty lunch boxes back to the *sushi* eatery; taking things forgotten on the grounds (two watches, three umbrellas, two handkerchiefs and a plastic mat) to the estate's meeting hall; sweeping out and washing the floor of the hall; and picking up all the remaining trash left around the grounds. By half past four – that is within only one hour – almost everything was finished.

During the last twenty minutes only officials of the sports com-mittee and the youth sports teams stayed on. They finished clean-ing the toilets in the sports hall and the cooking room in the school. As people finished, they gathered round the side of the school where the remainder of the coffee was served to them. A short discussion about the *undookai* ensued and everyone agreed that it had gone very well. At four forty it began to drizzle and all the people there were invited to the estate's meeting hall for a few drinks.

Drinks and reflection

About twenty men gathered in the small assembly hall for what one man elegantly defined as a sort of part meeting for reviewing and reflecting on the sports field-day (*hanseikai*), and part meeting for resting and relaxing (*tsukarekai*). This group of twenty was made up of most of the sports committee, the male coaches of the youth sports teams, and two men from Hieidaira's neighbourhood association who had helped throughout the day. Everyone sat on the matted floor next to low wooden tables that were arranged in the middle of the room in a square figure. People sat around the tables in more or less a random fashion with none of the usual congregation of Yamanakaites on the one hand, and groups of Hieidaira acquaintances on the other.

While we waited for the food and drinks that had been ordered by the sports committee to arrive, the *sushi* and rice crackers that remained from the *undookai* were passed around, and an open *sake* bottle began to be emptied. Soon, however, the procession of couriers bearing the refreshments began. Within five minutes the manager of the liquor store arrived with twenty large bottles of beer. A little while after that the supermarket owner turned up with a giant bottle of *sake* he said was his token of appreciation to the organizers of the *undookai*. Next, the wife of a Taiwanese immigrant who runs a Chinese restaurant in the estate came with a big plate full of fried chicken and pork. But as this didn't look as though it would be enough, one of the younger members of the sports committee quickly went out to a few of the local stores. He came back with sausages, salami, crisps, chips and other savouries made from fish and sea products.

One of the assistants to the head of the sports committee put all of the remaining prizes in a small side room just off of the main meeting hall. There he began to divide them up into individual packages to be given to all those people who had helped organize the *undookai*. In addition he prepared packages which included a jumping rope and a letter of thanks to be handed out to all of the local business establishments who had contributed to the sports day. As this man kept his glass of beer in the main room he would appear every five minutes or so and gulp down a few mouthfuls. After a few times people began to tease him. Some said he would never finish with the packages because no time would be left. Others quickly interjected that the real reason would be that he'd get too drunk to know what he was doing.

During the first three quarters of an hour this was very much the tone of things. People sat back, ate and drank, and talked of the things that had happened during the day. One of the villagers who had been in the sports committee when Yamanaka participated in the *undookai* of a larger district, talked with quite a bit of pleasure of the advantages the alliance with Hieidaira had brought:

> 'When we participated in the sports day of that district there was a strict limit on the number of people who could take part in each event. For example, if they wrote in the programme that only five heats would be run – say in the 100-metre dash – they kept to it. Now in our district we run as many heats as there are competitors. I know it's much more tiring for us who have to organize everything, but this way anyone who wants to participate can do so. Then there were always problems in having to choose who would run and who wouldn't.'

Other people recounted some of the more humorous incidents that had occurred during the day. One example was the funny running style of one of the heavier members of the sports committee (not me). Another, was the teasing one man had received when he was awarded cooking foil as a prize despite the fact that he barely knew how to prepare tea for himself.

Then, as the drink began to have its effect and people began to get flushed and grow just a bit drowsy, some of the difficulties and problems that had been involved in organizing the *undookai* began to be aired. This all began when the conversation turned to who had and who had not come to help in the preparations carried out on Saturday afternoon. The head of the sports committee turned to one of the functionaries from the neighbourhood association and spoke of the problems of – as he put it – communication (*renraku*) between the two organizations. The heads of the neighbourhood associations, he said, evidently didn't make enough of an effort at mobilizing the officials of the associations' base groups (*kumi-choo*) towards help in the *undookai*. He felt, he continued, that if it was anyone's fault, it was that of the head of the district's alliance of neighbourhood associations rather than anyone else. He hadn't even come to the *undookai*, he stressed, and in his stead the honorary head of the day was his deputy: the head of Yamanaka's association. 'It's as though', he finished, 'this man just does not care about what is happening in the two communities.'

In reply, one of the representatives of the neighbourhood associations pointed out that as far as he knew a circular asking people to help in the sports field-day had been published. One of the deputies of the sports committee next interjected that one has to always look at both sides of a story. You have to understand, he declared, the *jichikai* is an organization with numerous demands on it, and with central functionaries who are as a consequence of these circumstances extremely busy. Moreover, one must take into account, he went on, the fact that this head of the alliance of *jichikai* is an executive of one of the giant department stores in Kyoto, and thus has to work on Sundays as well. It's all very well to complain, he concluded, but with so many problems it's difficult for the man to be everywhere at all of the activities associated with the communities. The head of the sports committee stuck to his opinion, however. Turning now to everyone seated around the tables he said:

'Look, in all of the areas where there is some kind of tradition (*rekishi ga aru chiiki*), the heads of the neighbourhood associations put in an appearance at such events. It's part of their role, it's part their being the top official of these kinds of organizations. I understand very well that in his capacity he has an awful lot of work, and I understand that he wants to delegate some of the tasks and responsibilities out to other people. But there are certain functions, certain events, that I think he must appear in as the head of the alliance of neighbourhood associations.'

For all this, however, there was little feeling that these deliberations were intended to lead to any kind of systematic uncovering of the 'problematic' issues involved or to their solutions. Rather, each claim and argument were raised as though their actual declaration – their becoming part of public knowledge – was sufficient in itself. The atmosphere, then, was one in which each person could air his grievances in more or less a free way and be quite certain that they were noted by others present.

231

Another illustration of this point were the words of one committee member who belonged to the team who came in last place, and who related the difficulties that lay behind this somewhat embarrassing achievement. His complaints centred on two points: one related to the special problems of his ward, the other to the more general difficulties found in Hieidaira. He first explained the problems he had with the head of his ward's neighbourhood association and this man's two assistants. It turned out that all three had told him that they were too busy to help in recruiting people to the *undookai*, and he thus had to appeal to the *kumichoo* directly. Although these people proved helpful, he quickly added, if the head of the *jichikai* would have lent a guiding hand things would have become much easier.

When he began to talk of the more general problems of recruitment that he had encountered, many of the other people present nodded their agreement, or added comments confirming his observations. For the difficulties he found in mobilizing people towards participation in the *undookai* were shared by all the committee members from the estate. In his case, this second-warder stressed, such difficulties were compounded by the fact that he commutes daily all the way to Osaka. This brought about a situation, he said he felt, where despite living in Hieidaira for close to ten years, he really knew few people outside the neighbours in his immediate vicinity.

His comments prompted others into talking. One man echoed the general feeling among the people present when he said the following:

'Listen, over the years we've made constant and I might add quite successful efforts to bring people to the *undookai* and other sports events we organize. You know, if you compare the number of people who came this year to the number who came in previous years there is a notable growth. The biggest problem still remains, however, continuing to get more people to participate. In this respect, the biggest obstacle are those people with no children.'

A similar line of thinking is found in the following criticism raised by another man in relation to the parents who had set up the food stands. He noted:

'You should have seen all the mothers from the youth sports teams who slaved away at the food stands all day. It shouldn't be like that. The main thing is not to work for money, even if it is for a good cause. Much more important, I think, is that they should have had time to participate and see their kids running and taking part.'

Such deliberations often provided the Yamanakaites who were present with opportunities for contrasting the village and the esate. Some of them noted the high percentage of locals who generally came to the activities Yamanaka or its representatives take part in. Others contrasted the attitudes towards the local neighbourhood associations that are found in the two communities. Thus in the village – the Hieidairaites were told – when something important comes up, even the minor functionaries of the *jichikai* take time off from work in order to join the associations' drives.

A mixture of humour, self-criticism and optimism marked the last subject discussed. The head of the youth sports teams was asked about how the baseball team was doing. Flavouring his reply with funny anecdotes about missed balls, fumbles and strike-outs, he described how they had lost all of the four games they had competed in. They had even managed to lose the last game by a score of twenty to zero. No matter, he finally said good-naturedly, they are a new team and given time they'll find the right formula for success.

At about a quarter past seven, the chairman of the sports committee looked at his watch and said to the deputy sitting next to him that it was getting late. At this cue everyone stood up and helped clean the tables and hall. The people who had agreed to take the packages of prizes and jumping ropes did so, and the hall was closed and locked.

15 Concluding Considerations

The *undookai* is one of the most important public events carried out in the Hieidaira–Yamanaka school district. This event – which draws to it hundreds of local participants and tens of community organizers and city officials – is a blend of communal ceremonies and sports competitions. As such an important public event, the sports field-day clearly has to do with an attempt at creating or communicating a number of elements: a sense of local solidarity or unity in the district; a stress on the sharing of the experience of participation; a freedom for the locals to explore the nature of the ties linking them; and the definition of community activity as part of the quest for meaningful leisure. At the same time, however, the *undookai* is marked by a highly complex and problematical nature. This is because it is carried out in an artificially created territorial unit with a community identity that is open to question. Moreover it is based on the voluntary contributions and efforts of local organizations, and involves the partial participation of locals many of whom are strangers to each other. In this concluding chapter I explore some of the implications of these realizations. This, however, entails proceeding from the following point. If the *undookai* is a construct that somehow operates on the social order of and social relations between the local residents, then an examination of the logic by which it is put together is crucial to an understanding of how it works and what it is able to accomplish.

'A special time'

The construction of the *undookai* – again like the construction of all public events (Handelman, n.d.: 10) – is predicated upon a selection of themes or messages. One set of messages has to do with the unique character of the event itself. This set of messages – like that found in rituals or in drinking 'occasions' erects the special reality of the sports day. It does this through pointing to how the *undookai* is segregated from and opposed to everyday reality, and to how it is organized by rules different from those governing mundane activities. More specifically the 'special' character of the *undookai* is alluded to through a variety of inter-related features that have to do with the organization of time and space, the use of clothing and language, the order and systematiz-ation of the competitions and contests, and the kinds and numbers of participants.

Take the school grounds, for example. These are especially spruced up for the occasion. The tents, chairs, tables, sound system and other equipment are all carefully arranged around the running tracks so as to focus on the centre of attention: the main tent. The running tracks themselves are diligently marked out, raked, and outlined in whitewash. The flags and signs that are placed around the grounds lend an added aura of ceremoniousness and formality.

Similarly, people wear special clothing. Local and city dignitar-ies who do not participate in any of the competitions come dressed in dark dignified business suits and ties. The sports committee appear in a 'uniform': dark slacks, white T-shirts, and 'H' baseball hats. They, as well as most of the other organizers, wear ribbons denoting their status as officials of the sports field-day. Even the 'informal' wear of the residents shows a remarkable consistency: while most of the adults wear sports or track suits, the majority of children arrive dressed in the school's sports costume.

Temporal markers are examples that further underline the pecu-liar character of the day. First of all, the *undookai* is held on a Sunday, that is it is set apart from the normal work-a-day week. Moreover, the highly explicit declarations of commencement and completion sounded on the day itself serve to bound the event clearly. Finally, the contests and ceremonies themselves are bound to a tight and distinct schedule, and form a highly coherent and orderly series of activities.

All of these messages, then, serve to highlight the special reality of the *undookai*. Yet they are accompanied by another set of messages or themes. This latter set has to do with the nature of the 'ordinary' social context to which the event is related, and upon which it provides a commentary. The most important of these messages are the recurrent emphases on the potential unity, cohesion and common identity of the area and the accomplishment of these through participation.

Unity, co-operation and participation

These themes are expressed in discursive as well as non-discursive ways. On a discursive level one finds a recurrent emphasis either on how the day is based on the combined efforts of the people from the area, or on how participation in the *undookai* serves to create a sense of belonging to the district. Thus, for example, the honorary head of the sports-day related the event to the consolidation of local ties and the development of a potential for co-operation between the estate and the village. The mayor linked this to the gradual drawing together of the children of the two communities and their future collaboration in joint ventures. Other city officials spoke of the district as an integrated unit standing at the base of city and ultimately national sports projects. Finally, the head of the sports committee talked of the potential for friendship, and the fostering of ties that lie at the base of the *undookai*.

At the same time each stress on the potential of the *undookai* is accompanied by an emphasis on how the achievement of such a potential is contingent on the widest possible participation of the locals. This was evident both in the public speeches uttered, as well as in the private comments of the sports committee members. In both was noted the growth – and continual need for such growth – of the number of people taking part in the sports day.

In a sense the very noteworthiness of the need for participation serves to underline its precariousness in modern communities. This is no mean point in relation to localities marked by conditional and limited involvement in public affairs, and is most evident in the variety of non-discursive means that were used in order to express the day's main messages. Thus, for example, the choice of guests and dignitaries was designed to play up the theme of estate–village oneness. The honorary head of the *undookai* was asked to take up this role not in his capacity as the head of the village's neighbourhood association, but as the assistant head of the Hieidaira–Yamanaka alliance of *jichikai*. The presence of 'external' representatives from the municipality and other city-level organizations may be seen as a complementary aspect of this same point. For the presence of these outsiders represents the continuing external validation and recognition of some kind of estate–village identity.[1]

It is in a similar light that the invitation of functionaries from the local educational institutions and major community organizations should be understood. For given the partial participation of the locals, the presence of these people served to represent at least the organizational or associational unity of the district. In other words, despite the limited involvement of the local residents an effort was made to achieve an organizational representation of all the major segments of the local population.[2]

The internal structuring of the *undookai* itself followed much the same lines. On a rather simple level some events – the opening and closing ceremonies or the public exercise, for example – by including everyone served to underscore the themes of unity and oneness. On a more complex level the design of events for all age-groups and the constant alternation between spectators and participants in themselves carried the same messages.[3]

Another example of these realizations has to do with the prizes. Here note the very small differences between the prizes which are awarded for the first three places, and between these and the compensation prizes. These small differences seem to underline the stress on the importance of participation *per se* rather than on a specific individual's achievements.[4] The fact that everyone receives something, leads – as Brown (1979:30) most perceptively notes in relation to an *undookai* he witnessed – to a situation in which 'publicly everyone appears to be a winner, everyone contributes to the cause, and no one is isolated from the group.'

Implicit assumptions and the problematics of modern communities

An interpretation of the *undookai* in terms of its role in creating local unity and co-operation seems to fall squarely within the discussions found in the literature on sports and ritual (e.g. Birrel, 1981:357ff.; Cheek and Burch, 1976:207; Stone 1981:221). The basic emphasis within this literature – which is situated within a rather explicit Durkheimian approach to communal rites – is on the essentially integrative or solidary functions filled by games and rituals.

Along these lines, the sports field-day can be seen as providing for the people of Hieidaira and Yamanaka an occasion for experiencing and reminding themselves of their unity. The central messages of the day are reinforced through the active participation of all of the segments of the local population, and by the special sense of sharing that develops out of taking part together in the contests and ceremonies. The *undookai* then – like other public sports events marked by high levels of participation – appears to provide the experience of a highly charged social gathering through which the inculcation of the messages of unity and oneness is effected. Such a rendering illuminates both the importance of the emotional rapport needed for the transmission of messages, and the essentially dynamic nature of 'accomplishing' a sense of unity.

None the less, while such an interpretation goes beyond the more conventional accounts of rituals in 'traditional' Japanese villages (Embree, 1939), it fails to deal with the highly problematic peculiarities of public ceremonies in modern artificially created territorial units. For what is not stated about the wider context within which the *undookai* takes place seems as important as the constant stress on the unity and joint efforts of the locals. As Colson (1977:190) stresses in her analysis of an American public event, what is not said is often more suggestive 'than what *is* said, for silence betrays implicit assumptions about the participants' relationship to the larger society and the political and economic framework that provides the order.'

In this respect two features in the *undookai*'s wider context, which receive little explicit expression, seem to be of importance. The first is the slight but ever-present tension or disquiet that marks the relations between and joint identity of the estate and the village. The second involves the co-presence of strangers participating in the *undookai* and the difficulties in breaking down the barriers between them.

The tensions between Hieidaira and Yamanaka – like the strains found elsewhere between older areas and new communities that have been incorporated into new administrative units (Cornell, 1981:29) – are related primarily to the apprehensions of the villagers. These apprehensions revolve around the fear that the village as a separate social entity with a high measure of internal solidarity and intimacy will break down. These apprehensions, however, grow out of an ambivalent attitude. This is because the growing ties with Hieidaira represent for the villagers two kinds of potential. On the one hand such ties are seen as possibilities for building alternatives – social and organizational – to the at times restricting relationships found within the village. On the other, such ties are seen as potentially leading to a domination of joint district organizations by the estate, and the ultimate 'swallowing-up' of Yamanaka. The villagers thus constantly shift between claims about the positive contributions of the alliance with Hieidaira, and asssertions about their separate identity, organizational independence, and the fact that the alliance is one of separate and qualitatively different localities.

For their part, most Hieidairaites see the estate–village relationship less in competitive terms and more as a complementary tie. Most are clearly cognizant of the villagers' apprehensions and are willing to accept the qualitative 'uniqueness' of Yamanaka. Thus much of the sense of a two-sided rivalry is infused into the competitions by the villagers, who seem to take the whole matter of the *undookai* just that bit more seriously. For the Yamanakaites, then, each team victory represents an expression of the village's special potential for co-ordinated action and full use of the locals' athletic resources.

Yet the interesting thing is that the underlying competition or contest between Hieidaira and Yamanaka is expressed without it irreparably damaging or negating the sense of unity and combinedness that the *undookai* creates. An understanding of the way this is accomplished involves, again, referring to the way the *undookai* is constructed, and to the 'permissiveness' (Lawrence, 1982:165) it allows for the expression of the different external qualities of the participants.

In the first place, the Hieidaira–Yamanaka rivalry is given little formal recognition. Most of the team events, rather than being designed as two-opponent contests, are competitions between what are officially stipulated as five equal teams. Moreover, the village–estate division is muffled, as it were, by a division within Hieidaira itself: i.e. between the ward teams. In addition the

239

arrangement of the team bouts in between the individual competitions further assures that there is relatively little emphasis on team results. Finally, the sole competition in which the village– estate rivalry finds open expression (the fire brigades relay race) is slated just before an event stressing their joint efforts (the dance performed by the women's associations).

At the same time the *undookai* does include a possibility for the expression of the communities' differing qualities. In this respect the nature of sports events as contests with problematic or uncertain outcomes is important. On an individual level these uncertain outcomes create the possibility for the expression of differences between competitors. The point to note, however, is that this potential exists not only for the expression of individual differences, but for variations between teams as well. The achievements and results of the teams in the sports events are in this way related to their external features: i.e. to the qualities not directly related to them as participants in games. These qualities in turn include, for example, their potential for mounting co-ordinated efforts, or their success at selecting the right strategies which combine those people with the suitable skills for the right team events.

Along these lines it may be understood why the uncertainty of outcomes was important for the Yamanakaites: the team contests provided recurrent 'tests' of their communal qualities. In being able to pull the ropes in the tug-of-war in a concerted fashion, they 'proved' their ability to 'work together'. In choosing the right people for the races, they expressed their potential for making good use of their knowledge of every villager's athletic capabilities. Again, in mounting the loudest and most organized support for their team, the villagers showed their solidarity. And lastly in pointing to the successive victories of the village team in all of the *undookai* held to date, they underlined the continuity of all these 'characteristic' features of Yamanaka.

Thus it may now be understood how the *undookai* allows the demonstration of the Hieidaira–Yamanaka rivalry without permitting the infraction of the basic rules governing the organization of the day. The element of the tension inherent in the local social structure is thus given expression, but it is structured in such a way as to mute or muffle its potentially divisive effects.

The exploration of local ties

The explicit stress on another of the *undookai*'s qualities seems to underline – albeit circuitously – a second problematical feature of the social context within which the *undookai* takes place. The quality which is stressed is that of the sports day as a potential meeting ground for the people making up the two communities. The problematical feature that this quality implies – and that finds relatively little public recognition – is the difficulty in initiating acquaintanceships and creating ties between strangers or between people belonging to different social categories.

In a private discussion a man in his late twenties pointed to the background against which such ties emerge. We were talking of the different impact the amalgamation of Hieidaira and Yamanaka into one administrative unit has had on the two communities. He began by contrasting the two localities:

'In Yamanaka almost everyone knows everyone else. Thus even if the older people don't know the names of each and every child in the village, they at least know to which family they belong. In Hieidaira things are different. People in the new neighbourhood don't know each other, and thus are sometimes uncomfortable in each other's presence. Another problem that you find is that the adults of the village are sometimes hesitant to get to know the people in Hieidaira or even to start talking with them.'

Yet despite these difficulties the *undookai* provides a host of opportunities for the maintenance of existing ties, the introduction of spouses and children of acquaintances, or even the initiation of new relationships. It is in this regard that the similarity between the sports day and many Japanese 'drinking occasions' is important. For it is in both types of situations that people unfamiliar with each other – or familiar with each other only stereotypically – can get to know one another.

This potential is an outcome of the special rules and expectations that govern behaviour in such situations. Thus both in the *undookai* and in 'drinking occasions' are found – for the duration of the frame (Handelman, 1977) – the following: a disregard of *certain* external attributes of the participants and their levelling

241

down to an 'equal' footing; the breaking down of many everyday social barriers (Lebra, 1976: Moeran, 1984a); and an assumption that one is being caught up in something that goes 'beyond' any individual participant. It is under these kind of circumstances that people can experiment with and explore the actual or potential ties that bind them together.[5] Thus, for example, the Tokyo bank's boss and his subordinates (Rohlen, 1974:108ff.), or the political heads of a small hamlet in Kyushu (Moeran, 1984a) can during their bouts of imbibement engage in a direct and frank discourse about the relations that bind them together.

Behaviour during the *undookai* should be seen along much the same lines. For during the day Hieidairaite and Yamanakaite, truck driver and university lecturer, or simply locals unfamiliar with each other, can all engage in negotiations about their identities and ties and about the processes by which they can potentially grow closer. This is not, then, just a matter of the seating arrangement which facilitates the striking up of conversations, or the sharing of food and drink. Nor is it just the case of the sports day 'providing' ready conversational subjects for breaking the proverbial ice. For on another level the potential of the *undookai* is related to the set of assumptions which govern behaviour during the day: the 'bringing down' of the participants to an equal status, the temporary disregard of outside characteristics such as occupation or income, and the expectation that conduct is oriented to the special – albeit transient – collective entity that is created through participation.

Closely related to these features is another peculiarity of the *undookai* which aids new – and often anxious – residents to join in the activities. It appears that the set events, fixed teams, and structured activities – all appearing in a published programme – provide a more-or-less ordered and clear framework to which the newcomers can orient themselves, and within which they can interact with others. This peculiarity is reinforced by the facts that *undookai* taking place in different communities throughout the country follow the same general outline, and that within a specific community changes in the programme are usually small and incremental. Thus the familiarity with the programme and the feeling that one is 'in the know' seem to add a measure of freedom in the social exploration and experimentation that go on. As Sutton-Smith (1981:455) observes, there 'is a considerable consensus that the person who plays is at some ease with his environment and his fellows.'

Potentials and limits

The *undookai* in a newly created territorial unit such as the Hieidaira–Yamanaka district is far from being the only kind of instance in which a potential for the creation of cohesion and familiarity among a group of strangers is found. Vogel (1975:xxi), for example, notes that despite the popular and academic stereotypes of the Japanese as having one overriding allegiance to their closely knit and familiar work group, modern Japan offers a range of other cases where such cohesion and familiarity can arise quickly. This can be seen in a variety of ad-hoc groups made up of people previously unknown to each other. Thus, he cites the quite widespread but as yet little analysed phenomena of special task forces, study committees, or tour groups that are established by and mediate between different public and private organizations. When compared to such ad-hoc aggregates in the United States or Europe, Vogel concludes that such impermanent Japanese groups appear to have a number of social mechanisms – drinking, recreation activities, ceremonies – which facilitate a relatively quick and smooth creation of solidarity and a climate suited for close interaction.

It is these same or at least similar mechanisms, I contend, that operate both in the interstitial spaces between different organizations, and in artificially created territorial communities. In both kinds of situations such mechanisms make possible the creation of solidarity and identity among people with different backgrounds, diverging allegiances and diverse external ties.[6]

The growing importance of such mechanisms in modern residential localities should be seen as part of a general development in which the more 'traditional' symbolic modes of communication are being supplanted. In the past community solidarity, familiarity, and identity were created and re-created primarily through a variety of festivals, rites and functions which were carried out in local, territorially based, shrine Shinto. The post-war period, by contrast, has been the scene of a gradual but steady decline in

243

the importance of urban community shrines and in the practices performed there (Dore, 1958:295ff.; Norbeck, 1970:167). But this has *not* spelt the emergence of a highly alienated population with no ties of identity or solidarity with groups, although such people no doubt exist. Rather, one finds that the 'traditional' Japanese potential for the creation of a solidarity and closeness that transcends the individual (Kumon, 1982:20) has been transferred – albeit in a slightly different form – to a number of other frameworks. Apart from the company two of the more well known of these social loci are the new religions and the giant urban shrines. For in both types of framework one can sense the emergence of – to use a rather extreme term – the super-organic potential for the drawing together of strangers.

From our perspective, however, it should be noted that the transfer of the traditional localities' modes of creating solidarity and familiarity has not been limited to such extra-community frameworks. As Norbeck (1970:106) notes, 'community solidarity today is expressed more and more through identification with secular common-interest associations rather than through joint membership in the shrine community.' What this means is that such modern locality-based organizations are but one out of a number of frameworks to which the potential-that-transcends-individuals has shifted. In other words communal organizations now provide one viable mode out of a range of possibilities that have developed since World War II. Moreover, the emergence of this community alternative well fits the character of the modern locale. Just as common beliefs and joint rites centred about the tutelary spirit enshrined in the local shrine were functionally appropriate to communities in which unity was essential for survival, so too the voluntary and conditional nature of such activities now well fit the nature of the ties and local sentiments that characterize modern communities.

It must quickly be restressed, however, that the unity and identity and the fostering of local ties are all *potential* states that such activities as the *undookai* comments about or hints at through the participation of the locals. Whether unity or divisiveness, or intimacy or isolation will come about is dependent on other things such as the political and economic relations between the two communities. In other words, the relationship between participation in the *undookai* and the larger social context is not direct nor certain. As Sutton-Smith (1981:474) eloquently puts it:

Play potentiates; it does not itself actualize. Thus the Olympic Games make theoretically potential a universal world of cooperating nations. . . . They create a fantasy of unity. The relationship of that fantasy to what may actually happen is however determined, even overwhelmed, by many other variables. But at least the play is a communicative form that can be understood by many who were formerly completely entrapped within their more parochial boundaries.

What the sports field-day is, then, is a communicative form that can be understood by many of the locals who were previously 'just' strangers, or who formerly only knew each other through stereotypical or categorical labels: 'villager', 'estatian', 'neighbour' or 'stranger'. For it communicates – discursively, non-discursively, or through the actual experience of participation – such things as the potential unity of the district, or the breaking down of social barriers.[7]

The individual and the community

An examination of the social context within which the *undookai* takes place leads the argument back to the wider developments related to leisure in modern Japan, and to the place of the individual and the community within these developments. For crucial to an understanding of the *undookai* is the realization that the act of taking part in the day – as an organizer or simply as a participant – is basically an elective act. That there are quite a few people who choose not to participate is one expression of this.

Other indications have to do with the way the participants themselves view the *undookai*. Everyone – perhaps with the exception of a few city dignitaries – comes to the *undookai* to enjoy themselves, to have fun. As one member of the committee put it a few days after the sports field-day: 'the main aim is recreation. The whole day is organized so that people can come and relax and have a pleasant time.'

Recreation and enjoyment have a variety of meanings for people. One mother in her mid-thirties, for example, told me that the *undookai* was an opportunity for the whole family to get together and do something different from the usual Sunday outing. A young student attending a private Kyoto university said that it's an occasion for indulging in his favourite hobby of sports. An older woman from Yamanaka explained that for her just the opportunity of coming to the housing estate and meeting a few of the Hieidairaites is an enjoyable experience in itself. Finally, one older individual from the estate's third ward mentioned the pleasure he got from supporting his team and acting as 'head Kibitzer' of the sports day.

The fun people experience in the *undookai* extends to another type of enjoyment. For the organizers of the *undookai* seem to derive a special kind of satisfaction from orchestrating and bringing off a complex and involved affair. The organization of the field day – with its busy mix of participants, organizers, events and equipment – is a challenge which appears to excite many among the sports committee. As the committee's chairman once understatedly put it: 'I enjoy it when things go smoothly.'

This is not to deny that at times joining a community organization or participating in a local event like the sports day take on a certain obligatory character. Thus for some men, the act of going to the *undookai* may be little more than an extension of Sunday's family service (*katei saabisu*), i.e. a time devoted not to the company or workplace but to one's wife and children.[8] Nor is all of this to deny that taking part in the sports day involves being subject to a whole complex of organizational and social codes and regulations. But to overstress these aspects is to fail to be aware of the large measure of choice at the base of such activities. Turner (1977:42) brings this out – perhaps with a hint of overstatement – when he observes in a related vein, that:

Football, chess, and mountaineering are undoubtedly exacting and governed by rules and routines at least as stringent as those of the work situation, but being optional, they remain part of the individual's freedom, of his growing self-mastery, even self-transcendence.

Participation in the *undookai* thus appears to partake – albeit in different ways for different people – of an essential quest for a self-realization that is based on free choice.

What must be stressed, however, is that the holding of such activities on the local neighbourhood level is part and parcel of the post-war expansion of leisure *alternatives* which the modern individual or family face. These options may include more private or solitary pursuits such as gardening or collecting, or they may encompass family or group activities like clubs or outings. The point is that the sports day represents the growth of community alternatives in the past few decades. It represents, then, the growth of a whole variety of voluntary groups, and the development of a whole range of locality-based activities. The choices the individual or family now face, in other words, are not only choices between community and other options, but between different local activities as well.

Some Japanese social critics have seen in the trends away from work and towards more privatized modes of spending one's leisure time, a manifestation of an egoistic individualism sweeping the country (see Linhart, 1975:205). Others present a more balanced view. Tada (1978:217) sees this trend as an outgrowth of the 'my-homism' phenomenon with its stress on protecting people's individuality and integrity as against the workplace. Fukutake (1982:217) sees in the attempts at making a positive use of the lengthening periods of leisure a challenge best handled on the local community level. And Plath (1969:128) sees in the 'experimentation' with this variety of alternatives part of the process by which modern Japanese are searching for meaningful and worthwhile guidelines within the modern behavioural environment. As he (1969:128) puts it, the 'search is not some simple craving for personal or social paroxysm, though that may be part of it. It is a search for forms of play that an adult can take seriously. It is a continuing search for traditions.'

In this respect the *undookai* represents a search for creating and living in a new liveable residential environment. This is not to de-emphasize the difficulties of the search for community alternatives, nor to overemphasize the importance or prevalence of such a search. This is, however, to stress that community options or choices continue to be in constant competition with the possibilities offered by both the workplace and by more private concerns. Thus while we are witnessing a certain surge in the search for the potential of the new urban community, this search does not spell a return to the close-knit villages of the past. Rather, we are seeing the emergence of local communities that are marked by partial participation, voluntarism and a greater respect for individual preferences (Yamazaki, 1984:12–17).

Changing Japanese Suburbia

In this respect the 'operation' of the *undookai* extends beyond its power to create unity or familiarity. For the 'play' and 'exploration' that go on during the day potentiate a new kind of activity which is based on voluntarism and organization. It is through such activities that a gradual redefinition of the individual–group – or rather individual–social framework – ties is emerging. And it is to this and other issues that we now turn in the conclusion.

Part Six
CONCLUSIONS: IMPLICATIONS AND SUGGESTIONS

16 Conclusions

Rather extensive concluding chapters have been presented at the end of each of the book's preceding three parts. In this concluding section, therefore, I will try and highlight some of the wider implications – theoretical and comparative – of the issues and cases presented in the book. This will be done through showing how these issues and cases are related to a central theoretical controversy that has recently emerged in Japanese studies. Specifically this refers to the growing debate about the limits, utility and underlying assumptions of the leading and probably most widely known model of Japanese society: the 'group' or 'consensus' model.

In order to do this, a short explication of the main critiques of the model will first be presented. Then, through drawing out some of the problems and conclusions which are common to all of the case studies presented in the book, these critiques will be related to the utility and shortcomings of both the 'transfer of community' and the 'breakdown of community' approaches which were presented earlier. Finally a few comparative topics will be examined through contrasting Hieidaira and Yamanaka with other local communities both in Japan and in other advanced industrial societies.

The group model of Japanese society: critiques

The group model of Japanese society lacks a high measure of theoretical sophistication. Yet despite this, for many years it provided central foci for the controversies and concerns found in the social scientific literature on Japan.[1] It has not only provided the

251

central conceptual orientations for many of the analyses of social
and cultural phenomena in the country, but since the mid-1970s,
it has been at the centre of the development of a whole new
variety of counter-approaches. These have usually focused on the
assumptions and views of man and society that underlie the model,
and on its application in a monolithic fashion to explain all aspects
of Japanese behaviour (Befu, 1980:41; Sugimoto and Mouer,
1980).

The first major focus of criticism has been – to borrow from
Wrong (1961) – the oversocialized conception of the Japanese
individual. As Befu (1980:39) eloquently puts it, 'individuals are
portrayed by the group model as automatons or robots without
will and without any freedom of choice, simply acting out the
demands and the norms of the group. Nor is there any explanation
of how these demands and norms are created.' While basically
accepting the strength and importance of Japanese groups, such
a critical stance nevertheless stresses that Japanese people have
an ability to take an independent view of their roles and the
social order within which these roles are embedded. Moreover, it
suggests the importance of developing analytical tools for dealing
with the freedom, choice and will (and their limits) of individuals
in Japan.

This stance is also related to the second point. This is the
assertion that the group model is seriously flawed in its ability to
deal with the ways individuals decide among strategies, compete
for and manipulate resources, and create those 'ill-defined, non-
enduring forms of social life' (Boissevain, 1968:542ff.) as networks, factions, or quasi-groups. While a few of these elements
have been integrated into the group model through the analyses of
patronage or organizational factionalism (Vogel, 1975:xxi), many
theoretical issues suggested by these analyses have been left
untouched. These include, for example, questions about the ways
individuals work towards the formation of inter-group or inter-
organizational coalitions, or the effects of wider developments –
growing leisure or higher educational achievements, for example
– on the way the ill-defined forms of social life are created.

The third point is related to the growing realizations that the
Japanese may actually have a number of varying and coextensive
definitions of the collectivity or group (Befu, 1980:43). Here, for
example, one finds assertions that beyond an exploration of one
mode of group formation – that of recruitment of outsiders into

an existing collectivity which is vertically organized along patron–subordinate lines – little regard has been given to the possibility that groups may be constructed in different ways. Moreover little consideration has been given to the tensions individuals may face when belonging and being subjected to the requirements of a number of collectivities at one and the same time: say, for example, the workplace, residential community and old school group.

The fourth centre of critical attention has been most consistently highlighted by those scholars who have dealt with the manifold expressions of conflicts, frictions and struggles that are found in almost any area of Japanese society. The contentions of these scholars have been that the widely held view that Japan is a highly integrated society requires at least a partial reassessment (Sugimoto, 1978:281), and that consensus and integration are not the only aspects of Japanese society (Sugimoto and Mouer, 1980:8). When writings on conflicts or struggles in Japan have appeared, they have tended to portray particular events without yielding a comprehensive or systematic view of Japanese society (*ibid.*). Although not expressly formulated, these assertions seem to suggest a widening of theoretical concerns to deal with such questions as the problematics of political legitimacy and citizens' rights, the development of new modes of conflict resolution, the place of conflict and power in creating integration and change, or the social limits imposed by the growing organization of technology, government and bureaucracy.

The fifth point is related to the way the group model deals with change. Here the assertions have been that the stress on a relatively orderly modernization and the continuity of major cultural orientations has inclined many supporters of the model to overlook the possibility of further change (Burks, 1984:3). Included in this is not only a demand for dealing with the major contradictions in the model itself, and the ways Japan has moved beyond the 'modern' stage, but perhaps more importantly that many aspects of Japan be reconceptualized as social and cultural phenomena which have a dynamic of their own and which are constantly changing and being changed, on a variety of levels.

The last two critical points have to do with the comparative treatment of the Japanese experience. The growing awareness of the complexities of Japan as an advanced industrial democracy – for example the blurring of class lines, the ideological diversity, or unique historical legacy of different areas – is the starting point for the first. Here the primary assertion is that the group model is too restrictive in the place it grants to the multiformity and variety found in various parts of the country's society and culture, and to the different social arrangements and principles around which they are organized. The consequent conclusion has of course been the need to focus attention on variation *within* Japanese society.

An attack on the tendency to use 'unique' Japanese terms as explanatory principles is the starting point for the second criticism associated with the comparative treatment. The stress on the unique traits of the Japanese leads, according to this view, to much conceptual ambiguity and to difficulties in placing Japanese cases in a comparative context. As Sugimoto and Mouer (1980:11; see also Dale, 1986) put it:

> Many key terms like *tate shakai* (vertical social structures) or *amae* (dependency) are never precisely defined; instead their general usage is only illustrated, the result being that a particular word is sometimes used to represent a concept for cross-cultural comparison (an analytical category) while at other times it is used to express something peculiarly Japanese (as a descriptive category).

The primary demand in this respect has been for a more precise and rigorous delineation of such concepts, and the explication of just those aspects of Japanese social phenomena which can be compared cross-culturally.

All of these criticisms and critiques have not, on the whole, spelt a total rejection of the group model. Indeed, as is clear from the rendition presented here, most of the counter-approaches have largely been the outcome of attempts at elucidating the limits of the model, or coming to terms with the major issues it has raised. The rise of these approaches thus has led to an insistence on defining just those aspects of Japanese society which the model may help to explain, and on developing alternative models for those parts which the model does not explain (see, for example, Befu, 1980:43). In the remaining parts of this concluding chapter I set out to illuminate these themes in relation to modern Japanese localities in general, and specifically to Hieidaira and Yamanaka.

Communities and organizations: resources and interests

The central argument presented throughout the book is that the potential for community involvement – in political action, in the provision of care, or in the creation of local sentiments – is very much present in modern-day Japanese communities like Hieidaira and Yamanaka. For the citizens of these two communities have on the whole succeeded in struggling for a host of environmental and public facilities, in establishing new arrangements for the provision of aid and assistance to the elderly, and in contending with the generation of local solidarity, identity and belonging. The potential for community involvement thus obtains both for the achievement of rather concrete instrumental ends, as well as for the engendering of less tangible notions and affects.

All of this is not to deny that in attaining these things the residents of Hieidaira and Yamanaka had – and still have – to overcome a variety of difficulties such as recruiting activists and participants, setting up communication channels, or engaging government and other officials. These difficulties, however, point less to the inherent weakness of these localities than to their changed forms of community action, community care, and community sentiments, and to the complexity and scale of the environment within which they are embedded.

It is against this background that the importance of what have come to 'constitute' modern residential communities – local voluntary organizations – should be understood. It is these local organized groups which carry and produce the changed forms of community involvement, and mediate between the locality and its environment. The unique ability of these organizations lies both in their capacity to marshal and make good use of a community's resources, and in their power to manage its external relations. Thus, the neighbourhood association came to embody the estate as a political actor both in terms of it being the pool of Hieidaira's political resources and the representative entity with which the developer and government authorities entered into negotiations. Similarly the voluntary welfare workers and old-folks clubs embody the 'care' provided by the two localities, both in terms of their concentration of collective care-giving resources and their function as representatives of the communities' welfare interests. Yet again, the district's sports promotion committee embodies the potential identity, solidarity and co-operation of Hieidaira and Yamanaka both in terms of its being the organizational means for enacting and creating these potentials symbolically, and in its providing the concrete focus by which the validation and recognition of external bodies is effected.

Local organizations 'make good use' of resources because they are able, in Tilly's (1973:214) words, to store and dispose of the community's pooled resources and apply them towards collective goals. They can, in less abstract terms, bring together in an organized way precisely those people who have the relevant skills and commitment to act on behalf of the community as a whole. The success of the estate's neighbourhood association in securing various facilities and amenities, despite the participation of only about half the residents, is one example of this. Yet again the great amount of care provided by the voluntary welfare workers and the old-folks clubs is dependent on the time and efforts of only a small part of the communities.

Embarking on a community 'venture' in modern localities, then, need not be based on the solidarity or support of the whole community. Rather, as demonstrated in the case studies, such collective projects can be carried out on the basis of a more limited backing of only part of the locality. This means that the effectuation of such ventures is most often predicated upon the existence of one or more local groups or social categories who have a direct – and often active – interest in these projects. There is more to this observation than the rather trivial truism that in any community some local groups may use collective means in order to further their own specialized interests. The point rather is one central to an understanding of how most post-war Japanese localities have become communities of limited liability.

What seems to be emerging is an attitude on the part of local residents, that their attachment and commitment to the community are related to their rational material interests and social investment in the territory (see Guest, 1984:9). This suggests that in many cases interaction and ties with neighbours and involvement in local voluntary associations have come to be based on the perception of common interests which require collective organization and action. Such interests – as illustrated throughout the ethnography – may cover a whole variety of matters like childrearing, home ownership and environmental improvement, marketing of foodstuffs and household goods, or the management of dependency in old age.

The point, then, is that in one respect the preparedness of people to join locality-based organizations and activities is related to a sort of familial 'consumerism' – i.e. it is associated with the interests and investments of the households which make up the community.[2] This, in turn, suggests two further points. First, in contrast to the stress implied by the group model, today's Japanese may and do have interests and goals apart from the 'company'. In other words, they develop interests which cannot be reduced to those of only one overriding group. Second, and this stands in contrast to the predictions about the 'withering away of locality', some interests still continue to be served only on a territorial basis. That is, because certain services which serve local interests continue to be given primarily on the local community level, they will for the foreseeable future persist in being nuclei for potential activity and organization.

This awareness of how community concerns are to a large measure rooted in the interests and relevance of certain issues to local groups is related to a further realization. It is related to a recognition of the fact that such concerns constantly rise and wane, and change and develop. Community dealings, then, are things which take prominence for limited periods of time. Moreover, they are relevant to local groups which themselves are maturing and ageing, proceeding through different stages of the life-cycle, learning from their own experiences, and responding to the development of new expectations of public authorities.

Over and above this, the effectiveness of community involvement is dependent on two further preconditions: one related to wider trends in present-day Japan, and one related to the internal dynamics of modern communities. Recruitment into community activities is related first of all to such broad developments as the greater affluence and growth of leisure time, the expansion of the educational system, or the increase in the number of people who have been socialized to work towards solving their problems in an organized way: in political parties, labour unions, administrative and commercial frameworks, or student and citizen movements. Such developments provide a ready pool of people from which local communities enlist activists and functionaries.

Second, collective activity within communities is predicated on the continual creation of locality-based networks from which the resources and people are drawn. This is a point to which I will return to in a later section. Suffice it to say here that both Fuku-take's stress on the dissolution of community and Nakane's assertions about the transfer of community to the company fail to take into account the 'natural' growth of networks and ties on the basis of territorial contiguity. They fail to capture the reality of how interpersonal relations and group ties are constantly being fashioned and refashioned (Janowitz and Street, 1978:111).

Communities and organizations: consciousness and response

The emphasis on the role of local voluntary bodies in mobilizing and making use of community resources has been coupled with a stress on the ways the modern community's concerns are increasingly structured by, and dependent upon relations with external agencies and bodies: various branches of local government, public utilities, the media, the national bureaucracy, and other communities. The point is that almost any involvement with the locality involves coming into contact with the community's external 'advocates' and 'adversaries'. These considerations were hinted at in the ethnographic profile, and developed to a greater degree in each of the later chapters. Here a number of further points should be highlighted.

The first is the realization that in many cases the very creation of a modern locality and its identity are the direct outcome of actions undertaken by external organizations and agencies. These outside bodies – whether out of a wish to create a constituency or market and keep it intact, or out of a desire to establish organizational extensions of their services – attempt to produce a territorial unit whose name and boundaries are institutionally secure (Suttles, 1972:58). The case of Hieidaira and Yamanaka provides a good example of how a locality or its parts – community organizations, activities, facilities – are established because of the needs and interests of outside policy. Seen from this point of view, the estate's neighbourhood association was set up through municipal encouragement in order to facilitate the operation of city services. Similarly the opening of the old-folks clubs and the recruitment of the voluntary welfare workers should be viewed at least partly as city initiatives to extend its welfare services. Finally, the official recognition of the district's sports committee was to a great extent an outcome of the city sports department's desire to assure a smooth and responsible handling of the local sports facilities and grounds.

Such processes, however, should not be simplistically reduced to a stress on the all-powerful domination and fabrication of local communities by giant organizations outside them. Nor can they be accounted for by the inherent manipulability and subjugation of these weak communities. For to a great extent these processes are the outcome of a positive and active reaction of local individuals and associations to what they perceive as outside threats or opportunities. In more abstract terms – and this is the second point – this calls for conceptualizing and analysing the dynamics of local residential communities 'as a response of territorial populations to the environment' (Suttles, 1972:233; Guest, 1984:6).

Such responses may be individual or household-level reactions. Witness the decisions of certain families to move away from Hieidaira during the estate's first few difficult years, or the choice of certain people to manage their elderly relations' dependence on the basis of household resources. Yet for a population which is 'tied' to the local territorial community – out of a lack of options outside, a high investment in the area, or sentimental attachment to the locality – the most effective means of response is collective, i.e. it is organizational. This was the conceptualization that lay behind the analysis of the way Hieidaira's locals perceived their lack of amenities and facilities, compared strategies for dealing with and improving their situation, and acted upon the opportunities they saw for building a coalition with the city government and securing the lacking lands and services. By the same token again the initiative taken by the oldsters of the village and the estate in setting up the old-folks clubs was an outcome of their perception of the opportunities provided by the municipality – e.g. advice, budgets, medical services.

What we are witness to, then, is the increasing development of 'conscious communities' (Hunter, 1978:147). They are conscious in that such localities have increasingly come to possess formal organizations that mobilize local resources towards the creation of a collective definition of local interests and goals. This means that many of Japan's local communities are not just aggregations of people who happen to live together. Rather, the point is that local organizations – whether themselves the outcome of local initiative, or the result of reaction to external threats and opportunities – have contributed to the creation of communities which are marked by active purposiveness, self-awareness, choice and planning.

In the case of Hieidaira these issues were most clearly brought out in the discussion about how the estate emerged as a social and political fact. For the large amounts of communications – letters, leaflets, notices – disseminated by the neighbourhood association during the estate's first few years did not only convey a sense of territorial identity to a diverse array of strangers. Just as important was the contribution of these communicative efforts to the emergence of a collective definition of Hieidaira as a community with a common fate. Similarly, during the sports day, the stress was on the conscious self-perception by the two communities of their potential to work together, join in a common identity, and grow closer.

These considerations, in turn, imply a third point which is a more realistic appraisal of another derivative of the group model: the over-centralized view of Japanese government (Reed, 1982). According to this view – which is quite widely accepted both within and outside Japan (see, for example, Matsushita, 1980:10) – the country's government appears as a configuration of vertically linked structures. These structures, so the explanation goes, reach down from the central government through to the prefectural and municipal levels, and then on down the hierarchy to the level of neighbourhood and hamlet associations. The result is a situation which is characterized by an impeded development of pluralistic pressure groups, and the perpetuation of local groups which function as little more than auxiliaries of bureaucracy or as vote-getting machines for the ruling Liberal-Democratic Party.

Such an approach, however, not only lacks an appreciation of the problematics of extending government control in an all-embracing and homogeneous manner, it is also deficient in its awareness of the potentials for conflict, tensions or struggles that are part-and-parcel of any social system. The success of the Hieidairaites in mounting a highly effective struggle, or the achievements of the district's older inhabitants in setting up a local system of community care attest to the fact that local initiative and autonomous action can occur despite the greater dependence of today's localities on external agencies and organizations.

All of this, of course, is not to deny that there are serious limits to what the 'solitary' community can do. For as stressed throughout my account, the technological and bureaucratic structures of today's complex society often guide local action and activity according to their own organizational priorities. The stress, rather, has been on the dual potential of locality-based associations and organizations. On the one hand such local organized groups can and do act as administrative sub-contractors for government. But on the other hand, they can and do act as watchdogs and pressure groups that become active when local interests are seen as being threatened. Japanese government and community, then, are not necessarily antithetical nor congruent. The ties and relations between them take on a contentious or co-operative character according to the issues at hand and the wider historical situation.

For all this, however, it is not enough to trace out the internal dynamics of communities, and their interactions with external organizations. One must also take into account developments in the wider environment which place limitations on the scope and modes of local enterprise and activity, but which are at the same time analytically distinct from these two sets of variables. These developments are usually not the outcome of activity or action in any one specific community, but they nevertheless do become relevant by presenting specific localities with threats and opportunities. Two such examples are the financial situation of the municipality (itself dependent on certain national and international trends) and its implications for the construction of local amenities, and the evolution of official policies for social welfare and their significance for the establishment of community care systems.

Not surprisingly, many discussions of Hieidaira and Yamanaka's future revolve around these issues: the potential of the estate and village to meet the difficulties and chances posed by a changing environment. The villagers, for example, worry about the continued breakdown of Yamanaka's physical isolation through changed urban land-use laws and regulations. Most of them are cautiously optimistic about their capacity to deal with a new situation in which their locality will be but part of a much larger and undifferentiated territorial entity. A few also talk of the future opportunities that could be opened by the sale of communally owned land and the construction – with the monies received – of village leisure facilities like tennis courts or a new road.

Communities and environment: transformations and emergence

The new dynamism, initiative, and conflictual attitudes of Japan's modern 'conscious' communities and their representative organizations cannot be attributed solely to the formal and informal institutional physiognomy of Japanese government and administration. Of no less importance are the qualitative transformations that have accompanied the rejection of the negative consequences of the country's industrialization, and the questioning of this industrialization's accompanying ideology.

The milieu of public struggles and contestations within which the questioning of the 'growth first' policy arose was heavily influenced by a variety of groups: citizens' movements, environmental lobbies, consumer co-operatives, student fronts, civil rights and welfare groups, and some labour unions and political parties. These movements – many of which were led by and comprised of people who were born after World War II – have succeeded not only in placing new issues on the country's political agenda, but in changing the very premises on which public struggles are carried out. They have been instrumental in crystallizing the idea that Japan's modern citizens have something called 'rights' which the system owes them, and have taken the lead in pushing for the establishment of democratic procedures for expressing their demands and struggling for their acceptance (McKean, 1981:267–8). The emergence of these citizen groups, moreover, spells the acceptance of the inevitability of and increased tolerance for legitimate conflicts that are waged within accepted frameworks (*ibid.*).

Perhaps just as important as these effects has been the influence of these varied groups on the types of issues that are now placed before Japan's central institutions. Like other highly industrialized democracies (Eisenstadt, 1973:255) these issues are no longer related just to industrialization. Rather they entail such problems as the distribution of wealth, the carry-over costs of industry, the quality of life made possible by the high level of growth, the specialized needs of certain categories of the citizenry (Benjamin and Ori, 1981:76; Burks, 1984:11), and the uses to which the new leisure time is to be put.

For all this, however, the experience of these varied groups in Japan provides a contrast to other industrialized societies. This contrast is related first of all to the relative rootedness – organizational and structural – of citizens' movements, consumer lobbies and other such groups in local communities. In America or Europe similar organized groups tend to base much of their activities on religious, ethnic, class or professional affiliations. By contrast Japanese movements appear to draw more of their activists from and make use of the organizational networks and resources of community associations and local voluntary organizations.

But this 'rootedness' in local communities has not spelt a radicalization of locality based organizations and associations. For the contrast between the Japanese and the American, Australian and West European experience of protest and citizens' movements extends beyond the organizational realm. The contrast extends to the kinds of ideological and political images and orientations carried by such movements. In short, Japanese movements – in contrast to other 'post-modern' democracies – carried no counter-model of society. Thus, when community organizations and associations borrowed modes of protest and ways of expressing demands from citizens' and other movements they did not have to adopt a stance of rejection of the Japanese polity and society. Just as the demands and expressions of such movements were limited, so too were those of local organized groups.

This was brought out in the three case studies presented and in the placement of these instances against the wider backdrop of local oganizational activity in Japan. Thus, Hieidaira's neighbourhood association carried virtually no orientation towards basic changes to either local or societal power relations. This is also true of the old-folks clubs and voluntary welfare workers which, as we saw, hold no aspirations for substantive professional treatment, or for altering or reforming the basic welfare priorities set by the various levels of government. Yet again, the identity stressed in the *undookai* was not a separate one based on class, ethnicity or even historical legacy. It was rather a stress on an organic unity in which Hieidaira and Yamanaka form the lowest constituent parts, and which leads from the district to the city and prefecture and through them to the Japanese nation as a whole.

This does not imply that there was little or no influence of wider movements on community organization. Rather, this means that the influence was limited to modes of struggling and issues and expectations that could be adopted readily by local activists. They were adopted, that is, without the accompanying baggage of a radical commitment to transform society.

These considerations direct our attention back to the conceptualization of Japan's modern communities. For through an understanding of how members of community groups drew from and acted upon the experience of citizens' movements, the developmental nature of the community–environment relationship can be perceived. It is precisely through such a focus that the historical context within which these ties develop can be integrated into the analysis. This suggests more than an understanding of the actions of the locals as the outcome of their comparing their 'situation' to that of other communities or groups. This means – as stressed in the chapters on the estate's development and the local welfare organizations – that community activity is also the result of the locals' basing their demands on the assumptions and expectations that are part of the contemporary milieu of public issues and struggles. That is, in a community's response to the environment not only are threats or opportunities central, but also the wider cultural premises which defined these threats and opportunities.

A closely related point is perhaps best brought out in Kapferer's (1976) rendition of transactionalism. The point is that the decisions of the locals should not be viewed as the outcome of a fixed set of goals and opportunities, but as related to the continual changes in these factors themselves. This implies, moreover, that the changes in this set of goals and opportunities may themselves be products of either the emergent forms of the community–environment ties, or the results of trends wholly external to these ties.

A good illustration of changes which are related to the emergent forms of the relationships themselves is the way the label of '*interi*' was attached to Hieidaira. The label – the combination of highly educated and aggressive – initially emerged out of the negotiations between the estate's neighbourhood association and the city government. Yet later, in subsequent negotiations, this label itself was used as a resource. The effects of the rising national expectations of public life on the relationship that developed between the municipality and the two communities is an example of the way factors external to the relationship itself find expression within it. For on the basis of these changed expectations – formalized in new regulations, ordinances and laws – the locals could press for the establishment of local welfare and sports programmes or the construction of local facilities; could wage their struggles against a background in which the expression of citizen demands was increasingly accepted as legitimate; and could utilize many of the channels of neighbourhood–municipality communications which were incorporated into the formal machinery of government throughout the 1960s and 1970s.

In sum, then, communal change and continuity should not be seen as simple functions of external factors, or as mere results of changes in the decisions and strategies of individuals or organizations. Rather, they should be seen as products of both: 'strategies and decisions evolve as a response to one another and to external forces' (Kapferer, 1976:19).

Community as group: 'Groupishness' and instrumentality

In concluding the analysis of the Hieidaira–Yamanaka *undookai*, I noted that modern Japan seems to be characterized by the existence of a whole set of mechanisms – drinking, sharing of food, sports meets, ceremonies, recreation activities – which facilitate a smooth creation of solidarity and a climate suited for close inter-action among groups of relative strangers. These social-inter-actional mechanisms point to an underlying continuity in the group orientation of the Japanese, and to those aspects of modern life where the group model is still applicable. A short analytical excursion into the social-psychological roots of such mechanisms can best bring out these continuities.

On the whole, few middle-class Japanese have a primary group (except perhaps the family) to which they belong for their entire lives (Befu, 1980:39). What does seem to be the case is that most middle-class Japanese acquire through their socialization a learned capacity to move from and relate to a succession of groups throughout their lifetime (Keifer, 1970). This is related to the complex processes of (direct, anticipatory and vicarious) socialization, and an individual's procession from childhood to old age through a whole range of formal and informal groups: play and neighbourhood gangs, kindergarten and various school classes, sports teams, student clubs, coteries of friends, task and work groups, and so on.

Put in abstract terms, middle-class Japanese acquire – through a process Bateson (1972:167) terms deutero- or meta-learning – a capacity to move from one frame (Nakane, 1973:34), *waku* (Plath, 1969), or *soo* (Kumon, 1982) to another. They learn to relate to groups on a meta-level. That is, they learn to relate to a constant 'idea' or 'construct' of a group although they may move successively or *concurrently* through many actual groups. This means that in any specific group within which they may find themselves, Japanese people quite quickly settle into the patterns and peculiarities which are elucidated by the group model: co-operative work, solidarity and intimacy, comfort in group context, ritualized behaviour, and the creation of an entity that somehow goes 'beyond' the participants.

As I have tried to show through a number of examples, the experiences of people in Hieidaira and Yamanaka well mirror these assertions. For many members of the estate's old-folks club membership in the association represents a move into a new meaningful group *after* belonging throughout their lives to other such groups. For both the Hieidairaites and the Yamanakaites affiliation with the sports committee means joining a rather close and intimate group while *at the same time* belonging to similar groups such as the workplace or coteries of friends.

The centrality of such mechanisms as drinking for such groups as the old-folks clubs or the sports committee suggests a number of points. First, the special logic of such mechanisms seems to fit the 'traditional' notions of Japanese interactional behaviour. The unique features of these mechanisms – the levelling of status, the creation of an identity that goes beyond the participants, and most importantly their openness to mutual exploration and experimentation – appear well suited to the Japanese tenor and practices of social interaction. They seem to fit, in other words, those special Japanese peculiarities of refinement, circumspection, and high sensitivity in interpersonal relations (Smith, 1983:73; Plath, 1980). In a culture characterized by indirectness and inference in social intercourse and by problematic communication (Smith, 1983:53) such mechanisms facilitate or increase the probability of successful encounters and meetings.

Second, these mechanisms seem all the more important in today's Japan which is marked by a multiplicity of situations where strangers or people familiar to each other only as representatives of social categories have to co-operate, work or live together. That is, these devices facilitate the formation of groups or social frameworks in those modern circumstances in which strangers – whether voluntarily or out of necessity – find themselves together.

These social mechanisms, many of which are actually relatively recent inventions, have both instrumental and sentimental aspects. The former side of things is best brought out by Smith (1983:65–7; see also Atsumi, 1979) in his discussion of *tsukiai*: the socializing done by workers employed at the same large firm after hours. He relates his analysis to the contribution of *tsukiai* to the accomplishment of work tasks in such enterprises where the interaction and identity of the workers is problematical. Thus Smith (*ibid.*, 66) states the following:

> It is no exaggeration to say that *tsukiai* is an indispensable technique designed to make affairs of the firm run more smoothly, and that the larger the enterprise, the more necessary it becomes. This phenomenon is not a simple transfer into modern corporations of an established tradition; like the QC circles and the lifetime commitment, it too is a new device that meets the new needs of industrial society as the Japanese perceive it.

This is a point which appears to be sorely missed by many proponents of the group model: that devices for the creation of groups – and all their peculiarities – may be used for practical or utilitarian ends. As another commentator notes, such mechanisms should be seen as purposely created social techniques of interpersonal communication for the creation of 'warm' and empathic relations and 'smooth' transactions (Saito, 1982).

It can now be understood why these kinds of social devices seem no less indispensable – in the instrumental sense – in modern artificially created communities like Hieidaira or the Hieidaira–Yamanaka district. Such social practices facilitate the smooth running of local associations and organizations and through this, of course, the 'efficient' achievement of their goals. Thus in many local associations – such as the *jichikai* or other committees – and in meetings between local and city officials, such situations are consciously created. They are created in order to achieve goals other than the identity and intimacy of the participating groups themselves. In a similar vein such mechanisms are sometimes used in order gently to explore the preparedness of people to take on local public roles and functions. In this sense, in certain situations the feelings of togetherness and openness of communication are sentimental prerequisites for the effectuation of instrumental action.

Again, however, a reduction to instrumental intentions is too simple. For the creation of some sense or feeling of 'togetherness' or 'commonality' seems to be essential in modern communities not only for the emergence – as outlined throughout the ethnography – of networks of mutual aid and assistance, groups for political mobilization and action, or for other instrumental ends. The search for conjoint identity and a sense of solidarity seems to be part of a much wider quest for building a liveable environment.

Community as group: sentiments and their creation

For the majority of families and individuals who make up modern communities in advanced industrial societies, local territorially based sentiments of identity, solidarity and belonging continue to be important. This is indicated by a variety of discussions from different disciplines. Thus Hunter (1978), for example, demonstrates how the creation and maintenance of local sentiments in highly urbanized areas continue despite popular and theoretical stereotypes to the contrary. Tuan (1977) insists on the continued capacity of people to develop a sense of and attachment to place in spite of effects of modernization. Finally, Cohen (1982) shows how the valuing of local distinctiveness and the sense of belonging to a certain territory go on despite the increased integration of local communities into wider regional and national systems.

Yet the creation of such sentiments would seem to be especially difficult in 'contrived communities' (Suttles, 1972) – i.e. in artificially created locales like Hieidaira or the Hieidaira–Yamanaka district. This is because these communities are marked by: the presence of a population with a previous attachment or an attachment elsewhere; a lack of local 'natural' networks and informal ties; and by the existence of a local populace with a multiplicity of interests and orientations. One might expect these attributes to work against the generation of local sentiments.

In Japan this kind of expectation is reflected in much of the ongoing debate about the future of local communities. Thus for Fukutake (1982) this debate forms part of his assertions about the loss of the sentiments of the traditional locality, and about the search for new forms of community which will be able to generate them anew, albeit in changed ways. For Nakane (1973) it is part of the analysis of how community (i.e. group) sentiments have been transferred to the workplace, and how as a consequence local residential communities have become little more than places for housing workers and their families. Looked at more closely, however, such projections do not seem to fit the actual situation of many modern communities. Local sentiments develop in such localities, and they do so in a variety of ways.

In the first place the growth of such sentiments – in older as well as newer 'contrived' communities – is related to the interplay of two elements: territorial contiguity and ecological stability. Taken together these two requisites make possible the 'natural' maturation of local ties and the emergence of a sense of sharing a common experience and identity. As Guest (1984:16) states,

> Such simple acts as living for a long time in an area and interacting with nearby others make social claims upon us. . . . We become caught up in webs of social relationships which have no rational basis but are meaningful and important to us.

In this respect it is clear why the villagers are mindful of how lucky they are in that Yamanaka has experienced relatively little inward or outward mobility. For the village is marked by little rupture in the ways the local ties of exchange, emotional contact and a sense of togetherness are being constantly produced and reproduced. So too in the estate, there are places – mentioned in the ethnography – where people living next to each other have created their own little networks of support and security and attachment to each other.

In this regard it may be valuable to contrast Hieidaira with

269

those housing estates made up of massive apartment blocks which
Keifer (1976b) and White (1976) studied. The residents of these
latter apartments tend to view their stay in the housing estate as
a temporary situation – a way station – on their way to a fully
owned, detached dwelling. Hieidaira, however, *is* the final stage
for many such people who see their residence in the locality as a
long-term matter. Thus, while the residents of the big apartment
blocks tend to invest few emotional and sentimental resources in
local ties because of anticipated mobility, many Hieidairaites can
and do invest in such ties.

Local sentiments and meaningful relationships may also be the
unintended results of joint activity in a local association. Here co-
operation in an organized group devoted to the achievement of
instrumental goals gives birth to non-utilitarian ties. Thus many
of the people who mounted the estate's successful drive for local
facilities still remain close despite the fact that over a decade and
a half has passed since then, and in spite of living in different
parts of the estate. Similarly people – even from the different
communities of Hieidaira and Yamanaka – who have served
together in the PTA or children's committee retain a sense of
closeness and attachment many years later.

For all this, however, the 'natural' processes of growth and
maturation have their limits. On a scale of more than a few tens
of people other types of efforts seem to be required. This means
that in the case of relatively large communities such as Hieidaira
or the district there seems to be a need for much more planned,
conscious and intentional efforts for the creation and maintenance
of local sentiments. Such active efforts can be found the world
over in such local activities as ceremonies, festivals, parades,
sports teams, functions of religious centres, or the chronicling of
community histories. Yet the operation of such 'traditionalizing'
and 'sentimentalizing' elements is of course closely related to the
nature of different local communities and to the cultural and social
milieu within which they develop.

Norbeck (1962:77), writing in the early 1960s, astutely noted
the importance of Japan's local neighbourhood- and hamlet-level
organizations in this respect. Linking his assertions to the long
historical tradition of such organizations and their presence in
almost every local community, he forcefully argued that they
were becoming vehicles for the production and expression of local
solidarity. Later he (Norbeck, 1970:106) began to envisage – much

along the lines proposed by the 'dissolution of community' approach – a steady weakening of such organizational functions. Seen from the vantage point of the late 1980s, Norbeck seems to have had a partial appreciation of how local organizations were to change and adapt to their new communal circumstances.

Norbeck fully sensed the point made earlier about the emergence of conscious communities in Japan: i.e. communities which in many instances actively define and articulate certain 'images' of solidarity and identity of the area, and consciously seek a validation and recognition of these from external organizations and groups. Such communities consciously and purposively organize special moments like the *undookai* when the locals assemble and explore their potential unity and attachment to the locality. What Norbeck did not fully appreciate was that these conscious efforts are increasingly waged against a background in which communities have become communities of limited liability. The fact that modes of community activity were being transformed seems to have been interpreted by Norbeck as a sign that they were generally becoming weaker, rather than as an indication that they could emerge in more volitional, conditional and specialized forms.

Local sentiments, then, are not just persisting residual elements with limited significance for modern residential communities. They are not just vestiges of traditional communities which are in the process of dissolution, nor mere remnants of community notions and affects which have been transferred to other frameworks like the workplace. They should, rather, be seen as emergent social constructions of reality whose significance varies over space and time (Hunter, 1978:145).

These considerations suggest three further points. First, such 'objective' elements as the historic or cultural legacy of an area, its social characteristics, or its natural surroundings, may all be mobilized and symbolically stressed according to contemporary circumstances. Second, the creation of local identity, solidarity and a sense of belonging are always part of a process of negotiation which goes on among the locals themselves, and between them and external social entities. And third, the creation of new 'polities' – amalgamated neighbourhoods, school districts, or administrative units – always entails not only bureaucratic or organizational implications but also cultural and sentimental ones.

The stress on local sentiments as emergent phenomena casts

doubt on another one of the central elements of the group model of Japanese society: the proposition that the Japanese develop an overriding allegiance to, and identity with *one* group or social framework. Rather, analytical attention should be directed to the possibility that people may have multiple allegiances, senses of belonging, or feelings of identity with different groups at one and the same time. Some people may have strong sentimental attachments, at the same time, to social frameworks which are usually seen as mutually exclusive. This is the case of the feelings many Hieidairaites and Yamanakaites hold towards both the workplace and the residential community. But such plural senti-mental attachments may also be directed – as in Yamanaka which was incorporated into a larger urban unit – to frameworks which are joined in ever-growing circles of territorial inclusion (see also Cornell, 1981:29; Johnson, 1976:204). Such multiple allegiances and identities signal, I believe, a new pluralism in Japanese society.

This point, in turn, must be seen against the trend away from the 'traditional' pattern of creating local sentiments on the basis of the active participation of the whole community. For the pro-duction and maintenance of such sentiments is increasingly being carried out by limited segments of the local population: i.e. differ-ent local groups may be involved to varying degrees, and at differ-ent times in the production of local solidarity and identity. Let us trace out a few examples of these assertions.

In Hieidaira it is the older and middle-aged individuals (many of whom were born and raised in pre-war villages) who call for the construction of a Shinto shrine and a local cemetery in the estate. Pointing to the existence of these centres in Yamanaka, these people justify their claims in terms of the importance of ensuring the intergenerational continuity of the estate. Another segment – overwhelmingly parents of children at school – not only take an active part in organizing but are continually defending the holding of the summer's children's festival (*Jizoobon*). Their explanation is that without such religious practices the children will find it difficult to develop a notion of spiritual matters and an attachment to the area. Similarly, it is a small group of intellec-tuals – authors, social critics and journalists – who talk of the need to arrange for some kind of documented chronicle of the estate's beginnings and of its present character.

In Yamanaka the main difference is between the older and

younger generations. Among the older villagers the chief stress is on the importance of maintaining the locale's past sentiments – which often appear as idealized versions of the solidarity and intimacy of times gone by – through the continuation of the variety of ceremonies and rites held in Yamanaka. The younger adults – in an interesting inversion – point to Hieidaira and call for the development of the values of personal fulfilment and freedom which they see as characterizing the estate. What they want, however, is not just the weakening of the communal values of participation, loyalty and closeness which are now found in Yamanaka. Rather they seem to be seeking a balance between these values and the Hieidaira type of sentiments which mix a more conditional attitude to community affairs with a greater respect for personal choice.

The search for such a balance of values by Yamanaka's young people is indicative of much wider issues. For it touches upon the variety of contentions surrounding the definition – or redefinition – of the relations, needs, and obligations that tie today's modern middle-class Japanese to her or his group.

Communities and individuals: choice and conditionality

In recent years a growing number of observers have begun to note that individuals – and individual attributes and qualities – are being granted increasing importance in various sectors of Japanese society. Some of these assertions are phrased as the discovery of elements that have always been part of Japanese society, and that have received little analytical recognition because of the group model's theoretical blindness to the place of the individual and his actions. Others see the rise of the individual as the result of certain social and cultural developments that have unfolded since World War II (or sometimes since the Meiji Restoration), and that the group model is seriously limited in its capacity to handle.

Befu (1980:40), for example, asserts that he has uncovered a very definite conception of personhood in Japan. Moeran (1983), for his part, attributes the rise of modern individualism – and its attendant craving for the satisfaction of personal tastes and experience – to the effects of mass consumerism. Lebra (1979:342) observes that today's leisure activities have been transformed from mere pastimes into a search for individual *ikigai* (purpose of life) expressing a will to live based on personal goals. Finally, Yamazaki (1984:17–18) notes that today's Japanese are beginning to demand a re-evaluation of the importance of the individual and the ways people are treated by others as unique persons.

These and other statements (e.g. Keifer, 1976a:299, 1976b:22; Fukutake, 1982:214–15) suggest the emergence – however unclear as of yet – of new types of orientations to and expectations from social life and relations. Moeran (1983:105) – perhaps somewhat too strongly – asserts that this new individualism implies a threat to the very core of the Japanese stress on the priority and importance of the group over the individual. While this new individualism may not imply a full-blown threat to the cultural stress on groupism, it nevertheless points to the confusion that now surrounds the definitions governing the ties binding individuals to their groups.

The bearing of these realizations on an understanding of modern residential communities was hinted at throughout the analaysis of Hieidaira and Yamanaka. The first point to note is that in both communities, albeit to different degrees, people's lives are not 'exhausted' by their local communities. That is – and this again is true to different extents for different groups – friendships and ties exterior to the locality, affiliation with external frameworks (organizations, associations, clubs), and membership in working situations outside, all pose competing demands on community issues.

For the individual this is not just a matter of belonging to more than one group. Nor is it simply a matter of a situation in which people have alternative ways of improving or maintaining their material circumstances. This situation also implies the existence of a variety of options for personal attainment and fulfilment, and the co-presence of a multiplicity of loyalties and demands. In this sense, community alternatives for fulfilment – through local activism, for example – compete with options outside the locality.

This implies, in turn, that the emergence of a conditional attitude, a voluntaristic posture towards belonging to and membership in the modern community and its organizations and activities, is not just a matter of 'familial consumerism'. It is also a result of the kinds of satisfaction or fulfilment individuals find in different collectivities among which the community is but one. Rather than the image of an uprooted, lonely urban or suburban individual, should be placed one of a person moving between groups and basing his membership on the interplay of 'material' considerations and deliberations about more personal things like experiences and fulfilment.

These developments, then, are but part of a much wider milieu in which individuals are relating to different groups while maintaining a certain distance, and while identifying with them on a more rational and multivalent basis (Yamazaki, 1984:12). Membership in the local community – as in many other groups – is dependent now on the perception of individuals that they can find personal attainment and accomplishment there. As Cummings (1980:196–7) eloquently puts it,

> the new individualism does not mean a rejection of taking part in groups; rather it seems to involve a new orientation to the group. The group is viewed as a collection of individuals, each of whom is seeking self-fulfilment. A group is appreciated insofar as it is responsive to individual needs. In contrast a group that imposes rigid and non-negotiable demands on the individual is disliked.

The needs answered by today's group frameworks include more 'traditional' essentials – such as the enjoyment of togetherness, the exchange of sympathetic concern, or the comfort of a well defined collectivity – as well as more 'modern' ones – for instance the fulfilment of self, the expression of personal taste and desires, or the sensitivity to personal expectations of life.

It is these kinds of expectations that underlie much of the discussions about the building of *komyuniti* in Hieidaira and Yamanaka. In the village they underlie the quest for finding a balance between the social obligations incurred by membership in the locale, and the desire for a freedom to find personal fulfilment through this membership. In Hieidaira they rest under the sentiments – mentioned throughout the ethnography – of the right 'not to join' local organizations, and the right 'not to neighbour'.

For all this one must quickly add that it is very unlikely that we shall see a dramatic decline in the importance of the family or the work group. We are not witness to the development of a new type of (Western) individual, who is 'independent, autonomous, and thus essentially a non-social *moral* being' (Dumont, 1982:2, emphasis in original). Nor are we seeing the emergence of an image of society which is but an aggregate of such morally auton-omous, psychologically free individuals (Nisbet, 1953:228). What does seem to be the case is that the opportunities for self-affirmation in Japan will no longer be limited to the household or the company (Yamazaki, 1984:17). What appears to be developing is a greater pluralization of Japanese society, and the formation of social frameworks on the basis of more purposive and mindful considerations. In other words while the meta-level group orient-edness of many Japanese continues, it is in the concrete expressions of this orientation – in inter-group mobility, nego-tiation over group authority, or choice of membership, for exam-ple – that the changes are manifesting themselves.

Conscious communities: contrasts and comparisons

Although not explicitly formulated as such, many recent studies of residential localities in Japan seem to highlight their emergence as 'conscious communities': i.e. as local populations that are marked by a collective self-awareness, choice, and an active response to external forces (see Smith, 1978:chap.8; Moeran, 1981; Falconeri, 1976). At the same time, to judge by the recent experience of residential localities in other post-industrial societ-ies, the trend towards 'conscious communities' is far from being limited to Japan. Out of a very large body of studies witness the following few examples: the growth of neighbourhood associations as a response to the effects of city development in such American cities as Pasedena, California (Lawrence, 1982:172); the establish-ment of neighbourhood and community councils for the expansion of participation in local government decision-making throughout the United Kingdom (Smith and Jones, 1981); or the rise of urban social movements pressing for better facilities in French housing estates (Castells, 1977:chap.14).

A comparative perspective, however, suggests that middle-class Japanese localities have a relatively greater potential or predis-position for territorial 'consciousness'. This has to do with the (historical and contemporary) ubiquity, long-term durability, and territorial-rootedness of locality based associations and organizations in Japan. Historically, many of today's rural associations have their roots in the mid-nineteenth century organizations that cared for the control and maintenance of roads, lands and forests. The urban associations go back to that period's organizations for production, finance and marketing (Yoneyama, 1976a:234ff.; Norbeck, 1967:199–200). The bulk of local organizations, however, were established during this century, and were the result of both the encouragement of various levels of government, and the initiative of local communities themselves. This is brought out by the persistence of organized groups, at least some of which are found in *all* of Japan's rural, urban and suburban residential communities: neighbourhood and village associations, women's and children's committees, old-folks clubs, voluntary welfare councils and workers, parent–teachers associations, sports teams and committees, shop-owners' associations, voluntary fire brigades, shrine deputies, food and marketing co-operatives, traffic safety groups, self-education circles, or a variety of leisure clubs.

These varied groups contribute to the potential self-awareness and purposive action of local communities in two interrelated ways. First, the very existence and persistence of these frameworks provide – like the administrative structures of many Islamic urban neighbourhoods of the preindustrial era (Azarya, 1984:162ff.) – a relatively long-term focus for local identity, and a device for the utilization of local resources for the definition of the locality and its ends. Second, such frameworks provide a ready model for organized action. This is both in the sense of presenting familiar routines and patterns for action which can be applied to a variety of ends and purposes, and in the sense of being accepted as valid and legitimate social units for the achievement of these purposes.

The organizational potential of Japanese localities for 'consciousness', it must quickly be added, should not be taken as a suggestion that this potential is a *constant*. Rather the potential for local consciousness is a variable. Thus the case of the relatively strong self-awareness and active formulation of community problems as they are found in Hieidaira and Yamanaka should be contrasted to other instances in Japan. They may be constrasted, for example, to those communities where consciousness develops rather weakly (Falconeri, 1976) or along non-territorial lines (Taira, 1968–9).

In addition, the stress on consciousness should not be interpreted as a transformation of Hieidaira and Yamanaka into ideo-logical communities. They are not wholly inward oriented. True, they do possess – in comparison with middle-class residential neighbourhoods in other industrialized democracies – a strong organizational capability for mobilizing resources toward a rela-tively clear formulation of identity, solidarity and interests. But they are far from waging these efforts in the concerted and extreme way, and with the high personal commitment found in social movements or certain ideological communities.

On the other hand, although Hieidaira and the Hieidaira–Yam-anaka district are to an extent the creation of giant external bodies, they differ from other types of territorial units which are established by exterior structures. Thus, unlike Japanese company housing estates – and for that matter unlike frontier stockades, politically motivated settlements or monasteries (Azarya, 1984:chap.7) – they were not brought together in order to fulfil part of an overall plan designed according to the official aims and priorities of the external developer or local government bureauc-racy. Nor are they simply appendages of these external structures. In fact – as outlined in the previous section – local residential communities may be one of those alternative loci where interests and values are cultivated *as against* the workplace.

Finally the trend towards a raising of consciousness of local Japanese communities should not be taken as portending the transformation of the locale into an organized totality, of its turn-ing into little more than an organization of organizations. This is for three reasons. First, the local community continues to be the site of a wealth of social life that goes on without being organized. It continues to encompass all sorts of groups and quasi-groups: small and large, formal and informal, ill-defined and clear. Second, the very conditionality and voluntarism that underlie people's attitudes to the community will go on to create a plural-ism of social forms and frameworks – among them organizations – through which people will act. And third, as Sakuta (1978:248–9) astutely observes, for a true 'citizen consciousness' to arise, the divergence of home and work lives is essential. Self-consciousness and a critical stance towards one's social framework, in other words, will continue to be heightened by membership and partici-pation in diverging groups.

The near future, then, signals the development of what Cornell (1981:31) terms 'urbanism in a different style'. It will most probably be marked by the exploration and expression of greater regional diversity, and a search for more personally satisfying pursuits. This experimentation and searching, however, will, I am sure, be much more aware, purposeful and planned than before.

Komyuniti: multiple images of Japanese society

The nature and quality of the nation's modern communities have been at the heart of one of Japan's central political and intellectual controversies since the early 1970s (Kelly, 1986). Since that period academics and intellectuals, government officials and party activists, planners and social service professionals, as well as ordinary citizens have begun to talk about such concepts as *mai taun* (my town), *furusato tsukuri* (the creation of a 'home-town'), or *machi tsukuri* (the creation of locality). Yet the most commonly used concept in official and academic publications as well as in the media and popular conversation is one borrowed from English – *komyuniti*. But like its English equivalent, *komyuniti* is open to a variety of interpretations and suggestions which often cross-cut distinctions between the political left and right, which are based on differing theoretical perspectives.

For many of the ruling Liberal-Democratic party's politicians, for example, *komyuniti* provides an important symbol of the modern quest for the spirit of the traditional community and its emphasis on self-help, self-reliance and solidarity (see the anlayses found in Nihon Fujin Dantai Rengokai, 1980). In a related vein, for Tokyo's former left-wing governor (Tokyo Metropolitan Government, 1982; Nagashima, 1981:296) this concept denotes a growing awareness of community identity, and the search for 'roots' in territorial units. In both renditions, *komyuniti* is linked to an image of the past territorial group – the 'traditional' village – and its character as a closely knit framework marked by relative unity and mutual assistance.

Takayose (1979b) stresses the role of *komyuniti soshiki* (community organizations) in enabling local communities to react to the problems posed by an evergrowing administrative and governmental apparatus. According to him such organizations achieve this through their being the prime agents of community control

279

over services, and the vehicles through which communities act. Here local associations are viewed at the same time both as positive devices for the articulation and expression of local demands and interests, and as ameliorative mechanisms designed to cushion the effect of external forces.

Other more radical scholars like Taira (1978) view the creation of *komyuniti* as a means to counteract – and perhaps triumph over – the Japanese state and its extention. This approach is similar to that of the 'neighbourhood utopians' (see Hunter, 1978:159) who see localities as loci for the strengthening of societal 'underdogs', and as centres for the transformation of the basic structural arrangements of a society.

Finally, Fukutake (1982:137) suggests that underlying the concept of *komyuniti* is a feeling that it is necessary to find new ways to organize today's citizens democratically, and still evoke a sense of local solidarity and co-operation. His image too is utopian or visionary, but it is rooted less in the inherent conflictual nature of society than in what can be seen as the potential of Japanese social frameworks eventually to produce new altruistic forms of collective action for, and identification with, the locality.

Underlying each of these examples are different ideological and theoretical assumptions about and images of Japanese society and man. There seem to be at least one axis along which these assumptions and images can be arranged. This axis runs between a 'conservative' view and a 'radical' view of the potential of Japanese society. The conservative view combines a stress on the possibility of nurturing local self-help and reliance and a return to some kind of past communitarian spirit, with an emphasis on the ameliorative potential of localities for correcting some of the excesses of today's urban society. The radical view stresses the potential of local communities for strengthening local control, developing advocacy roles and influencing the structural arrangements of Japan's society and polity.

Present-day Japanese society, then, seems to present a number of contrasting and at times conflicting semblances of the potentialities and realities of local residential communities. Each interpretation of *komyuniti* in turn draws upon these different semblances of properties and possibilities according to its underlying images and guiding assumptions. The emergence of this theoretical and analytical pluralism is important not only because it highlights the variety of potentials inherent in Japanese society.

From the viewpoint of Japanese studies in general this signals the emergence of a more realistic view of the group model of Japanese society, and the rise of an awareness that they are other ways of understanding the Japanese world. This development has not spelt a wholesale rejection of the group model. Nor has this meant the emergence of a plurality of theoretical approaches with little mutual impingement and cross-fertilization. Rather, in ways akin to developments in social studies in general, there is a trend towards searching for the topography of possibilities and constraints in Japanese society and culture. Possibilities and constraints because these include not only the broad – and slowly changing – contours of continuity and persistence, but also the potentials for choice, uncertainty and confusion. Thus, as I have been trying to make clear, the dynamics and qualities of present-day communities like Hieidaira and Yamanaka must be understood against the background of and as the specific playing out of the wider field of social constraints and possibilities.

If I seem to have been stressing a rather cautiously optimistic view of the potential for community involvement in such localities, it is not just a reflection of my own personal attitudes. It is also a theoretical and ethnographic counter-stress to both the 'loss of community' and the 'Japanese company as community' approaches. This is because both stress the relative weakening of the modern locality and its limited potential for action, mutual help and identity.

Finally, I would like again to emphasize that only a balanced recognition of the local community's limits can best bring about an awareness of its potential. For community involvement can make a difference. As I have tried to show, inherent in such involvement is a very real potential for improving the quality of the living environment and everyday life. And that is not such a bad thing.

Appendix A: Fieldwork

Beginnings

Fieldwork was carried out between July 1981 and August 1983.
Throughout this period, with the exception of a number of trips
to other parts of the country, my family and I lived in Hieidaira.
We lived in a nice two-storey detached dwelling that is characteristic of many new residential areas in Japan. The house itself had
four rooms – two of which had the traditional *tatami* floors – and
a relatively spacious garden.

Although I had studied some Japanese before arriving, I felt
that my knowledge at the beginning was insufficient for full-
fledged fieldwork. In deciding to further my study of the language,
however, I had to choose what type of Japanese to concentrate
on. I decided to devote most of my efforts at first to the spoken
language, and to keep the written and read forms on a low fire.
After about fourteen months in the country I switched the emphasis and began to devote much more of my time to reading a
variety of texts. My first eight months were thus devoted chiefly to
language studies at a Kyoto language school; at Osaka University
where I began to learn Japanese social science jargon and to read
a bit of sociological literature; and with two local residents, one
with whom I exchanged an hour of English each week for an hour
of Japanese, and one with whom I exchanged Hebrew. Studying
a language in this way inevitably brings about a situation in which
one is more advanced on one level or type of discourse than in
others. Thus I found at a certain stage that I could say things like
'social stratification' or 'political autonomy and domination' but
had trouble expressing myself at the local barber. During this time
my wife also studied at the language school and exchanged lessons
with a few local women. Our son, who began to attend the local

day-care centre three weeks after we arrived – he was two-and-a-half at the time – picked up his Japanese very quickly.

This initial period of study proved advantageous not only in terms of developing my linguistic skills, but also in that it allowed me very gradually to become familiar with some of the estate's residents as well as with our son's day-care centre and its PTA. Perhaps more importantly it provided an opportunity for many of the estate's citizens to become familiar with my family and me. At the time I did not realize how important this was. Quite a few people later told me that initially I was a bit of a threatening figure. This had to do I think both with my size (190 centimetres and over 110 kilograms) and booming voice and with my initial Israeli penchant for directness and frankness. Within a few months, however, both elements were somewhat softened. First I began to be sensitive to – and master in a very rudimentary way – the variety of indirect and delicate modes of interpersonal communication. Second being a family man probably helped even more. My daily outings with our son – to the day-care centre, to local playgrounds or just for walks – gave an impression of someone 'human' with personal concerns that the locals could relate to.

During these first few months I also discovered that the neighbouring village of Yamanaka was joined with Hieidaira in one school or administrative district. I thought at the time that studying Yamanaka would represent little more than an additional marginal effort, and that this kind of study would provide a good comparative perspective on what was happening in Hieidaira. I was right about the comparative aspect. The contrast between the two communities provided a host of insights and raised many questions that would not have been encountered in a study of one community. I was wrong, however, about the marginal effort. This is because it proved difficult to overcome the problems of not living permanently in the village: I found I was missing the wealth of information gathered by just living in a place, and thus had to try and make this up by conscious and intentional efforts (for example tape recording every interview, taking a large number of photos and slides, or planning visits to the village at different times of the day). I also missed the information one gathers through chance meetings and the knowledge and insights I gained in the estate through the remarks and observations of my wife and our son. Finally, especially at the beginning, I had difficulties in understanding the local dialect spoken by the elderly villagers, which the youngsters would often translate for me into standard Japanese.

Methods

Two major analytical realizations guided the types of questions and problems I set out to study. The first was that an understanding of modern communities involves being actively aware of their larger social, economic and political situation. With this in mind I strove to relate local affairs and issues to their wider context. Thus in interviews and through the examination of government and historical documentation, I tried to stress such questions as the relation between Hieidaira and Yamanaka and other communities, the different perspective city and prefectural level officials hold on local matters, or the manifestation of contemporary dilemmas facing Japanese society in the two communities (for example educational competition, or control of urban growth).

The second realization was that of the importance of local organizations to community and extra-community ties. Thus I chose to approach people through local organizational networks. That is, I initially approached residents in the two communities through their capacity as local activists and functionaries. Only after I had covered most of the local associations and groups did I begin to 'tap into' the more informal social networks. By that time too, my Japanese had improved, and I was more accepted in the area as a researcher.

A mixture of methodologies were used to gather data.

Interviews

About 200 interviews were carried out. In every case I made a date ahead of time (through a personal visit or by phone). Often I had to change my plans because of the limits of other people's times and schedules. It must be emphasized that, while structured, these interviews nevertheless tended to be conversations rather than straightforward question and answer sessions. Moreover, I tried whenever possible to meet people in their own 'circum-stances'. Thus the overwhelming majority of interviews were held in people's homes, in shop-keepers' shops, in teachers' insti-tutions, and in bureaucrats' government offices. This proved ben-eficial in that I gathered much information from observation of and questions about the 'material' surroundings. These rather concrete questions were an added advantage when there was a long pause in the conversation or when the interviewee was shy.

Except for the visits to the City Office and the local educational institutions I always took along a small gift, a cake my wife or I had baked or a small set of postcards of Jerusalem. These proved to be good 'conversation pieces' for breaking the social ice, and were not so expensive as to put the people I gave them to in an awkward position. I was often – but not always – given things in return such as oranges, strawberries, cookies, chocolates or vegetables grown in people's gardens.

About half the interviews were tape recorded and then tran-scribed. I chose to record conversations with people who were extremely busy (like city or prefectural officials) and all of the interviews in Yamanaka. All in all people seemed happy to be interviewed, and I had only one refusal during the whole period of fieldwork. Most Japanese are well educated and familiar with accounts of academic research and techniques, and the ones I studied were no exception. A few, however, had trouble under-standing that I was interested not only in the 'traditional' side of things but in modern mundane customs as well. Indeed five or six Hieidairaites even suggested that the estate was not really worthy of academic interest, and that I had better stick to Yamanaka or some other traditional area.

An interesting point is the place of anthropology in the popular mind. As anthropology in Japan is usually associated with primate studies, at the suggestion of some of my university friends I pres-ented myself initially as a sociologist. Then if someone was interested enough to pursue the matter I would go into an expla-nation of the nature of social anthropology.

The types of interviews carried out were the following:

(1) Family interviews: these included demographic data, family history, kin and neighbour relations, participation in local and extra-local organizations, political attitudes, religious practices, and patterns of use of services (shopping, medical, etc.). The

interviews usually lasted about two or three hours. While 60 family interviews were completed in the estate (including 15 local shop-keepers), 15 were completed in the village.

(2) Organizational officers: this refers to activists in local organizations. These interviews included going over organizational charts, official and unofficial divisions of labour, relations between members, recruitment into the organization, and detailed questions about activities carried out. About 40 such interviews were completed. As I often turned these meetings into partial family interviews (that is gathered some data on the interviewee and his household) the totals given in some tables in the text sometimes add up to more than one would expect for 60 households.

(3) 'Officials': this refers to people who work in the two areas on a day-to-day basis but do not reside there (the biggest group in this category being school and nursery teachers). With this group I went over such questions as the formal and informal opportunities to meet with parents and representatives of local bodies. When the official had experience in other parts of the city or prefecture, I tried to talk about the differences and similarities with the local situation. About 35 of these interviews were completed (including 6 former principals and teachers no longer working in the communities).

(4) 'Externals': this category includes people who live and work outside the area but deal with it in a more or less regular way (heads of administrative units in the city and prefectural administrations, and heads of voluntary organizations on the city level). Interviews were designed to throw light on city and regional problems and developments, and on the place of Hieidaira and Yamanaka in this wider context. About 45 such interviews were held.

Local participation

During the two years, I joined as an active member the area's sports committee, the day-care centre's PTA, and the biggest calligraphy club. Other than that I regularly attended meetings of the neighbourhood association, and tried to put in an appearance at at least one meeting of all the other local organizations (about 15 of them). Finally, I made an effort to be at most of the local activities: for instance singing clubs, religious festivals, sports meets, graduation ceremonies, or concerts.

During the first few weeks people in the sports committee and the neighbourhood associations seemed to feel a bit constrained in my presence. But soon when most had some idea of what I was studying, things loosened up and my presence appeared to have less of a disruptive effect. It was as if – as one of the *jichikai* activists put it – I had become part of the furniture. An added element had no doubt to do with the fact that I was willing to contribute actively to local community activities: for example carrying equipment on the sports day, setting up the lighting for the summer children's festival, or selling balloons and water pistols at the day-care centre's annual bazaar.

It took a while longer for the members of the day centre's PTA where almost invariably I was the only male out of 30 or 40 women. But when one day after about 14 months in the field a group of 4–5 mothers began in my presence to talk about pregnancy and childbirth I felt I knew that this was some sign of acceptance. I readily joined in the conversation talking of my wife's pregnancy and our son's birth at which I was present, and heard with sympathy about the difficulties of Japanese women in childbirth (narrow pelvis and relatively long labour periods).

In terms of the informal side of social life, my wife and I initiated reciprocal relationships with people – couples and singles – in the estate and the village, and joined a number of informal social circles. Much of the socializing revolved around food and drink. We often served middle-eastern and Mediterranean things and were treated in return with an array of Japanese and Chinese dishes. In addition we often went out with families we had become familiar with to drives, picnics, parties and American suburban-style barbecues.

For all this, however, my wife and I often felt the need to get away from the Japanese and things Japanese. In this respect the detached house and the privacy it offered were important. In addition we made friends with other English-speaking Westerners in and around Kyoto and found our ties with them both pleasant and interesting. Finally with another Israeli couple living in Kyoto we chanced upon quite a number of (American and Australian) Jews with whom we celebrated the main religious festivals of Judaism (Passover or the New Year, for example).

Statistical data

Three main sources were used.

(1) Official statistics: Japanese social statistics are gathered on many levels (national, prefectural, local), and by many organizations. They are of high quality and are published at frequent intervals. In my case parts of the national census pertaining to Hieidaira and Yamanaka (held eight months before I arrived) provided a good background for more detailed data I gathered. An especially good source was the city statistical yearbook which provides data down to the sub-blocks within my communities.

(2) Data drawn from my interviews: Some of the information I collected on such matters as family make-up, educational achievements or shopping patterns has been turned into descriptive statistical data. The 60 families interviewed in the estate comprise about 10 per cent of the total households. Although I did not approach these families in a random way, both the data provided by Motoyama (see next paragraph) and the national census provide a good check on my results.

(3) Geographical research: In the summer of 1982 a geography student from Ritsumeikan University in Kyoto carried out a small project on Hieidaira (Motoyama, 1982). The data he gathered concerned family composition, occupations, commuting and use of shopping and services. His was a random sample (every third occupied household in alternate blocks throughout the wards), and of the 88 questionnaires he distributed, 76 were returned.

Literature and documentation

Wherever possible I sought out written material pertaining to the two communities. This included secondary historical sources (city and prefectural histories), previous studies (primarily on the village's shrine and festivals), correspondence (between local organizations and the city), government documentation (policy statements, regulations), proceedings and announcements of local organizations and clubs, personal diaries and notebooks, and the letters and booklets sent to parents by the local educational institutions. In addition I collected a variety of advertisements placed by local commercial establishments in newspapers, and the pamphlets, visiting cards and announcements found in our post-box. Finally I took many slides and snapshots of a variety of views, events, meetings, people, and streets and houses.

When I arrived back in England with a mountain of documented material, I began to envy my fellow students who had worked in illiterate societies, or at least in countries where photo-developing and photo-copying facilities were not so cheap or accessible. I had come back with 1,600 pages of fieldnotes, over 600 cards indexing the notes, over 1,000 slides and pictures and 2 notebooks detailing the contents of these, 30 one-and-a-half-hour long tapes, 20 folders full of letters, pamphlets and other documents collected, and a tea chest full of journals, books, research and position papers and other material I had gathered from local government (I am most probably a bureaucrat at heart). But as soon as I began to write up I found the great advantage of having multiple sources of information. It was much easier to cross-check accounts, and to try and differentiate between gossip, public knowledge, documented data, opinions or secrets.

Changes

Fieldwork has a dynamic of its own which is often difficult to get down on paper. The presentation of the 'methods' each with its own contents, details and kind of data gathered does not do justice to their mutual influence and development. Nor does it do justice to the ways one develops and changes along the way. Perhaps – to judge by certain currents in contemporary anthropology – in some not too distant future a different manner of writing ethnography will be developed. Here, however, a few comments – technical, theoretical, and personal – may be in order.

First, on a rather 'technical' level, I have begun to appreciate how as my command of the language improved and the mutual trust between the locals and myself deepened, I could begin to explore those more sensitive issues it would have been impossible to tap into at the beginning. This relates to such things as an appreciation of the nuances of meaning which conveyed intimacy and closeness, or conflict and strain. But it also involves discussions with people about such things as corruption (dealt with in the text), mental health in the family, or attitudes to the outcast or ethnic minority problems.

The second point pertains to the changes in my own theoretical biases. Before going to Japan I had already had opportunities to read about the country and its history and society. The picture I got, however, was constructed along the lines of the 'group' model. Thus I expected and initially interpreted everything according to such principles as group orientation, harmony, loyalty and consensus. It took me time to gradually see other sides of Japanese society: the conflicts and strains, individualism and the pursuit of personal experiences, or the distance people put between themselves and the groups to which they belong.

The third point is probably related to the general anthropological realization that one learns about oneself and one's society through a study of others. On one level this struck me through the almost endless discussions we had when we tried explaining what a Jew and Israeli are. We usually ended up with our Japanese friends summing it up nicely as, 'Jews are actually Christians who believe only in the Old Testament.' On another level these problems arose when I began to understand how terribly unproblematical – especially when compared to Israelis – a national and social identity is for the Japanese.

Towards the end of fieldwork our son – who was then a few months past four – came home one afternoon. My wife and I were suddenly unsettled at realizing how his Hebrew had deteriorated at the expense of an increasingly natural command of Japanese. We both felt that it was time to leave.

Appendix B: The Yamanaka–Hieidaira Sports Field-Day – the Programme

8.00   Gathering of the *undookai* management committee and related sub-committees

9:30   Opening ceremony
- General assembly
- Declaration of opening
- Greetings by the head of the sports field-day
- Introduction of guests
- Words of welcome by guests
- Safety and security arrangements
- Public exercises

10:00   Commencement of competitions

12:30   Lunch break
- Gateball exhibition
- Raffle for oil containers

13:00   Continuation of competitions

15:00   Closing ceremony
- General assembly
- Announcement of results
- Presentation of victory cups
- Concluding remarks by the head of the sports field-day
- Declaration of closing
- Exit of participants

Appendix C: The Competitions

No.	Competition	Contestants	Particulars
1	50-metre dash	Primary school boys and girls, grades 1,2,3	
2	Ball-dribbling race	Primary school boys and girls, grades 4,5,6	
3	Obstacle course	Middle- and high-school boys and girls	
4	Obstacle course	Men	
5	Grandma and Grandpa 'put up a good show'	Men and women over 60 years of age	
6	Inter-ward relay race	Primary school boys and girls	Grades 1 and 2, 50 metres; grade 3 and up, 100 metres
7	Gather round tiny tots	Infants and children	
8	Date with a card	General public	10 groups of men and women
9	Pull some candy by your teeth	Primary school boys and girls	
10	Inter-ward tug of war	Men	Each team 20 members
11	Inter-ward chuck-the-ball	Women	Each team 20 members
	LUNCH BREAK		
12	Exhibition drills	Youth sports teams	
13	Voluntary fire brigades relay race	Yamanaka and Hieidaira brigades	
14	Traditional dance	Women's groups	
15	Catch a fish	Primary school children, women, and over 60s	

No.	Competition	Contestants	Particulars
16	Gather round tiny tots	Infants and children	
17	Light a cigarette and run	Men	
18	100-metre dash	Middle and high school boys and men	
19	Inter-ward relay race – local organizations	Representatives from each organization	Neighbourhood association (head and 2 officials), women's group, PTA, sports committee, children's association
20	Funny runs and hops	Men and women	
21	Inter-ward relay race – by age groups	Middle school pupils and over	Men – middle-school, 19, 29, 39, and over 40 Women – middle-school, 19, 29, and over 30
22	Beautification		Everyone to pick up garbage from the grounds

Notes

Preface

1 In Otsu as in many other Japanese cities, administrative districts are based on and congruent with school districts. The terms are thus used interchangeably in this book.

1 Introduction: Approaches and Problems

1 Other scholars (cited in Johnson, 1963:218) use the term *shizen sonraku* (natural village) in much the same way.
2 Other factors that Fukutake cites were a uniform and levelling educational system, a national and unified mass media, and widely accepted middle-class aspirations and living standards.
3 The group model has also been formulated within a number of other conceptual schemes. These include for example cultural (Benedict, 1967; Maraini, 1975), interactional (Kumon, 1982), or psychological (Doi, 1973) approaches.
4 Allinson (1978:458) points to the underlying links between their theoretical assertions of community breakdown, and the personal experiences of anomie and isolation many Japanese intellectuals have undergone in the post-war period.
5 Later studies show how other groups have been pulled into participation. Thus for example McKean (1981:126–31) in a study of citizens' movements documents how different sets of activists were recruited into local movements and organizations, once they perceived the urgency of certain issues.
6 Similarly, Norbeck (1977:56) notes in relation to a suburban village that while interest in company-sponsored clubs and activities has grown, local associations in which men are active still persist.

7 Short historical overviews can be found in Norbeck (1962:74–5) and Yoneyama (1967a:234ff.).

8 An indicator of this quality is found in Rochon's (1983:356) comparative analysis of citizens' movements in Western Europe, Australia and Japan. He concludes that Japanese activists seem much more rooted in their communities, and tend to rely on local community organizations much more than their counterparts elsewhere.

9 Two examples of organizations that can be found almost anywhere in the country well illustrate the peculiar attributes of local organized groups in Japan. For both – neighbourhood associations and old-folks clubs – are territorially based, and have strong links to local government. A recent study of neighbourhood or self-government associations (Shin Seikatsu Undo Kyokai, 1982) noted that these organizations – which function as the lowest rung of city administrations – exist in almost every urban, rural or suburban region in the country. It further stated that their number – of 1980 – was 270,000 throughout Japan. Linhart (1981) observed that today about 50 per cent of all people aged sixty or over are affiliated with community-based old-folks clubs that number over 100,000 nationwide. These clubs – which carry out leisure activities as well as welfare work – were mostly set up through governmental encouragement and allocation of subsidies.

10 By 1980 (Asahi Shinbunsha, 1983:42), the primary sector accounted for only 11 per cent of the labour force, the secondary for 34.7 per cent, and the tertiary sector for a significant 54.3 per cent. Within the latter, the proportion of sales workers has increased from 1955 to 1980 by about half, while the proportion of professional and technical workers has more than doubled (Fukutake, 1982:108).

2 The Two Communities: An Ethnographic Profile

1 While Kyoto is the nation's fifth largest city in terms of population, Otsu is the ninetieth (Otsu-shi, 1982:290–1).

2 In Japan addresses are given not in terms of street numerals, but rather as ward, block and plot numbers. This necessitates the constant use of maps or the giving of very specific directions in order to get anywhere.

3 There is as yet no direct bus line between Yamanaka and Otsu proper.

4 The name of this district is written with different characters than

those used in Shiga Prefecture, and is based on Shiga village which lay to the north of the historical Otsu.

5   American policy dictated that because of the cultural and historical treasures found in the city, Kyoto would not be bombed.

6   The national average for 1981 was 3.24 (Japan Foundation, 1982), and for the city of Otsu it was 3.15 (Otsu-shi, 1982:12).

7   These conclusions are reinforced when data about school attendance is examined. Primary school children (aged 6–12) make up 11.4 per cent of Yamanaka's population, 11.8 per cent of the first ward, 14.7 per cent of the second ward, and 13.4 per cent of the third ward's populace.

8   An account of the methodology used by both Motoyama and myself is given in the appendix.

9   Although there are a number of controversies surrounding the precise definition of 'Kansai' (roughly the Kobe–Osaka–Kyoto region), in this context it is used to include the following prefectures: Hyogo, Osaka, Kyoto, Nara and Shiga.

10   In the city 67.5 per cent of dwellings are owned, 8.4 per cent rented from public housing authorities, and 24.4 per cent rented from private and company landlords (Otsu-shi, 1982:105). The national figures are respectively 61.3 per cent, 5.2 per cent and 33 per cent (Asahi Shinbunsha, 1983:106).

11   The most apparent discrepancy between the figures Motoyama and I give can be attributed to a slightly different type of categorization. That is, I added the categories of 'housewife' and 'pensioner' which together account for a similar proportion to Motoyama's 'no answer'.

12   Kirkpatrick (1975:238ff.) deals with the origins and political implications of the National Association of Consumer Co-operatives (*Seikyooren*).

13   The deputies also attend – as representatives of the local branch – meetings of the regional (*Kansai*) and national co-operative associations, and occasionally participate in these organizations' political struggles (for example against the use of certain chemicals in foodstuffs).

14   Motoyama (1982), using much more specific categories than the ones I used, found a similar trend towards the use of Kyoto's facilities.

15   This figure does not include, however, bars, cabarets and nightclubs. If these were included, Hieidaira would probably be ranked behind the entertainment districts in the centre of the city and in Ogoto.

16   Under the three-tiered Japanese system, primary schools encompass the first six years of education, middle schools the next three, and high schools the final three years.

17   Villagers often observed that it is exceptional to find so many temples in a relatively small settlement like Yamanaka. Although unclear

about it, a number of the older residents attributed the temples' existence to schisms that occurred within the Buddhist church in the sixteenth and seventeenth centuries.

3 Introduction

1 For example, reflecting this trend, university enrolment quadrupled between 1950 and 1975 (Tsurutani, 1977:172), and the share of the tertiary sector of the national total employed persons rose from 30 per cent in 1950, to 52 per cent in 1975 (Nagashima, 1981:289–92).
2 In common Japanese usage 'conservative' or 'conservative parties' (*hoshu seitoo*) refers to the Liberal-Democratic Party and its affiliated politicians and political groups. 'Progressive' or 'progressive parties' (*kakushin seitoo*) is used to denote the Japan Socialist Party, the Democratic–Socialist Party, and the Japanese Communist Party. I follow this usage.

4 Development of the Estate

1 In other contexts (Embree, 1939:24–6) the term *aza* is distinguished from the more common *buraku*: the former is used in a geographical while the latter in a social or political sense. In the case of Shiga Village these divisions seem to have been congruent and the terms used interchangeably. The six hamlets had more or less a permanent size of a little less than 100 households and comprised: Yamanaka, Minami Shiga, Shiga Sato, Nishikori, Yamagai and Sazanami.
2 Actually this is the newer name of the association. It was previously known as the Shiga Common Forest Association (*Shiga Kyooyuu Sanrin Kumiai*), and was set up in 1932 when the village was amalgamated into Otsu City. The reasons for its establishment seem to have been the quite real apprehensions of the villagers that such an amalgamation would open the way to an appropriation of their common land by government authorities. By organizing themselves in a legally recognized association, they hoped, such a possibility would be curtailed.
3 According to the criteria used by Kamachi (1971), this company would rate as one of the smaller of the large realtors. With a capital

base of 300 million Yen (Tonan Shoji Kabushiki Gaisha, 1973), it was far from being a small firm.

4   Bennett (1976:n.12), who studied a lumbering area in another part of Japan, noticed a similar process. There the post-war market pressures, need for cash, and an interest in profits led to excessive cutting of the forests. As he notes, traditional values, such as 'reverence for forests as the home of important spirits and aesthetic values . . . alone does not tell very much about what people are likely to do with natural resources.'

5   Overviews of the structure and operation of Japanese local government can be found in Shindo (1982), and Ministry of Home Affairs (1982). In very general terms government in Japan is divided into three tiers. The bottom tier (cities, towns and villagers) and the intermediate one (prefectures) are usually referred to as local government. The topmost tier is made up of the national government ministries and affiliated organizations.

6   Allinson (1979:150–1) contrasts the differing reasons for moving to suburbia in America and in Japan. In the United States among the prime considerations were anxieties about crime, race relations and educational opportunities in the inner cities, and the pull towards the image of a leisured life-style of the suburbs. the Japanese suburbanite by contrast chose his abode on the basis of more practical considerations like the proximity to jobs or the price and availability of land.

7   The difficulty of uncovering the occurrence and scope of corruption in the building industry has also been noted in regard to Britain (Pinto-Duschinsky, 1977; Drewry, 1977). I was helped in my case by the facts that the affair at the time of fieldwork was already fifteen years old, and that the main participants were dead or dying.

8   As will become evident further on, although the Hieidaira affair was never investigated formally, it was linked directly to the general situation in Shiga politics. The published material cited in the text therefore relates to the general situation and not to the specific affair of Hieidaira.

5   The Rise of Citizen Activism

1   Although I have no precise statistical data about their total number, I was told of four or five families who did manage to leave Hieidaira during this period.

2   McKean (1981:7–8), basing her calculations on a survey done by the

Asahi newspaper in May 1973, states that a conservative estimate would put the number of citizens' movements that had arisen throughout the country by 1973 at 3,000; the number of core activists between 60,000 and 135,000 people; and the number of more peripheral rank-and-file members at 6 million (or about 5 per cent of the nation's total population).

3 Accounts of this successful movement were published in contemporary editions of both the regional (*Kyoto Shinbun*, 20 June 1973) and national newspapers (*Asahi Shinbun*, 7 June 1973).

4 The prime source for the information given here are two very lengthy interviews held with the young university lecturer who was a prominent member of the ad-hoc study group. The benefit of hindsight contributed no doubt to the systematic and rather academic-sounding way that the dilemmas of organization were presented to me. Interviews with three other members of this group, as well as material written at a time closer to the events (Watanabe, 1977), show that these were problems that the locals discussed and thought about.

5 Although I gathered very little data on this point, two elements would seem to have worked against the integration of the estate's residents into a city or prefectural politician's personal support network (*kooenkai*). For both the mobility and diversity of the Hieidairaites, and the post-war tendency to build *kooenkai* on the basis of functional rather than territorial organizations (Allinson, 1979) would have made an effort at such political recruitment in the estate likely to fail.

6 An historical account of these associations is given in Nakagawa (1980) and Braibanti (1947). Nakamura (1982) presents a dissenting opinion: he sees no historical continuity between the forms of the Tokugawa period and modern associations. Curtis (1971:111ff.) gives a very detailed account of the role of *choonaikai* of old urban neighbourhoods in the personal support network of a Liberal-Democratic Diet member.

7 Opposition to the revival of the neighbourhood associations was not limited only to academics or social critics. Allinson (1979:114) gives an account of the efforts of well educated white-collar suburbanites in the Tokyo area to dissuade city officials from resurrecting these local organizations which they found to be 'troublesome intrusions on their private lives'.

8 Although I have no information with regard to the change of names these associations underwent in Otsu, Allinson's (1979:114) remarks about a similar change in Fuchu city are illuminating. He states that city officials were sensitive to the complaints that *choonaikai* (lit. ward associations) were 'odious' artifacts of the war period and that they urged all local associations to abandon this term in the early

1960s in favour of the word *jichikai* (lit. self-government association) with its more modern and democratic connotations.

9 According to a later official of the neighbourhood association between 90 and 95 per cent of the households in the estate (excluding summer homes) belonged to the *jichikai*. Present-day estimates put the figure for the *whole city* at 84.2 per cent (Otsu-shi, 1982:61).

10 Since 1973 the *jichikai* has added many more functions and committees to this basic structure. These include a fire brigade, voluntary welfare workers, a social welfare council, a group helping run public elections (city, prefectural and national) and an anti-delinquency group.

11 I was rather fortunate with regard to the varied sources of data for this section. These were interviews with three of the neighbourhood association's officers, two City Office officials who participated in the first contacts with Hieidaira, and two officials from Tonan Shoji (one of whom has left the company and felt freer to speak); the documentation relating to the estate which is on file in the municipality; and *jichikai* reports about the association's activity which were lent to me by a local resident.

12 On the prefectural level such concrete administrative reforms as the opening of new citizens' affairs bureaux and departments were accompanied by a strong stress on 'an age of localism' (*chihoo no jidai*) (*Shiga Janqaru*, 1982:2), and the encouragement of government-sponsored citizens' movements for the prevention of pollution. Later (Ikemi, 1982:224; Watanabe, n.d.), as a consequence of the intense activity by citizens' groups, this prefectural administration achieved national notoriety when it drafted strict ordinances banning the use of certain detergents polluting Lake Biwa.

6 Concluding Considerations

1 Allinson (1979:14) also notes in passing how the image attached to a suburb he studied (Musashino) – that of an expensive upper-class area – also oversimplified its social complexity.

2 Although this is probably the most important way, such familiarity need not be achieved only through direct participation. Vicarious experiences of organized action may contribute greatly to what sociologists call anticipatory socialization to an organizational role.

3 It may well be that because citizens' groups in Japan posed rather limited demands, it was relatively easy for government to meet them. Much easier, that is, than meeting the more general aims of the

European movements: disarmament, women's rights, nuclear energy, or regional autonomy (Rochon, 1983:358).
4 Similarly it is easy to overestimate the importance or impact of citizens' movements. No less important is the economic and political context within which such organizations act.
5 Ironically, the current revenue crisis in local government is blamed by the ruling conservatives on overspending by local progressives during the 1970s.

7 Introduction

1 It seems that Japan is not unique in this respect. As Walker (1982a:6) notes in regard to Britain, the 'current concern about community care and dependency is almost exclusively a concern about dependency in old age and about care of the elderly.'

8 Community Care: Policies and Administration

1 In this section I rely heavily on the discussions found in Campbell (1979), Ernst (1982), and Koseisho (1982). Overviews of the prewar system of social welfare can be found in Taira (1967), and Linhart (1983).
2 This is not to deny that substantial problems still remain. For example, the health and pension schemes are actually made up of a number of independent systems varying according to local government authority, economic sector, size of firm, and type of employment. The basic heterogeneities and inequalities found in these schemes have persisted till today (Ernst, 1982:555). At one end of the scale are the elite employees of the large firms and institutions which are relatively well protected. At the other are millions of women, temporary workers and employees of small firms with much less protection.
3 This stands in contrast to the successful professionalization in Japan of the other semi-profession – teaching (Cummings, 1980:54ff.).
4 It is hard to overstress the contrast between Japan and the United States and Britain in this respect. In these latter two countries the fields of social welfare policy, running of institutions and the

301

initiation of schemes and programmes are dominated by professional social workers. These people are trained in special schools of social work; organized into powerful institutions and societies; issue their own specialist journals and publications; and (although there are a number of approaches propagated) share a basic orientation towards their own role, the agencies they serve, and the clients they deal with.

5   The aim of this rotation, according to the testimony of local bureaucrats, is twofold: to widen the officials' knowledge about the variety of City Office affairs, and to broaden their orientation from one limited to a specific department to one directed at the whole municipality. One can add, however, that this system may also ensure that the personnel of the City Office are rendered more manipulable to those directing them, but also less liable to corrupt practices.

6   See Townsend (1975: chaps 13–15) for examples of the extreme variation in social welfare programmes found in English and Welsh local councils.

7   These differences should not be overstressed. For, as Maeda (1978:57) notes, about one-half of those living separately from their children in Western countries live geographically very close to them. It seems that Westerners prefer what Sussman (1976:222) calls 'intimacy at a distance'.

8   Most Japanese women seem to enter the labour force in their thirties after the childrearing stage is finished. They do so for a number of reasons: increasing household income, increasing personal disposable income, involvement with work, or the search for meaning through participation in activities outside the family (Takenaga, 1983:56–62).

9   In Britain, by contrast, the emergence of community care policies was much more the outcome of professional critiques of institutionalization (lack of freedom, disconnection with kith and kin) and a backlash against the lack of citizen participation in determining social policy (Townsend, 1975:218ff.).

10   In a similar vein a ministry official states that, 'the family is the basic venue of human life, and it is desirable for the aged to live in their own home and in their native neighbourhood aided and comforted by their own loved ones and compassionate neighbours.' (Ministry of Health and Welfare, 1982:18).

9   The Voluntary Welfare Workers

1   The official translation of the term *minsei-iin* is 'welfare com-
    missioner'. Commissioner, however, with its implications of power
    and authority, is a term more apt for the *minsei-iin* of the pre-war
    and immediate post-war periods. As will become evident from the
    text, the scope of *minsei-iin* power has since that period become
    much more limited. It seems preferable, then, to follow Smith
    (1978:70), and give them a politically more neutral name like public
    welfare workers, or voluntary welfare workers.
2   The *minsei-iin* also serves concurrently as a *Jidoo-in*, a voluntary
    child welfare worker under the Child Welfare Law. This responsi-
    bility is to enable him or her to have a knowledge of the living and
    environmental conditions of children as well as expectant mothers
    in the district. In this capacity *minsei-iin* are expected to co-operate
    with Child Guidance Centres, health centres, and welfare offices
    (Ministry of Health and Welfare, 1974:34).
3   This was a general trend among the Buddhist churches in the post-
    war period. Following Christian establishments, they too began to
    initiate such welfare-related activities as creches, hostels, orphanages
    or convalescence homes (Dore, 1958:346).
4   Not to be confused with the regular national pensions (*Kokumin
    nenkin*).
5   For lack of space, I cannot go into an examination of the fascinating
    concepts of health in Japanese culture. An especially interesting
    treatment of apprehensions about deterioration in health and death
    among old women is found in Woss (1982).
6   Taira (1967:99–101) traces the beginnings of the political role of
    minsei-iin to the 1930s. During that period they emerged as a major
    force that was partially successful in getting the pre-war government
    to institute a number of welfare assistance programmes.
7   The management of the welfare departments – like that of all
    bureaucracies – is marked by a prevalence of rules and regulations.
    Officials are thus bound by prefectural and central government laws,
    city ordinances and standing rules, and a host of more specific intra-
    divisional and intra-departmental instructions and directives.

10 The Old-Folks Clubs

1 As Wagatsuma (1977) so astutely notes, it is not at all clear to what degree pre-war patterns were consistent with this model. What is significant, however, is that this model, and the construction of the past it entails, is what is compared with present circumstances.

2 *Karaoke* (lit. empty orchestra) first became commercially available around 1976. It developed first in Japanese bars and pubs as a means by which to encourage customers to sing. Essentially it consists of singing to a background of pre-recorded music while the singer adds the vocals. This is done through an electronic echo chamber, so that it is very difficult to distinguish the quality of the singing. *Karaoke* is now popular on such diverse occasions as home gatherings, television programmes (where 'stars' and sumo wrestlers compete), post-wedding banquets, taxis and public tournaments.

3 These associations seem to have existed in varying degrees all over rural Japan, and had names like *toshiyorigumi*, *roojingumi* or *inkyogumi* (Linhart, 1981:3).

4 In 1981 workers aged sixty-five and over accounted for 28 per cent of the workforce. The comparable figures for the US and UK are 12.6 per cent and 11.3 per cent respectively (Prime Minister's Office, 1981:6).

5 This seems to be a marked change from the situation in 'Village Japan' (Beardsley *et al.*, 1959:63–4) in which older people 'reach out gladly and thankfully to old age' rather than fear it.

6 This pattern of ageing underlines the realization that there are multiple pathways towards a successful adaptation in later life. Although not common, this disengaged life-style as it is called (Maddox and Wiley, 1976:15) seems to be a continuation from adulthood rather than a product of later life.

7 The case of Hieidaira seems in this respect to be typical of many old-folks clubs throughout the country. A number of authors (Campbell, 1979; Palmore, 1975:139; Maeda, 1978:65) have noted that the local political activity of *roojinkai* finds its parallels on prefectural and national levels as well. Linhart (1981:14), for example, argues that the high level of organization of the old-folks clubs has facilitated mounting large demonstrations and other forms of political pressure on the central government in Tokyo.

8 Maddox and Wiley (1976:39) remark that the emergence of the elderly as a 'leisure class' is a phenomenon found throughout all post-industrial societies.

9 Again this kind of emphasis is not limited to the city of Otsu alone. The aim of creating social networks that can be mobilized for every-

day needs as well as in times of crisis is one that is promoted by such organizations as the National Social Welfare Council (Kitani, 1981:283–9).

11 Concluding Considerations

1 These calls for more volunteers are echoed on a national level as well. See for example the statements of a Ministry of Home Affairs official cited in Isomura and Sakata (1981:65).
2 In essence I am arguing that the *minsei-iin* and *roojinkai* provide, from the city's point of view, some of the positive functions of what Landau (1969) calls organizational overlap and redundancy.
3 In the rather abstract terms of organizational theory, I am saying that the old-folks clubs are 'loosely-coupled' (Weick, 1976; Aldrich, 1979:76–84).
4 This example well echoes Glennerster's (1983:7) conclusions about the growing role of volunteer groups in the modern welfare state: 'the more widespread lay involvement and voluntary action there is, the more knowledge there tends to be about the needs of dependent groups, and . . . the *more* demand for services there is' (emphasis in original).
5 By the same token these community-based welfare organizations are least successful in innovating new treatment or therapeutic methods. But according to one social worker working in the city of Kyoto the lack of such innovations is a general weakness of the social welfare field in Japan, and not just of community groups.

13 Preparations and Expectations

1 While the school ranks only in 21st place in terms of the number of pupils, the grounds are the 8th largest in the city (Otsu-shi Kyoiku Iinkai, 1982:40).
2 Like sports committees all over the city (Otsu-shi, 1982:172), the district's association also receives a yearly subsidy of 300 Yen for each household belonging to the neighbourhood associations.
3 The food stands at the *undookai* represent only a small part of the entrepreneurial activities of these people. The greatest source of

income for the youth sports team is the money received once every three months when this organization mounts a collection of old newspapers and paper products which are sold to an Otsu recycling plant.

15 Concluding Considerations

1   Colson (1977:193) makes much the same point in relation to the guests invited to an old-age day centre she studied. She notes that even 'though only a few guests are present at any one time, it appears to be important that some outsiders be present to underline the common identification of Center members.'

2   The choice of the sports field-day as the forum for the 'introduction' of the youth sports teams and gate-ball activities reinforces this point. For at the base of this introduction is the assumption that the *undookai* constitutes *the* occasion on which the communities are assembled publicly and can be appealed to as some kind of united entity.

3   This is not to deny a point which Metheny (1970) makes in relation to women but which can be extended to other groups such as the elderly. Essentially this is related to the way women are constantly encouraged to participate while at the same time being subjected to a number of assumptions about the suitability of certain events for them. Examples are the general exclusion of women from the tug-of-war and light-a-cigarette contests and the barring of married women from running the obstacle course.

4   The fact that no finals were held between those people who came in the first places in different heats – i.e. there was no case of someone being the best in the whole district – is a variation on the same theme.

5   Turner (1977:40) brings out the potential of such situations when he talks of the way 'parts of liminality may be given over to experimental behavior. I mean here by "experiment", any action or process undertaken to discover something not yet known, not scientific experimentation. . . . In liminality, new ways of acting, new combinations of symbols are tried out, to be discarded or accepted.'

6   Such cases may not be all that new. The juxtaposition of strangers, their levelling down to an equal status, and the creation of sentiments of unity and communities can be found in such historical practices as the Shikoku pilgrimage.

7   All of this amplifies Moeran's (1984a:84) point about the relationship

between drinking 'occasions' and everyday reality. He rightly stresses that the usual Japanese assertion that 'all things said and done during drinking bouts are forgotten afterwards' must be rejected. Rather, as he continues to note, it is precisely because people remember what is said and done during such situations – that is they are changed by the experience – that upon a return to everyday life they make use of what they have learned.

8   Linhart (1975:205) observes in this regard that,

> Sunday is usually the only day the *sarariiman* (salaried worker), be it blue or white collar spends in the company of his family; and the activities of men on Sunday are commonly called *katei saabisu* (family service). . . . Spending the Sunday with one's children (naturally including the company of the wife) has become almost a norm for many Japanese men. This children-centred leisure on Sunday might consist of a visit to a department store, where lunch is taken and the children are allowed to play in the toy department, or an excursion to a children's play land, or simply playing catch-ball on a nearby open ground.

16 Conclusions

1   The group model is closely related and at times strongly structured by the academic and popular Japanese view of their culture and society as unique. This is most evident in the vast literature on what can be termed as Japanism (*Nihonron*) or Japaneseism (*Nihonjin-ron*). For lack of space I cannot go into these issues, but short reviews of the 'sociology of Japanology' are found in Smith (1983:110ff.) and in Sugimoto and Mouer (1980).

2   It is interesting to see both the development of the 'my-homism' phenomenon (Tada, 1978) and Dore's (1967:17) earlier comments in this light:

> Quite clearly there has been a change toward greater individu-ation. Sometimes the change can be concealed in the persistence of traditional behavioral forms. Marriages may continue to be arranged, but the arrangers are less concerned that 'the house of Tanaka' should receive a worthy future mistress than that their Taro should get a girl who will look after him and make him happy.

References

Abrams, P. *et al.* (1981), *Action for Care: A Review of Good Neighbour Schemes in England*, The Volunteer Centre, Berkhamstead.

Akamatsu, T. and S. Yamamoto (compilers) (1971), *Kyoto-Fu no Rekishi* (A History of Kyoto Prefecture), Yamakawa Publishers, Tokyo.

Aldrich, H.E. (1979), *Organizations and Environments*, Prentice-Hall, Englewood Cliffs, NJ.

Allinson, G.D. (1978), 'Japanese cities in the industrial era', *Journal of Urban History*, 4(4), 443–76.

Allinson, G.D. (1979), *Suburban Tokyo: A Comparative Study in Politics and Social Change*, University of California Press, Berkeley.

Allinson, G.D. (1980), 'Opposition in the suburbs', in K. Steiner *et al.* (eds), *Political Opposition and Local Politics in Japan*, Princeton at the University Press, 95–130.

Ames, W.L. (1981), *Police and Community in Japan*, University of California Press, Berkeley.

Anderson, R.T. (1971), 'Voluntary associations in history', *American Anthropologist*, 73, 209–22.

Asahi Shinbun (1977), *Gendai no Kao: Kokoku no Hyakunin* (Today's Faces – A Hundred People from Shiga), Asahi Shinbun, Kyoto.

Asahi Shinbunsha (ed.) (1983), *83 Minryoku* (National Manpower 83), Asahi Shinbun, Tokyo.

Atsumi, R. (1979), '*Tsukiai* – Obligatory personal relationships of Japanese white-collar company employees', *Human Organization*, 38(1), 63–70.

Azarya, V. (1984), *The Armenian Quarter of Jerusalem: Urban Life Behind Monastery Walls,* University of California Press, Berkeley.

Banton, M. (1957), *West African City: A Study of Tribal Life in Freetown*, Oxford University Press, London.

Barry, B. (1974), Review article: 'Exit, Voice, and Loyalty', *British Journal of Political Science*, 4, 79–107.

Bateson, G. (1972), *Steps to an Ecology of Mind*, Chandler, San Francisco.

Bayley, D.H. (1976), *Forces of Order: Police Behavior in Japan and the United States*, University of California Press, Berkeley.

Beardsley, R.K. *et al.* (1959), *Village Japan*, Chicago at the University Press.

Beattie, W.M. Jr (1976), 'Aging and the social services', in R.H. Binstock *et al.* (eds), *Handbook of Aging and the Social Sciences*, Van Nostrand, New York, 619–42.

Bedford, Y.N. (1980), 'The grass-roots modernization in a Japanese village', *GeoJournal*, 4(3), 259–66.

Befu, H. (1974a), 'Power in exchange: Strategy of control and patterns of compliance in Japan', *Asian Profile*, 2(6), 601–22.

Befu, H. (1974b), 'Gift-giving in a modernizing Japan', in T.S. and W.P. Lebra (eds), *Japanese Culture and Behavior*, University of Hawaii Press, Honolulu, 208–21.

Befu, H. (1980), 'A critique of the group model of Japanese society', *Social Analysis*, 5/6, 29–43.

Benedict, R. (1967), *The Chrysanthemum and the Sword: Patterns of Japanese Culture*, Routledge & Kegan Paul, London.

Benjamin, R. and K. Ori (1981), *Tradition and Change in Postindustrial Japan: The Role of Political Parties*, Praeger, New York.

Bennett, J.W. (1976), *The Ecological Transition*, Pergamon, New York.

Bennett, J.W. and S.B. Levine (1976), 'Industrialization and social deprivation: Welfare, environment, and the postindustrial society in Japan', in H. Patrick (ed.), *Japanese Industrialization and its Social Consequences*, University of California Press, Berkeley, 439–92.

Berger, P.L., B. Berger, and H. Kellner (1973), *The Homeless Mind: Modernization and Consciousness*, Penguin, Harmondsworth.

Berry, B.J.L. (1973), *The Human Consequences of Urbanization*, Macmillan, London.

Birch, A.H. (1975) 'Economic models in political science: the case of "Exit, Voice, and Loyalty" ', *British Journal of Political Science*, 5, 69–82.

Birrell, S. (1981), 'Sport as ritual: Interpretations from Durkheim to Goffman', *Social Forces*, 60(2), 354–76.

Boissevain, J. (1968), 'The place of non-groups in the social sciences', *Man*, 3, 542–56.

Braibanti, R.J.D. (1947), 'Neighborhood associations in Japan and their democratic potentialities', *Far Eastern Quarterly*, 7, 136–64.

Bring, M. (1978), 'Trains and townscape in the Kyoto corridor', *Architectural Association Quarterly*, 10(4), 16–19.

Brown, K. (1979), Introduction, to his (trans.) *Shingo: The Chronicle of a Japanese Village*, University Center for International Studies, Ethnology Monographs No. 2, University of Pittsburgh.

Burks, A.W. (1981), *Japan: Profile of a Postindustrial Power*, Westview, Boulder, Colorado.

Burks, A. W. (1984), 'Postindustrial Japan: A comparison with Korea and Taiwan', *American Asian Review*, 2(3), 1–15.

Campbell, J.C. (1979), 'The old people boom and Japanese policy making', *Journal of Japanese Studies*, 5(2), 321–57.

Castells, M. (1977), *The Urban Question: A Marxist Approach*, MIT Press, Cambridge, Massachusetts.

Cheek, N.H. Jr and W. R. Burch Jr (1976), *The Social Organization of Leisure in Modern Society*, Harper & Row, New York.

Clark, R. (1979), *The Japanese Company*, Yale University Press, New Haven.

Cohen, A.P. (1982), 'Belonging: The experience of culture', in his (ed.) *Belonging: Identity and Social Organization in British Rural Cultures*, Manchester at the University Press, 1–17.

Cole, R.E. (1979), *Work, Mobility and Participation: A Comparative Study of American and Japanese Industry*, University of California Press, Berkeley.

Colson, E. (1977), 'The least common denominator', in S.F. Moore and B.G. Myerhoff (eds), *Secular Ritual*, Van Gorcum, Assen, 189–98.

Cornell, J.B. (1967), 'Individual mobility and group membership: the case of the *Burakumin*', in R.P. Dore (ed.), *Aspects of Social Change in Modern Japan*, Princeton at the University Press, 337–72.

Cornell, J.B. (1981), 'Urbanization in Japan today: An anthropologist's view', *Nucleus*, 34(1), 16–31.

Cummings, W.K. (1980), *Education and Equality in Japan*, Princeton at the University Press.

Curtis, G.L. (1971), *Election Campaigning Japanese Style*, Columbia University Press, New York.

Dale, P.N. (1986), *The Myth of Japanese Uniqueness*, Croom Helm, London.

De Vos, G. and K. Mizushima (1967), 'Organization and social function of Japanese gangs: Historical development and modern parallels', in R.P. Dore (ed.), *Aspects of Social Change in Modern Japan*, Princeton at the University Press, 289–325.

De Vos, G. and H. Wagatsuma (1966), *Japan's Invisible Race*, University of California Press, Berkeley.

Doi, T. (1973), *The Anatomy of Dependence*, Kodansha, Tokyo.

Dore, R. (1958), *City Life in Japan: A Study of a Tokyo Ward*, Routledge & Kegan Paul, London.

Dore, R. (1959), *Land Reform in Japan*, Oxford at the University Press.

Dore, R. (1967), Introduction to his (ed.), *Aspects of Social Change in Modern Japan*, Princeton at the University Press, 3–24.

Dore, R. (1973), *British Factory, Japanese Factory*, University of California Press, Berkeley.

Dore, R. (1978), *Shinohata: A Portrait of a Japanese Village*, Allen Lane, London.

Dore, R. (1982), Foreword to T. Fukutake, *The Japanese Social Structure*, Tokyo at the University Press, ix–xiv.

Downs, A. (1979), 'Key relationships between urban development and neighborhood change, *Journal of the American Planning Association*, 45(4), 462–72.

Drewry, G. (1977), 'Corruption: The Salmon report', *Political Quarterly*, 48, 87–91.

Dumont, L. (1982), 'A modified view of our origins: The Christian beginnings of modern individualism', *Religion*, 12, 1–27.

Dunleavy, P. (1980), *Urban Political Analysis*, Sage, Beverly Hills.

Economic Planning Agency (1972), *The Japanese and their Society*, Tokyo.

Eisenstadt, S.N. (1973), *Tradition, Change and Modernity*, J. Wiley, New York.

Embree, J.F. (1939), *Suye Mura: A Japanese Village*, Chicago at the University Press.

Ernst, A. (1982), 'A segmented welfare state: The Japanese approach', *Journal of Institutional and Theoretical Economics*, 138, 545–61.

Falconeri, G.R. (1976), 'The impact of rapid urban change on neighborhood solidarity: A case study of a Japanese neighborhood association', in J.W. White and E. Munger (eds), *Social Change and Community Politics in Urban Japan*, The Institute for Social Research, University of North Carolina, Chapel Hill, 31–59.

Fischer, C.S. (1976), *The Urban Experience*, Harcourt Brace, New York.

Flanagan, S.C. *et al.* (1980), 'The partisan politicization of local government: Causes and consequences, in K. Steiner *et al.* (eds), *Political Opposition and Local Politics in Japan*, Princeton at the University Press, 427–69.

Frankenberg, R. (1965), *Communities in Britain: Social Life in Town and Country*, Penguin, Harmondsworth.

Fukutake, T. (1982), *The Japanese Social Structure: Its Evolution in the Modern Century*, Tokyo at the University Press.

Gans, H.J. (1972), *People and Plans: Essays on Urban Problems and Solutions*, Penguin, Harmondsworth.

Garrick, R.J. (1981), 'The problems of the aged', *Center News* (Japan Studies Center – The Japan Foundation), 6(5), 6–7.

Glennerster, H. (1983), 'Reappraisal', in his (ed.), *The Future of the Welfare State: Remaking Social Policy*, Heinemann, London, 1–9.

Glickman, N.J. (1979), *The Growth and Management of the Japanese Urban System*, Academic Press, New York.

311

Graburn, N. (1983), 'To pray, pay and play: The cultural structure of Japanese domestic tourism', *Centre des Hautes Etudes Touristiques*, Série B, No. 26.

Greer, S. (1972), *The Urbane View*, Oxford University Press, London.

Guest, A.M. (1984), 'Robert Park and the natural area: A sentimental review', *Sociology and Social Research*, 69(1), 1–21.

Handelman, D. (1977), 'Play and ritual: Complementary frames of meta-communication', in A.J. Chapman and H. Foot (eds), *It's a Funny Thing, Humour*, Pergamon, London, 185–92.

Handelman, D. (n.d.), 'Presenting, re-presenting, and modelling the world: Toward the study of public events and media events', mimeo, The Hebrew University of Jerusalem.

Hendry, J. (1981), *Marriage in Changing Japan: Community and Society*, Croom Helm, London.

Hendry, J. (1986), *Becoming Japanese: The World of the Pre-School Child*, Manchester at the University Press.

Hill, M. (1980), *Understanding Social Policy*, Blackwell, Oxford.

Hirschman, A.O. (1970), *Exit, Voice, and Loyalty: Responses to Decline in Firms Organizations and States*, Harvard University Press, Cambridge, Mass.

Hirschmeier, J. (1973), Preface, in M. Murakami and J. Hirschmeier (eds), *Politics and Economics in Contemporary Japan*, Kodansha, Tokyo, vii–x.

Hudson, R.B. and R.H. Binstock (1976), 'Political systems and aging', in R.H. Binstock *et al.* (eds), *Handbook of Aging and the Social Sciences*, Van Nostrand, New York, 369–400.

Hunter, A. (1978), 'Persistence of local sentiments in mass society', in D. Street *et al.* (eds), *Handbook of Contemporary Urban Life*, Jossey-Bass, San Francisco, 133–62.

Ikemi, T. (1982), *Mizu Senso – Biwako Gendaishi* (Water Wars – A Modern History of Lake Biwa), Ryokoku Shupan, Tokyo.

Inoue, T. (1972), 'Gozenmochi', in S. Tsuboi (ed.), *Kaisetsu 20 Shunen Kinen*, Bukkyo Daigaku, Kyoto.

Irokawa, D. (1978), 'The survival struggle of the Japanese community', in J.V. Koschmann (ed.), *Authority and the Individual in Japan*, Tokyo at the University Press, 250–82.

Ishida, T. (1986), 'The introduction of Western political concepts into Japan', *Nissan Occasional Paper Series*, 2.

Isomura, E. and M. Okuda (1966), 'Recent trends of urban sociology in Japan', *Sociological Review Monograph*, No. 10, 127–50.

Isomura, E. and K. Sakata (eds) (1981), *Asu no Toshi – Toshi to Fukushi* (Tomorrow's Cities – Cities and Welfare), Chuo Hoki Shuppan, Tokyo.

Ito, T. and C. Nagashima (1980), 'Tokaido – megalopolis of Japan', *GeoJournal*, 4(3), 231–46.

References

Ito, T. *et al.* (compilers) (1979), *Jinko Ryudo no Chiiki Kozo* (The Regional Composition of Population Flows), Taimeido, Tokyo.

Iwanami, I. (1980), 'Toshi zaisei no genjo to kadai' (Issues in the state of city finances), *Toshi Mondai Kenkyu*, 33(9), 2–14.

Janowitz, M. (1967), *The Community Press in an Urban Setting*, Chicago at the University Press.

Janowitz, M. and D. Street (1978), 'Changing social order of the metropolitan area', in D. Street *et al.* (eds), *Handbook of Contemporary Urban Life*, Jossey-Bass, San Francisco, 90–128.

Japan Foundation (1982), 'Results of polls and surveys', *Japan Foundation Newsletter*, 10(4).

Japan Foundation (1983), 'Results of polls and surveys', *Japan Foundation Newsletter*, 11(2).

Johnson, E. (1963), 'Perseverance through orderly change: The "traditional" *buraku* in a modern community', *Human Organization*, 22(3), 218–23.

Johnson, E. (1976), *Nagura Mura: An Ethnohistorical Analysis*, Cornell East Asia Papers, Ithaca.

Kamachi, N. (1971), 'Minkan deberopaa no jitai to Kozo' (The character and reality of private developers), *Juristo*, 476, 75–85.

Kansai Gorfujo Gaido Mappu (1982), *Kansai Gorufojo* (Golf Courses of the Kansai), Kokusai Chigaku Kyokai.

Kapferer, B. (1976), 'Introduction: Transactional models reconsidered', in his (ed.), *Transaction and Meaning: Directions in the Anthropology of Exchange and Symbolic Behavior*, ISHI, Philadelphia, 1–22.

Katagiri, A. (1981), 'Toshi zaisei no kadai' (Problems of city finance), *Toshi Mondai Kenkyu*, 33(9), 44–53.

Kelly, W.W. (1986), 'Rationalization and nostalgia: Cultural dynamics of new middle-class Japan', *American Ethnologist*, 13(4), 603–18.

Kiefer, C.W. (1970), 'The psychological interdependence of family, school, and bureaucracy in Japan', *American Anthropologist*, 72, 66–75.

Kiefer, C.W. (1976a), 'The *danchi zoku* and the evolution of metropolitan mind', in L.A. Austin (ed.), *Japan: The Paradox of Progress*, Yale University Press, New Haven, 279–300.

Kiefer, C.W. (1976b), 'Leadership, sociability, and social change in a white collar *danchi*', in J.W. White and F. Munger (eds), *Social Change and Community Politics in Urban Japan*, The Institute for Social Research, University of North Carolina, Chapel Hill, 15–30.

Kirkpatrick, M.A. (1975), 'Consumerism and Japan's new citizen politics', *Asian Survey*, 15(3), 234–46.

Kitani, Y. (1981), 'Chiiki fukushi to borantia katsudo' (Community welfare and volunteer activities), in E. Isomura and K. Sakata (eds), *Asu no Toshi – Toshi to Fukushi*, Chuo Hoki Shuppan, Tokyo, 277–93.

313

Kitazawa, Y. (1986), 'An aging society: Who will bear the burden?', *Ampo* (Japan–Asia Quarterly Review), 18(2), 55–64.

Koschmann, J.V. (1978), 'Introduction: Soft rule and expressive protest', in his (ed.) *Authority and the Individual in Japan*, Tokyo at the University Press, 1–30, 144–51.

Koseisho, (1982), *Kosei Hakusho* (Welfare White Paper), Tokyo.

Koshiro, K. (1979), 'Japan's labor unions: the meeting of the white and blue collar', in M. Hyoe and J. Hirschmeier (eds), *Politics and Economics in Contemporary Japan*, Kodansha, Tokyo, 143–56.

Krauss, E.S. and B.L. Simcock (1980), 'Citizens' movements: The growth and impact of environmental protest in Japan', in K. Steiner *et al.* (eds), *Political Opposition and Local Politics in Japan*, Princeton at the University Press, 187–227.

Kumar, K. (1978), *Prophecy and Progress: The Sociology of Industrial and Post-Industrial Society*, Penguin, Harmondsworth.

Kumon, S. (1982), 'Some principles governing the thought and behavior of Japanists (contextualists)', *Journal of Japanese Studies*, 8(1), 5–29.

Kusaka, K. (1985), 'What is the Japanese Middle Class?' *Japan Echo*, 12(3), 40–6.

Lakoff, S.A. (1976), 'The future of social intervention', in R.H. Binstock *et al.* (eds), *Handbook of Aging and the Social Sciences*, Van Nostrand, New York, 643–67.

Landau, M. (1969), 'Redundancy, rationality, and the problem of duplication and overlap', *Public Administration Review*, 29, 346–58.

Lauritsen, H. (1982), 'Washimi: A Japanese Mountain Village', mimeo, Kyoto University.

Laver, M. (1976), ' "Exit, Voice, and Loyalty" revisited: The strategic production and consumption of public and private goods', *British Journal of Political Science*, 6, 463–82.

Lawrence, D. (1982), 'Parades, politics, and competing urban images: Doo Dah and Roses', *Urban Anthropology*, 11(2), 155–76.

Lebra, T. S. (1976), *Japanese Patterns of Behavior*, University of Hawaii Press, Honolulu.

Lebra, T.S. (1979), 'The dilemma and strategies of aging among contemporary Japanese women', *Ethnology*, 18, 337–53.

Leonard, P. (1973), 'Professionalization, community action and the growth of social service bureaucracies', in P. Halmos (ed.), *Professionalization and Social Change*, Sociological Review Monograph No. 20.

Linhart, S. (1975), 'The use and meaning of leisure in present-day Japan', in W.G. Beasley (ed.), *Modern Japan*, G. Allen, London, 198–208.

Linhart, S. (1981), 'The search for meaning in old age: The Japanese case', Paper presented at the XIIth International Congress of Gerontology, Hamburg, July.

Linhart, S. (1983), 'Social security versus family ideology: The state's reaction to the consequences of early industrialization in Japan', *Rivista Internazionale di Scienze Economiche e Commerciali*, 30(8), 703–15.

Lipsky, M. (1968), 'Protest as a political resource', *American Political Science Review*, 62, 1144–58.

Lipsky, M. and M. Levi (1972), 'Community organization as a political resource', in H. Hahn (ed.), *People and Politics in Urban Society*, vol. 6, Urban Affairs Annual Reviews, 175–201.

Lock, M.M. (1984), 'East Asian medicine and health care for the Japanese elderly', *Pacific Affairs*, 57(1), 65–80.

Lowenthal, M.F. and B. Robinson (1976), 'Social networks and isolation', in R.H. Binstock *et al.* (eds), *Handbook of Aging and the Social Sciences*, Van Nostrand, New York, 432–56.

McCarthy, J.D. and M.N. Zald (1977), 'Resource mobilization and social movements: A partial theory', *American Journal of Sociology*, 82(6), 1212–41.

McKean, M.A. (1981), *Environmental Protest and Citizen Politics in Japan*, University of California Press, Berkeley.

Maddox, G.L. and J. Wiley (1976), 'Scope, concepts and methods in the study of aging', in R.H. Binstock *et al.* (eds), *Handbook of Aging and the Social Sciences*, Van Nostrand, New York, 3–34.

Maeda, D. (1978), 'Aging in Eastern Society', in D. Hobman (ed.), *The Social Challenge of Ageing*, Croom Helm, London, 45–72.

Maki, S. (1976), 'The postwar consumer movement: Its emergence from a movement of women', *Japan Quarterly*, 23, 135–9.

Maraini, F. (1975), 'Japan and the future: Some suggestions from nihon-jin-ron literature', in G. Fodella (ed.), *Social Structures and Economic Dynamics in Japan up to 1980*, Institute of Economic Studies for East Asia, Luigi Borroni University, Milan.

Matsumoto, H. (1982), 'Evolution of land and urban policies in Japan', Paper presented at the International Seminar on Urban Development Policies, Nagoya, Japan, 13–18 October.

Matsumoto, S. (1978), 'The roots of political disillusionment: "Public" and "private" in Japan', in J.V. Koschmann (ed.), *Authority and the Individual in Japan*, Tokyo at the University Press, 31–51.

Matsushita, K. (1980), 'Decentralization and political culture: Wither Japan', *Center News* (Japan Studies Center, The Japan Foundation), 5, 7–10.

Matsushita, K. (1978), 'Citizen participation in historical perspective', in J.V. Koschmann (ed.), *Authority and the Individual in Japan*, Tokyo at the University Press, 171–88.

Metheny, E. (1970), 'Symbolic forms of movement: The feminine image in sports', in G.H. Sage (ed.), *Sport and American Society: Selected Readings*, Addison-Wesley, Reading, Mass., 291–303.

Changing Japanese Suburbia

Minami, R. (1976), 'Introduction of electric power and its impact on the manufacturing industries: With special reference to smaller scale plants', in H. Patrick, (ed.), *Japanese Industrialization and its Social Consequences*, University of California Press, Berkeley, 299–326.

Ministry of Health and Welfare (1974), *Social Welfare Services in Japan*, Tokyo.

Ministry of Health and Welfare (1982), *Annual Report on Health and Welfare 1982*, Tokyo.

Ministry of Health and Welfare (1983), *Outline of Basic Survey on Welfare Administration in 1982*, Tokyo.

Ministry of Home Affairs (1982), 'Local Administration and finance in Japan', *International Review of Administrative Sciences*, 2, 144–79.

Moeran, B. (1981), 'Japanese social organization and the Mingei movement', *Pacific Affairs*, 54(1), 42–56.

Moeran, B. (1983), 'The language of Japanese tourism', *Annals of Tourism Research*, 10, 93–108.

Moeran, B. (1984a), 'One over the seven: "Sake" drinking in a Japanese Pottery Community', *Journal of the Anthropological Society of Oxford*, 15(2), 83–100.

Moeran, B. (1984b), 'Individual, group and *seishin*: Japan's internal cultural debate', *Man*, 19, 252–66.

Moeran, B. (1985), 'Confucian confusion: The good, the bad and the noodle western', in D. Parkin (ed.), *The Anthropology of Evil*, Basil Blackwell, Oxford, 92–109.

Moore, B. and B.G. Myerhoff (1977), 'Introduction: Secular ritual: Forms and meanings', in their (eds), *Secular Ritual*, Van Gorcum, Assen, 3–24.

Motoyama, H. (1982), 'Hieidaira danchi – sono chiikisei to seikatsuken' (Hieidaira estate – area life and characteristics), Department of Geography, Ritsumeikan University.

Murakami, N. (1978), *Nihon no Fujin Mondai* (Women's Issues in Japan), Iwanami Shinsho, Tokyo.

Nagashima, C. (1981), 'The Tokaido megalopolis', *Ekistics*, 289, 280–301.

Nakagawa, G. (1980), *Chonaikai: Nihonjin no Jichi Kankaku* (The Neighbourhood Association: The Japanese Sense of Self Government), Chuo Koron, Tokyo.

Nakagawa, Y. (1979), 'Japan, the welfare super-power', *Journal of Japanese Studies*, 5(1), 5–51.

Nakamura, H. (1968), 'Urban ward associations in Japan', in R.E. Pahl (ed.), *Readings in Urban Sociology*, Pergamon, Oxford, 186–208.

Nakamura, H. (1982), 'The historical development and function of *chonaikai* in a comparative perspective', *Tsukuba Journal of Sociology*, 6(1–2), 1–7.

Nakane, C. (1973), *Japanese Society*, Penguin, Harmondsworth.

Naoi, M. (1980), 'Rojin mondai to rojin no fukushi' (Problems of the elderly and their welfare), in K. Aoi and M. Naoi (eds), *Fukushi to Keikaku no Shakaigaku*, Tokyo at the University Press, 105–27.

Nihon Fujin Dantai Rengokai (1980), *Fujin Hakusho* (White Paper on Women), Tokyo.

Nisbet, R.A. (1953), *The Quest for Community*, Oxford at the University Press.

Norbeck, E. (1962), 'Common-interest associations in rural Japan', in R.J. Smith and R.K. Beardsley (eds), *Japanese Culture*, Aldine, Chicago, 73–85.

Norbeck, E. (1967), 'Associations and democracy in Japan', in R.P. Dore (ed.), *Aspects of Social Change in Modern Japan*, Princeton at the University Press, 153–84.

Norbeck, E. (1970), *Religion and Society in Modern Japan: Continuity and Change*, Rice University Studies, 56(1).

Norbeck, E. (1977), 'Changing associations in a recently industrialized Japanese community', *Urban Anthropology*, 6(1), 45–65.

Office of the Aged (Prime Minister's Secretariat) (1981), *International Comparative Survey of the Life and Perception of the Old: An Outline*, Tokyo.

Omori, M. (1976), 'A process of ubanization: Economic and social innovations in a suburban village in Fukuyama, Japan', in A. Rapaport (ed.), *The Mutual Interaction of People and their Environment*, Mouton, The Hague, 431–40.

Orbell, J.M. and T. Uno (1972), 'A theory of neighborhood problem solving: Political action *vs.* residential mobility', *American Political Science Review*, 66, 471–89.

Oshio, Y. (1981), *Nihon no Toshi Keikaku Ho* (Japan's Urban Planning Law), Gyosei, Tokyo.

Otsu-shi (1973), *Otsushi Jichikai Soshiki Unei Kijun* (Standards for the Management of Otsu City's Self-Government Associations), Otsu-shi, Shiminbu Jichika.

Otsu-shi (1978), *Shinshu Otsu Shishi* (Otsu City History – A New Compilation), vol. 3.

Otsu-shi (1981), *Shuyo na Shisaku no Seika Setsumeisho* (Description of the Results of the City's Major Policies).

Otsu-shi (1982), *Shisei Gaiyo* (Outline of City Administration), Gikai Jimukyoku.

Otsu-shi (1983), *Fukushi no Gaiyo* (An Outline of Welfare), Fukushi Hokenbu.

Otsu-shi Kyoiku Iinkai (1982), *Otsu No Kyoiku* (Otsu's Education).

Palmore, E. (1975), *The Honorable Elders: A Cross-Cultural Analysis of Aging in Japan*, Duke University Press, Durham, NC.

Parkin, F. (1968), *Middle Class Radicalism: The Social Bases of The*

British Campaign for Nuclear Disarmament, Manchester at the University Press.

Passin, H. (1975a), 'Changing values: Work and growth in Japan', *Asian Survey*, 15(10), 821–50.

Passin, H. (1975b), 'Intellectuals in the decision-making process', in E.F. Vogel (ed.), *Modern Japanese Organization and Decision-Making*, Tuttle, Tokyo, 251–83.

Patrick, H. (1976), 'An introductory overview', in his (ed.), *Japanese Industrialization and its Social Consequences*, University of California Press, Berkeley, 1–18.

Pharr, S.J. (1976), 'The Japanese woman: Evolving views of life and role', in L. Austin (ed.), *Japan: The Paradox of Progress*, Yale University Press, New Haven, 301–27.

Pinto-Duschinsky, M. (1977), 'Corruption in Britain: The Royal Commission on Standards of Conduct in Public Life', *Political Studies*, 25(2), 274–84.

Plath, D.W. (1969), *The After Hours: Modern Japan and the Search for Enjoyment*, University of California Press, Berkeley.

Plath, D.W. (1972), 'Japan: The after years', in D.O. Cowgill and L.D. Holmes (eds), *Aging and Modernization*, Appleton-Century-Crofts, New York, 133–50.

Plath, D.W. (1980), *Long Engagements: Maturity in Modern Japan*, Stanford at the University Press.

Prime Minister's Office (1981), *Population and Household Finances of the Elderly in Japan*, Tokyo.

Prime Minister's Office (1983), *Public Opinion Survey on Social Welfare*, Tokyo.

Reed, S.R. (1981), 'Environmental politics: Some reflections based on the Japanese case', *Comparative Politics*, 13, 253–70.

Reed, S.R. (1982), 'Is Japanese government really centralized?', *Journal of Japanese Studies*, 8, 133–64.

Rochon, T.R. (1983), 'Review article: Political change in ordered societies – the rise of citizens' movements', *Comparative Politics*, 15(3), 351–73.

Rohlen, T.P. (1974), *For Harmony and Strength: Japanese White Collar Organization in Anthropological Perspective*, University of California Press, Berkeley.

Rohlen, T.P. (1975), 'The company work group', in E.F. Vogel (ed.), *Modern Japanese Organization and Decision Making*, Tuttle, Tokyo, 185–209.

Saito, M. (1982), 'Nemawashi: A Japanese form of interpersonal communication', *Et cetera, A Review of General Semantics*, 3, 205–14.

Sakuta, K. (1978), 'The controversy over community and autonomy', in

J.V. Koschmann (ed.), *Authority and the Individual in Japan*, Tokyo at the University Press, 220–49.

Samuels, R.J. (1982), 'Local politics in Japan: The changing of the guard', *Asian Survey*, 22(7), 630–7.

Samuels, R.J. (1983), *The Politics of Regional Policy in Japan: Localities Incorporated?*, Princeton at the University Press.

Sargent, J. (1975), 'Regional development policy in Japan: Some aspects of the plan for remodelling the Japanese Archipelago', in W.G. Beasley (ed.), *Modern Japan*, G. Allen, London, 227–43.

Scott, W.R. (1969), 'Professional employees in a bureaucratic structure: Social work', in A. Etzioni (ed.), *The Semi-Professions and their Organization*, The Free Press, New York, 82–140.

Shiga Ken (1880), *Shiga Bussanshi* (A History of Production in Shiga Prefecture), Shiga Prefecture.

Shiga Janaaru (1976), 'Ueda Kimmyaku Tokushu' (Special issue: The Ueda gold vein), *Shiga Janaaru*, 1(1).

Shiga Janaaru (1982), 'Roundtable: The next elections on Shiga Prefecture', *Shiga Janaaru*, 2(2), 1–7.

Shimode, K. (1968), *Nihon no Toshi Kukan* (Japan's Urban Space), Eikoku-sha, Tokyo.

Shimpo, M. (1976), *Three Decades in Shiwa: Economic Development and Social Change in a Japanese Farming Community*, University of British Columbia Press, Vancouver.

Shindo, M. (1982), 'Relations between national government and local government in Japan', *International Review of Administrative Sciences*, 2, 180–6.

Shin Seikatsu Undo Kyokai (1982), *Jichikai, Chonaikai nado no Genjo to Tenbo* (The Present Situation and Outlook for Neighbourhood Associations), Shin Seikatsu Undo Kyokai, Tokyo.

Smith, H.D.II (1979), 'Tokyo and London: Comparative conceptions of the city', in A. Craig (ed.), *Japan: A Comparative View*, Princeton at the University Press, 49–98.

Smith, L. and D. Jones (eds) (1981), *Deprivation, Participation and Community Action*, Routledge & Kegan Paul, London.

Smith, R.A. (1970), 'Crowding in the city: The Japanese solution', *Landscape*, 19(1), 3–10.

Smith, R.J. (1978), *Kurusu: The Price of Progress in a Japanese Village, 1951–1975*, Stanford at the University Press.

Smith, R.J. (1983), *Japanese Society: Tradition, Self and the Social Order*, Cambridge at the University Press.

Smith, R.J. and E.P. Reyes (1957), 'Community interrelations with the outside world: The case of a Japanese agricultural community', *American Anthroplogist*, 59, 463–72.

Stein, M.R. (1960), *The Eclipse of Community: An Interpretation of American Studies*, Tokyo Princeton at the University Press.

Steiner, F. (1981), *The Politics of New Town Planning: The Newfields Ohio Story*, Ohio University Press, Athens.

Steiner, K. (1965), *Local Government in Japan*, Stanford at the University Press.

Steiner, K. (1968), 'Popular participation and political development in Japan: The rural level, in R.E. Ward (ed.), *Political Development in Modern Japan*, Princeton at the University Press, 213–48.

Steiner, K. *et al.* (eds) (1980), *Political Opposition and Local Politics in Japan*, Princeton at the University Press.

Stockwin, J.A.A. (1982), *Japan: Divided Politics in a Growth Economy*, Weidenfeld & Nicolson, London.

Stone, G.P. (1981), 'Sport as a community representation', in G.R.F. Luschen and G.H. Sage (eds), *Handbook of Social Science of Sport*, Stipes, Champaign, Ill., 214–45.

Sugimoto, Y. (1978), 'Quantitative characteristics of popular disturbances in post-occupation Japan (1952–1960)', *Journal of Asian Studies*, 37(2), 273–91.

Sugimoto, Y. and R. Mouer (1980), 'Reappraising images of Japanese society', *Social Analysis*, 5/6, 5–19.

Sussman, M.B. (1976), 'The family life of old people', in R.H. Binstock *et al.* (eds), *Handbook of Aging and the Social Sciences*, Van Nostrand, New York, 218–43.

Suttles, G.D. (1972), *The Social Construction of Communities*, Chicago at the University Press.

Sutton-Smith, B. (1981), 'The social psychology and anthropology of play and games', in G.R.F. Luschen and G.H. Sage (eds), *Handbook of Social Science of Sport*, Stipes, Champaign, Ill., 452–78.

Tada, M. (1978), 'The glory and misery of "my home" ', in J.V. Koschmann (ed.), *Authority and the Individual in Japan*, Tokyo at the University Press, 207–17.

Taira, K. (1967), 'Public assistance in Japan: Developments and trends', *Journal of Asian Studies*, 27, 95–105.

Taira, K. (1968–9), 'Urban poverty, ragpickers and the "Ant Villa" in Tokyo', *Economic Development and Cultural Change*, 17, 155–77.

Taira, K. (1978), 'Modernization, uglification, and an urban revolution in Japan', *Asian Profile*, 6(2), 135–52.

Takabatake, M. (1978), 'Citizens' movements: Organizing the spontaneous', in J.V. Koschmann (ed.), *Authority and the Individual in Japan*, Tokyo at the University Press, 189–99.

Takayose, S. (1979a), 'Chiiki jumin soshiki-ron' (Local residents organizations), in his (ed.), *Chiho Jichi to Jumin Jichi*, Genbunsha, Tokyo, 49–84.

Takayose, S. (1979b), *Komyuniti to Jumin Soshiki* (Community and Residents Organizations), Keiso Shobo, Tokyo.

Takenaga, N. (1983), 'Working mothers and their children in Japan, with special reference to three surveys on school children, teachers, and mothers', in Y. Muramatsu (ed.), *Proceedings of '83 Tokyo Symposium on Women: Women and Work*, Tokyo, 56–63.

Takeuchi, A. (1982), 'Chiiki to keizai' (Region and economy), in K. Itakura *et al.* (eds), *Nihon Keizai Chiri Tokuhon*, Tokyo Keizai Tokuhon Shirizu 25, Tokyo.

Tanaka, Y. (1979), 'The plight of the elderly: Scenes of indigence in an affluent society', *Japan Quarterly*, 16(1), 63–71.

Tilly, C. (1973), 'Do communities act?', *Sociological Inquiry*, 43(3–4), 207–40.

Tokyo Metropolitan Government (1982), *Tokyo Tomorrow: Report Prepared by the My Town Concept Consultative Council*, Tokyo at the Metropolitan Office.

Tonan Shoji Kabushiki Gaisha (1973), *Kaisha Gaiyo* (An Outline of the Company), Tokyo.

Tornstam, L. (1982), 'Gerontology in a dynamic society', in T.K. Hareven and K.J. Adams (eds), *Ageing and Life Course Transitions*, Tavistock, London, 183–220.

Townsend, D. (1983), 'Local diversity without local neglect', in H. Glennerster (ed.), *The Future of the Welfare State: Remaking Social Policy*, Heinemann, London, 173–84.

Townsend, P. (1975), *Sociology and Social Policy*, Penguin, Harmondsworth.

Tsurumi, K. (1970), *Social Change and the Individual: Japan Before and After Defeat in World War II*, Princeton at the University Press.

Tsurutani, T. (1977), *Political Change in Japan: Response to Postindustrial Challenge*, David Mckay, New York.

Tuan, Y.F. (1977), *Space and Place: The Perspective of Experience*, Edward Arnold, London.

Turner, V. (1977), 'Variations on a theme of liminality', in S.F. Moore and B.G. Myerhoff (eds), *Secular Ritual*, Van Gorcum, Assen, 36–52.

Vogel, E.F. (1963), *Japan's New Middle Class: The Salary Man and his Family in a Tokyo Suburb*, University of California Press, Berkeley.

Vogel, E.F. (1975), 'Introduction: Toward more accurate concepts', in his (ed.), *Modern Japanese Organization and Decision-Making*, Tuttle, Tokyo, xiii–xxv.

Vogel, E.F. (1979), *Japan as Number One: Lessons for America*, Harvard University Press, Cambridge, Mass.

Wagatsuma, H. (1977), 'Some aspects of the contemporary Japanese family: Once Confucian, now fatherless?', *Daedalus*, 106, 181–210.

Walker, A. (1982a), Introduction, to his (ed.), *Community Care*, Blackwell, Oxford, 1–10.

Walker, A. (1982b), 'The meaning and social division of community care', in his (ed.), *Community Care*, Blackwell, Oxford, 13–39.

Watanabe, M. (n.d.), *Biwako Jorei Zakkan* (Miscellaneous Impressions of Lake Biwa Regulations), Koen Shirizu.

Watanabe, S.J. (1980), 'Planning history in Japan', *Urban History Year-book*, 63–75.

Watanabe, T. (1977), 'Jumin undo kara miru ningen no pataan' (Citizens' movements and social patterns), *Jissen no Toei*, October, 1–5.

Watanuki, J. (1966), 'Political attitudes of the Japanese people', *Socio-logical Review Monograph*, No. 10, 165–82.

Watanuki, J. (1975), 'Japan', in M. Crozier *et al.*, *The Crisis of Democ-racy*, New York University Press, New York, 119–65.

Weick, K. (1976), 'Educational organizations as loosely coupled systems', *Administrative Science Quarterly*, 21, 1–19.

White, J.W. (1976), 'Social change and community involvement in metro-politan Japan', in his and F. Munger (eds), *Social Change and Com-munity Politics in Urban Japan*, The Institute for Social Research, University of North Carolina, Chapel Hill, NC.

Whyte, W.H. Jr (1956), *The Organization Man*, Doubleday, New York.

Wicks, M. (1982), 'Community care and elderly people', in A. Walker (ed.), *Community Care*, Blackwell, Oxford, 97–117.

Wildavsky, A. (1974), *Politics of the Budgetary Process*, Little Brown, Boston.

Woss, F. (1982), 'Escape into death: Old people and their wish to die', Paper presented at a conference of the European Association of Japanese Studies, Den Haag, September.

Wrong, D. (1961), 'The oversocialized conception of man in modern sociology', *American Sociological Review*, 26(2), 183–93.

Yamada, T. (n.d.) (1973), *Shimin Fukushi no Kojo o Mezashite* . . . (On the Way to an Improvement of the City Citizens' Welfare . . .), Otsu-shi.

Yamanda, T. (1983), *Hajime ni* (Introduction), to Otsu-shi (1983).

Yamazaki, M. (1984), 'Signs of a new individualism', *Japan Echo*, 11(1), 8–18.

Yoneyama, T. (1967a), 'Kaminosho: A farm village suburban to Osaka in South Central Japan', in J.H. Steward (ed.), *Contemporary Change in Traditional Societies: Vol. II. Asian Rural Societies*, University of Illinois Press, Urbana, 187–257.

Yoneyama, T. (1967b), 'Comparison of two Japanese villages', in J.H. Steward (ed.), *Contemporary Change in Traditional Societies: Vol. II. Asian Rural Societies*, University of Illinois Press, Urbana, 329–44.

Yoshida, T. (1964), 'Social conflict and cohesion in a Japanese rural community', *Ethnology*, 3(3), 219–31.

Yoshizawa, E. (1981), 'Fujin to borantia' (Women and volunteers), in E. Isomura and K. Sakata (eds), *Asu no Toshi – Toshi to Fukushi*, Chuo Hoki Shuppan, Tokyo, 326–37.

Yusa, K. (1975), *Biwako o Wakaseta Otoko* (The Man Who Brought an Uproar to Lake Biwa), Kodansha, Tokyo.

Index

aged, *see* elderly
agriculture, xii, 4, 7, 15, 27, 33, 40, 67–8, 173
agricultural co-operative, 42, 115
Allinson, G. D., 4, 14–16, 64, 126, 130, 294, 298–300
amae, 254
American occupation, 28, 67, 91
ancestors, 70
aspirations, 47
Atsumi, R., 192, 267
authority, 7, 65, 84–5, 107–8, 115–17, 119, 185, 188, 257, 263–5

Befu, H., 252, 254, 265, 273
Bennett, J. W. and Levine, S. B., 66, 115, 133, 141
Board of Education, 43, 63, 75, 107, 198, 206, 215
Bon dances, 163
boonenkai (forgetting the year parties), 197
'breakdown of community' approach, ix, 3–7, 9, 13, 16, 64, 251, 258, 269, 294
Buddhism, 22, 53, 57, 60, 73, 149, 175, 303
buraku, 11
Butsudan, 59

Campbell, J. C., 129, 133–4, 143, 301, 304
central government, *see* national government
ceremonies, 182, 234, 265, 270
children, 22, 30, 52, 56, 75, 77, 150, 163, 214, 217, 222, 232
children's association, xii, 50–1, 77, 163, 176, 191, 206, 209, 228, 270, 277
choonaikai, 91–3, 115, 299

Christianity, 59
citizens' movements, 11–14, 17, 65, 85, 93, 100, 111, 115–16, 134, 257, 262–3, 299–301
city office, xiii, 17, 28, 63, 71–121, 125–6, 130, 143–5, 147, 154, 158–9, 165, 176–88, 214, 222, 234, 259–61, 264–5, 278, 300–2
city assembly, 89–90, 101, 119, 139, 155, 176, 206, 215
clubs, 34, 48–53, 91, 98, 126, 184, 194, 277
commerce, 37, 153
communal land, 67–71, 262, 297
community action, 3, 10, 16–17, 63–121, 185, 255, 261, 268, 281
community care, 3, 17–18, 125–88, 255, 260–1, 268, 281, 301–3
community history, 60, 270, 272
'community of limited liability', 9–11, 17, 131, 247, 256–7, 271
community identity, 3, 18, 55, 112, 167, 174, 194–5, 203, 207, 215, 218, 227, 234, 236–45, 255–6, 260, 263–73, 277–81, 306–7
company and workplace, 4, 8–10, 15–16, 35, 192, 244, 253, 269, 271, 275, 278, 281
conflict, 83–4, 107, 115, 117, 262–3
consumer co-operatives, 39–40, 86, 262–3, 277, 296
consumer movements, 65, 110–11
Cornell, J. B., 85, 239, 272, 278
corruption, 79–81

danchi, 15
day-care centres, 22, 24, 42–3, 50, 63, 75, 78, 106, 172, 176, 192
demography, *see* population

Index